Victor W. Watton
& Diane Kolka

Catholic Christianity

for Edexcel **THIRD EDITION**

HODDER
EDUCATION
AN HACHETTE UK COMPANY

For Richard, my husband, and my children Hannah, Laura, Ben and Rachel.
Thank you for your love and patience.
Diane Kolka

For my wife Jill and grandchildren Benjamin, Kisa, Jasmine, Phoebe and Thomas.
Victor Watton

The authors would also like to thank Michael Corcoran, Our Lady's RC Primary School,
Chesham Bois; Bishop Peter Doyle, RC Bishop of Northampton, St Columba's Parish,
Chesham and Father Patrick Bailey, Parish Priest; Frs. Peter Conley and Joseph Quigley.

This material has been endorsed by Edexcel and offers high quality support for the delivery
of Edexcel qualifications.
Edexcel endorsement does not mean that this material is essential to achieve any Edexcel
qualification, nor does it mean that this is the only suitable material available to support any
Edexcel qualification. No endorsed material will be used verbatim in setting any Edexcel
examination and any resource lists produced by Edexcel shall include this and other
appropriate texts. While this material has been through an Edexcel quality assurance process,
all responsibility for the content remains with the publisher. Copies of official specifications
for all Edexcel qualifications may be found on the Edexcel website – www.edexcel.org.uk
http://www.edexcel.org.uk

Photo credits and acknowledgements can be found on page 210.

Although every effort has been made to ensure that website addresses are correct at time
of going to press, Hodder Education cannot be held responsible for the content of any
website mentioned in this book. It is sometimes possible to find a relocated web page by
typing in the address of the home page for a website in the URL window of your browser.

Hachette UK's policy is to use papers that are natural, renewable and recyclable products
and made from wood grown in sustainable forests. The logging and manufacturing processes
are expected to conform to the environmental regulations of the country of origin.

Orders: please contact Bookpoint Ltd, 130 Milton Park, Abingdon, Oxon OX14 4SB.
Telephone: (44) 01235 827720. Fax: (44) 01235 400454. Lines are open 9.00–5.00,
Monday to Saturday, with a 24-hour message answering service. Visit our website at
www.hoddereducation.co.uk

© Victor W. Watton, Diane Kolka 2009
First published in 2003 by
Hodder Education,
An Hachette UK Company
338 Euston Road
London NW1 3BH

First edition published (2003)
Second edition published (2007)
This third edition published (2009)
Impression number   5 4
Year   2013 2012

Cover photos © Giulio Napolitano/AFP/Getty Images; © Reuters/Corbis;
© Royal Observatory, Edinburgh/AATB/Science Photo Library
Illustrations by Steve Evans
Typeset in 12pt Electra LH Regular by Ian Foulis
Printed in Dubai

A catalogue record for this title is available from the British Library.
ISBN: 978 0340 975 534

Catholic Christianity

for Edexcel THIRD EDITION

Contents

How to use this book

This book covers the content requirements of the Edexcel GCSE Religious Studies in Roman Catholic Christianity (Units 3 and 10).

Each section of the book is one of the four sections of the units in the GCSE specification (3.1, 3.2, 3.3, 3.4 and 10.1, 10.2, 10.3, 10.4), and every sub-topic within the sections of the specification (11 for each section) is covered as a separate topic in the book. The main body of the text gives you all the information you need for each topic. The sources in the margin give you extra information for greater understanding of the topic.

Although the specification is called Roman Catholic Christianity, and this term will appear in the exam questions, this book uses the more preferred form of 'Catholic Christianity'.

In each examination (one for Unit 3 and one for Unit 10), you will have to answer four questions: one question on Section 1, one question on Section 2, one question on Section 3 and one question on Section 4. Each question is divided into sub-questions a) for 2 marks, b) for 4 marks, c) for 8 marks and d) for 6 marks. Examples of b), c) and d) sub-questions are given for each topic, and a tip is given on how to answer one of them.

- Work through the Introduction which will help you to understand the relationship between the Catholic Church and the other Christian Churches.
- Work through each topic. Words that you might not understand are in bold type so that you can look up their meanings in the glossary at the end of the book.
- Answer the exam tip question at the end of the topic. The exam tip gives you hints as to the approach which will gain you full marks. The other questions are to help you see what other types of question can be asked on the topic.

Quotations from the Catechism of the Catholic Church are identified by their paragraph numbers in the Eighth Edition. Scriptures quoted are from the New International Version.

Introduction

The specification requires you to study Catholic Christianity in the context of Christianity as a whole. This introduction explains what the different Christian groups are, and why they are different.

Historical background

Christians believe that God created the world and made humans, in his image, to be his stewards of the world. They believe that God chose the Jewish people to be his special people who were to show the rest of the world (the Gentiles) how to live. When the Jews failed to do this properly, God sent his son, Jesus, to show people how to live and to save them from their sins.

Jesus and the early Christians were Jews, but most Jews did not become Christians, and so Christianity began to develop as a separate religion which was soon mainly Gentile.

Christians believe that Jesus is alive in the Christian Church which has developed since his death and resurrection and which is now the most numerous and widespread world religion.

Why there are differences of opinion among Christians

- Christianity developed in different places in different ways. By the time Christianity became the official religion of the Roman Empire in 356AD, there were several different traditions within Christianity. They were organised mainly by bishops and councils of bishops, but in the West, the Bishop of Rome (the Pope) gradually became accepted as leader. In 1054, the Eastern Churches (Orthodox) ruled by councils of bishops split from the Western Church (Roman Catholic) which accepted the leadership of the Pope.
- In the sixteenth century, men like Martin Luther and John Calvin decided that the Western Church had deviated from the Church of the New Testament. They protested and demanded reforms (the Reformation). This led to Protestant or Reformed Churches, which believed in the Church being ruled democratically (all Christian believers being equal and sharing in the priesthood of Christ) and in the absolute authority of the Bible (individual Christians to interpret the Bible for themselves).
- The Church of England, established by Henry VIII and Elizabeth I, is a mixture of Protestant and Catholic ideas. English Protestants who wanted to reform the Church in England after the Reformation and would not join the Church of England are called Nonconformists.
- Another cause of difference since the nineteenth century has been liberal Christians who believe Christianity needs to take account of science and reason. They do not believe that the Bible should be taken literally as the word of God and reject many traditional beliefs.

The key features of non-Catholic Churches

The Orthodox Churches

These are national Churches led by a chief bishop called a Patriarch. Most of them are based in Eastern Europe (Greece, Russia, Romania, Serbia). They have priests who may marry, but their bishops must be celibate. Their worship is very elaborate and they revere icons and use incense.

The Church of England

This is the established Church in England. The Queen is the head of the Church and appoints bishops. The Church of England has branches in all the English-speaking parts of the world. These Churches are independent but meet together at the Lambeth Conference which is always chaired by the Archbishop of Canterbury. These Churches are known as either Anglican or Episcopalian. Some are very Protestant and are called Low Church; others are very Catholic and are called High Church.

Nonconformist Churches

These are Churches which thought the Church of England was not Protestant enough. Instead of bishops or priests they have ministers who are regarded as no different from lay people. They are governed by democratically elected bodies and their services are Bible-based rather than communion-based. The main Nonconformist Churches are the Methodist, the United Reformed (URC), the Baptist (who baptise adults rather than babies), the Society of Friends (Quakers), Pentecostals and a variety of Black Churches.

How Christians make moral decisions

All Christians believe that moral decisions should be based on the teachings of Jesus in the New Testament and the Ten Commandments in the Old Testament.

- **Roman Catholics** believe that these teachings are best interpreted by the Church, especially the head of the Church, the Pope, and the bishops. Therefore, to guide and direct their moral decisions, they refer to the teachings of the Church contained in the *Catechism of the Catholic Church* (1999) or the teachings of the Pope together with the bishops in the Encyclical letters. They would also ask their local priest.
- **Orthodox Christians** would base their decisions on how the Bible has been interpreted by councils of bishops, or simply ask advice from their priest.
- **Protestants** (Church of England, Methodist, Baptist, Pentecostal, etc.) believe that each individual should make their own decisions on the basis of what the Bible says, but most would also be guided by decisions made by democratically elected bodies of Church leaders (for example, the General Synod of the Church of England or the Conference of the Methodist Church).

Section 3.1 Believing in God

Introduction

This section of the examination specification requires you to look at the issues surrounding belief in God.

Reasons why some people believe in God
You will need to understand the effects of, and give reasons for your own opinion about:
- the main features of a Catholic upbringing
- religious experience
- the argument from design
- the argument from causation.

Reasons why some people do not believe in God
You will need to understand the effects of, and give reasons for your own opinion about:
- scientific explanations of the origins of the world
- unanswered prayers
- evil and suffering.

How Catholics respond to the reasons why some people do not believe in God
You will need to understand the effects of, and give reasons for your own opinion about how Catholics respond to:
- scientific explanations of the world
- the problem of unanswered prayers
- the problem of evil and suffering.

The media and belief in God
You will need to understand the effects of, and give reasons for your own opinion about how two television or radio programmes about religion may affect attitudes to belief in God.

Topic 3.1.1 The main features of a Catholic upbringing and how it may lead to belief in God

A Bishop laying on hands at a Catholic confirmation ceremony. Why might being confirmed lead to, or support, belief in God?

There are many reasons for believing in God. Some people are led to believe in God by one reason only, others find that a number of reasons taken together make it difficult not to believe in God. The next four topics investigate the following reasons for believing in God:

- Religious upbringing
- Religious experience
- The argument from design
- The argument from causation.

The main features of a Catholic upbringing

Children of Catholic parents will often be baptised when they are babies or young children. **Baptism** is the 'basis of the whole Christian life ... the door which gives access to the other **sacraments**' (**Catechism** 1213). As part of this sacrament, the parents will promise to bring up their children as Catholics and provide them with a Christian home of love and **faithfulness**. To bring their children up as Catholics, the parents are likely to:

- teach their children **prayers** and about the saints and the Church
- take their children to church – in many parishes, the children would go to the **children's liturgy** during Sunday **Mass** and on other special days where worship would be child friendly and help them to understand about God
- send their children to a Catholic school where the National Curriculum and RE are taught in a Catholic Christian environment.

As part of fulfilling their **vows** at baptism, Catholic parents will encourage their children to make their first **confession** and Holy **Communion** and later be confirmed as full members of the Church. These sacraments are likely to involve a religious experience in the liturgies themselves with children feeling the presence of God through prayers, vows and anointing with oil.

How a Catholic upbringing may lead to, or support, belief in God

A Catholic religious upbringing helps make belief in God seem natural because:

- A child's parents will have told them about God as part of their promises to bring them up as a Catholic and young children believe what their parents tell them.

- Catholic parents teach their children how to pray to God and about the lives of Jesus' disciples and other saints of the Church. This shows that prayer is a natural and important part of their lives and encourages children to believe in God.
- Going to church and seeing so many people praying to God and worshipping God is likely to make them think that God must exist.
- Going to Children's Liturgy would support belief in God because children would learn why Catholics believe in God and what they believe about him.
- Going to a Catholic school would have a similar effect, as God and Christianity would be a normal feature of school life. The school children have RE lessons which teach them that God exists and the children are likely to believe it because their teachers tell them it is true.
- Being confirmed would be likely to support their belief, as they learn more about God in the **confirmation** lessons, and possibly have a **religious experience** when the bishop lays his hands on them.

Why might attending a Catholic school lead to, or support, belief in God?

SUMMARY

Having a Catholic upbringing is likely to lead to belief in God because children are taught that God exists and they spend most of their time with people who believe that God exists.

Questions

b Do you think children should follow the same religion as their parents? Give two reasons for your point of view. **4**

c Explain how a Catholic upbringing can lead to, or support, belief in God. **8**

d 'A Catholic upbringing leads children to believe in God.'
  i Do you agree? Give reasons for your opinion. **3**
  ii Give reasons why some people may disagree with you. **3**

Exam Tip

c 'Explain' means give reasons. To answer this question you should name four features of a Catholic upbringing and explain, in two or three sentences for each, how they might lead to belief in God For tips on Quality of Written Communication see opposite.

Exam focus

Quality of Written Communication

'Explain' questions (part c in the examination) are where your Quality of Written Communication is tested, so you should answer these questions in a formal style of English, be careful with your spelling and try to use some specialist vocabulary (in this topic baptism, sacrament, prayer, worship, confirmation, bishop would all be specialist vocabulary).

Topic 3.1.2 How religious experience may lead to belief in God

KEY WORDS

Conversion – when your life is changed by giving yourself to God.

Miracle – something which seems to break a law of science and makes you think only God could have done it.

Numinous – the feeling of the presence of something greater than you.

Prayer – an attempt to contact God, usually through words.

Religious experience is an event that people feel gives them direct contact with God. You need to know four types of religious experience: **numinous**, **conversion**, **miracle** and **prayer**.

1. The numinous and belief in God

The numinous is a feeling of the presence of God. When people are in a religious building, in a beautiful place or looking up at the stars on a clear night, they may be filled with the awareness that there is something greater than them, which they feel to be God. It is often described as an experience of the transcendent (something going beyond human experience and existing outside the material world).

If someone has a numinous experience, it may lead them to believe in God because the experience will make them feel that God is real. If you become aware of a presence greater than you, you are likely to believe that that presence is God and so you will believe in him.

Example of the numinous

Father Yves Dubois has had numinous experiences while praying before a statue of Our Lady.
'Twice I have experienced the certainty of the presence of the Mother of God, which was an awareness of purity, holiness and love unlike anything I have ever known. Her holiness would have been frightening, but for the strong feeling of love and **compassion**.'
Source: Quoted in Christians in Britain Today, Hodder, 1991

Do you think Father Yves Dubois could doubt the existence of God after these numinous experiences?

2. Conversion and belief in God

Conversion is the word used to describe an experience of God, which is so great that the person experiencing it wants to change their life and commit themselves to God in a special way. It can also be used to describe an experience, which causes someone to change their religion or change from **agnosticism** or **atheism** to belief in God. It is sometimes called a regenerative experience because it gives a feeling of being '**born again**'. If someone has a conversion experience, that will lead them to believe in God because they will feel that God is calling them to do something for him. When **St Paul** was on the road to Damascus (Acts 9:1–19) and Jesus spoke to him from a bright light in the sky, telling him to become a Christian, the experience was so powerful that Paul decided to convert to Christianity.

Example of a conversion

During the Civil War in the Lebanon, Raymond Nader was a commander in the Christian militia who led the fighting against Muslim militias. On a cold November night in 1994, he went to pray at the shrine of St Charbel. Suddenly the night got warmer and he felt surrounded by a great light. He reached out to touch the light and his arm was burned by what he, and the Church authorities, believed was the presence of St Charbel. The vision made him give up his work in the militia to work for Tele Lumiere, the only Christian television station in the Middle East. Tele Lumiere and Nader are dedicated to spiritual peace, the defence of human rights and dignity as a way of challenging the violence and horror of the Middle East.

Do you think that Raymond Nader would have been able to be an atheist after this conversion experience?

3. Miracles and belief in God

A miracle is an event which seems to break a law of science and the only explanation for which seems to be God. Miracles are recorded in most religions and usually involve a religious experience.

This painting, by Augustin Cranagh in 1560, shows St Paul on the Road to Damascus. Saul was a persecutor of Christians and was on his way to Damascus to arrest the Christians there, when he had a vision of Jesus which blinded him. After this conversion experience, his sight recovered and he became a great Christian missionary and changed his name to Paul.

Example of a miracle

On Thursday 11 February 1858, fourteen-year-old Bernadette Soubirous saw a beautiful young girl in a niche at a rocky outcrop called Massabielle near Lourdes. The apparition beckoned to her, but Bernadette did not move and the girl smiled at her before disappearing. Bernadette later described how she had seen a young girl of about her own age and height, clothed in a brilliant and unearthly white robe, with a blue girdle round her waist and a white veil on her head. This was the beginning of eighteen apparitions during the spring and early summer of 1858. During one of these, Bernadette asked the lady her name and she said, 'I am the **Immaculate Conception**.' During another, the lady led Bernadette to a grotto where a miraculous spring appeared. Since these miraculous appearances of the Virgin Mary, Lourdes has become a great place of pilgrimage for Catholics and many healing miracles have taken place there which have been verified by an independent bureau of scientists and doctors. Many people say that while not all people who go to Lourdes are cured through their religious expereience, they receive great inner strength to cope with their illnesses and other problems of life.

The shrine at Lourdes.

> *'If you knew the gift of God!'* *The wonder of prayer is revealed beside the well where we come seeking water: there,* **Christ** *comes to meet every human being. It is he who first seeks us and asks us for a drink. Jesus thirsts; his asking arises from the depths of God's desire for us. Whether we realise it or not, prayer is the encounter of God's thirst with ours. God thirsts that we may thirst for him.*
>
> **Catechism of the Catholic Church 2560**

> *In the New Covenant, prayer is the living relationship of the children of God with their Father who is good beyond measure, with His Son Jesus Christ and with the Holy Spirit;... Thus the life of prayer is the habit of being in the presence of the thrice-holy God and in communion with him.*
>
> **Catechism of the Catholic Church 2565**

Miracles can lead to belief in God because, if a miracle has really happened, it means that God has acted on the Earth and that the people witnessing it have had direct contact with God. If an atheist or agnostic witnesses a miracle, their first reaction will be to look for a natural explanation. However, if they cannot find one, it might lead them to believe in God.

Miracles are a major part of Catholic belief. The process of declaring someone a new saint (canonisation) depends on being able to establish two miracles connected with the proposed saint. In the **Bible**, miracles are linked to people's faith and help faith to grow.

4. Prayer

All Catholics believe they can communicate with God through prayer. The Catechism teaches that human beings are born searching for God and that prayer is a way to complete the search. Prayer is the way to encounter God; it is a gift from God because God is waiting to hear human prayers. Although people may not always know how to pray properly, the Church teaches that if prayers come from the heart they are acceptable to God and allow communion with God. The importance of prayer for Catholics can be seen in the fact that one quarter of the Catechism is about Christian prayer.

There are many different types of prayer, from the formal prayers offered in worship, such as the prayers said during Mass, to the very informal prayers where a believer makes their own prayer to God in their own private place or as they go about their daily activities.

How religious prayer may lead to belief in God

If the person praying to God feels that God is listening to the prayer, then they have a religious experience through prayer and are sure that God exists. Perhaps the biggest religious experience anyone can have is when their private prayer is answered, for example when someone prays for a sick loved one to recover and they do. During prayer, a person may experience a sense of joy and peace, the closeness of God, or not feel anything in particular. The desire to pray is in itself a religious experience. Christians believe no prayer is ever wasted, though prayer is answered in God's time and on God's terms. As Jesus prayed 'thy will be done'.

Example of prayer leading to belief

About ten years later, I began to pray for my children's safety, and this became a habit which I have never lost, and often the answer to such prayer is spectacular. I find it best to live as if the soul of man were in communion with a superhuman force which makes for righteousness. May I add that since this belief grew in me, I feel that I had grown, as if my mind had stretched to take in the vast universe and be part of it.

Source: Alister Hardy Trust, Oxford

Any religious believer who has any form of religious experience will find that the experience supports their belief in God and makes it stronger because they now have more direct evidence for God's existence.

Catholic Christians in the Democratic Republic of Congo praying for fair elections in July 2006.

The caption for this cartoon reads: 'He never prayed, except for rain.' Why is this humorous?

Questions

b Do you think miracles prove that God exists? Give two reasons for your point of view. **4**

c Explain how religious experience can lead to, or support, belief in God. **8**

d 'Religious experiences prove that God exists.'
  i Do you agree? Give reasons for your opinion. **3**
  ii Give reasons why some people may disagree with you. **3**

Exam Tip

b You should already have thought about this, and you just have to give two reasons for your opinion. For example, if you think miracles prove God's existence, you could use these two reasons:
  • if a miracle happens there is no explanation for it except that God caused it to happen
  • Christians believe that Jesus rising from the dead proves he was God's Son because only God could rise from the dead.

Exam focus

What do you think?
In these questions (part b) in the examination) you must decide what you think about the issues and ideas you study. For this topic you need to think about whether:
• there is such a thing as the numinous and whether it means God exists
• conversions really happen and whether they prove God exists
• you believe in miracles and whether a miracle would prove that God exists
• prayer is valuable.
The questions are meant to be quite easy and to get full marks you just need to give two reasons.

SUMMARY

People experience God in the numinous, conversion, miracles and answered prayers. Religious experience makes people feel that God is real.

Topic 3.1.3 The argument from design and belief in God

What is design?

Any complex mechanism is designed for a purpose. **Design** involves things working together according to a plan to produce something that was intended. If you look at a car you can see that the fuel powers an engine which turns a shaft which turns the wheels and so makes a self-propelled vehicle to allow people to travel further and more easily. A look at any part of the car makes you think that the car has been designed.

Evidence of design in the world

Laws of science
A main reason why some people think the universe has been designed is because the universe works according to laws. The laws of gravity, electricity, magnetism, motion, bonding, gases, etc., all involve complex things working together.

DNA
DNA seems to be another piece of evidence of design in the world. DNA is a nucleic acid which forms the material of all living organisms.
- DNA is made up of two strands that form a ladder-like structure, which forms a right-hand spiral called a double helix.
- The DNA molecule replicates by unzipping and using each strand as a template to form a new strand.
- These new DNA strands are then passed on to daughter cells during cell division.

The structure of DNA and its formation of templates seem to indicate a design or blueprint for the structure of organisms.

Evolution
Some scientists also see evidence of design in the process of evolution where complex life forms develop from simple ones.

Beauty of nature
Artists see evidence of design in the beauties of nature where sunsets, mountains and oceans appear to have beauty which an artist would have to spend a long time designing.

How the appearance of design may lead to, or support, belief in God

Using the appearance of design to lead to belief in God is often called the argument from design (the most famous version is Paley's Watch). It goes like this:

Could this car have been made without a design?

Paley's Watch

If you came across a watch in an uninhabited place, you could not say it had been put there by chance. The complexity of its mechanism would make you say it had a designer. The universe is a far more complex mechanism than a watch, and so, if a watch needs a watchmaker, the universe needs a universe maker. As the only being that could design the universe would be God, it follows that God must exist.

Paley's Watch Argument for the Existence of God

- Anything that has been designed needs a designer.
- There is plenty of evidence that the world has been designed (laws of science, DNA, evolution, beauties of nature).
- If the world has been designed, the world must have a designer.
- The only possible designer of something as beautiful and complex as the world would be God.
- Therefore the appearance of design in the world proves that God exists.

This argument shows how the appearance of design in the world can lead people who are not sure about God to believe that he exists; and how it will give extra reasons for believing in God to those who already believe.

How the appearance of design may not lead to belief in God

Many people think the argument from design does not lead to belief in God because:

- The argument ignores the evidence of lack of design in the universe, for example volcanoes, earthquakes, hurricanes, diseases.
- All the evidence for design can be explained by science without needing even to think of God (see Topic 3.1.5).
- The argument does not refer to the existence of dinosaurs, which must have been a part of design, but no one thinks they could have been part of a design plan for the world.
- The argument only proves that the universe has a designer, not God. The designer could be many gods, an evil creator, a God who used this universe as a trial run so that he could create a better one.

Exam focus

Evaluation questions
- Decide what you think about the statement.
- Give at least three brief reasons, or two longer reasons, or a paragraph reason, supporting your point of view.
- Look at the opposite point of view and give at least three brief reasons, or two longer reasons, or a paragraph reason, for why people have this view.

The evaluation questions mean that you must always be aware not only of your own point of view about a topic, but also about the opposite point of view.

REMEMBER
One of your points of view should always be a Catholic one.

Questions

b Do you think God designed the world? Give two reasons for your point of view. **4**

c Explain why the design argument leads some people to believe in God. **8**

d 'The design argument proves that God exists.'
  i Do you agree? Give reasons for your opinion. **3**
  ii Give reasons why some people may disagree with you. **3**

Exam Tip

d Use the evaluation technique from this page. Arguments for design would be the argument itself. Arguments against would come from why some people disagree with the design argument.

SUMMARY

The universe seems to be designed. Anything that is designed must have a designer. Therefore God must exist because only God could have designed the universe. Some people disagree because things like volcanoes and earthquakes show a lack of design, and the argument does not prove God, only a designer who could be evil.

Topic 3.1.4 The argument from causation and belief in God

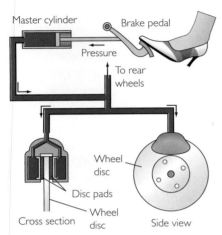

Putting your foot on the brake when driving a car causes hydraulic pressure in the brake pipes, which causes the brake pads to put pressure on the discs, which causes the wheels to stop turning, which causes the car to slow down.

What is causation?

Causation is the process whereby one thing causes another. It is often known as cause and effect; in the example in the diagram, the cause would be pressing the brake pedal and the effect would be the car slowing down.

Evidence of causation in the world

Cause and effect seem to be a basic feature of the world. Whatever we do has an effect. If I do my homework, I will please my parents and/or teachers. If I do not do my homework, I will annoy my parents and/or teachers. Modern science has developed through looking at causes and effects and in particular looking for single causes of an effect. Just as my parents' happiness may be caused by other things than my doing my homework, so the increase in someone's heart rate may be caused by other things than exercise. So when a scientist tries to discover the cause of increase in heart rate, he/she tries to reduce all the variables (for example the arrival of girl/boyfriend) so that a single cause can be identified. Science seems to show that, when investigated sufficiently, any effect has a cause and any cause has an effect.

The argument from causation

The appearance of causation in the world is often called the First Cause Argument and goes like this:

> If we look at things in the world, we see that they have a cause; for example, ice is caused by the temperature falling and water becoming solid at below 0°C.

> Anything caused to exist must be caused to exist by something else because to cause your own existence, you would have to exist before you exist, which is nonsense.

> You cannot keep going back with causes because in any causal chain you have to have a beginning; for example, you have to have water to produce ice.
> So if the universe has no First Cause, then there would be no universe, but as there is a universe, there must be a First Cause.

> The only possible First Cause of the universe is God, therefore God must exist.

This argument makes people think that the universe, the world and humans must have come from somewhere, they must have had a cause. As God is the only logical cause of the universe, it makes them think that God must exist, or it supports their belief in God if they already believe.

People who believe that causation proves that God exists often use the example of a goods train. Each wagon is caused to move by the wagon that is pulling it. But although each wagon is caused to move by another wagon, which is caused to move by another wagon, etc., the whole process can only be explained if there is an engine that is not moved by something in front but is 'an unmoved mover'. In the same way, the process seen in the world – of things being caused or moved by something else – can only be explained if there is an Unmoved Mover causing it all to happen and this could only be God.

Does the universe need a First Cause? If so, and that First Cause is God, does God need a cause?

Why some people disagree with the argument

Some people may think the argument from causation does not prove that God exists because:

- Why should the causes stop at God? If everything needs a cause then God must need a cause.
- A better explanation is that the matter of the Universe itself is eternal and so the process of causes goes on for ever.
- Even if the First Cause were to exist it would not have to be God, it could be any sort of creator.

Whatever is moved must be moved by another. If that by which it is moved, be itself moved, then this also must needs be moved by another, and that by another again. But this cannot go on to infinity, because then there would be no first mover, and consequently no other mover ... Therefore it is necessary to arrive at a first mover, moved by no other; and this everyone understands to be God.
From *Summa Theologica* by St Thomas Aquinas

◄ People who believe in the First Cause often use the example of a line of railway wagons, claiming that just as the wagons need an engine to explain how they are moving, so the universe needs God to explain how it is working.

Questions

b Do you think God is the cause of the universe? Give two reasons for your point of view. **4**

c Explain how the argument from causation may lead to belief in God. **8**

d 'The argument from causation proves that God exists.'
 i Do you agree? Give reasons for your opinion. **3**
 ii Give reasons why some people may disagree with you. **3**

Exam Tip

c To answer this question, you need to outline the argument and make sure you emphasise the conclusion (the last step in the flowchart and the first paragraph after the flowchart) so that you show exactly how it might lead to belief in God. For tips on Quality of Written Communication, look at page 3.

SUMMARY

The way everything seems to have a cause makes people think the universe must have a cause, and the only possible cause of the universe is God, so God must exist.

Topic 3.1.5 Scientific explanations of the world and agnosticism and atheism

KEY WORDS

Agnosticism – not being sure whether God exists.

Atheism – believing that God does not exist.

An alternative to the Big Bang?

Scientists from Princeton University claim that the universe began not with a Big Bang but a collision with another universe.

According to the scientists, a weak attraction brought two universes together, creating a collision that made particles and energy. The scientists claim that the theory explains many observations of the universe better than the Big Bang.

Recent observations of background radiation from the 'edges' of the cosmos, relics of early moments of the universe, reveal a startling homogeneity in all directions.

The Big Collision would have created almost instantaneously the energy and matter in all regions of the newly blossoming universe. This explains the consistency or smoothness of the universe. The new model allows for the slight ripples in the cosmic fabric that created the seeds for the formation of galaxies and large-scale structure in the universe, the researchers said.

***Science Journal,** April 2002*

Science explains how the world came into being in this way:

- Matter is eternal, it can neither be created nor destroyed, it can only be changed (scientists call this the law of thermo-dynamics).
- About 15 billion years ago, the matter of the universe became so compressed that it produced a huge explosion (the Big Bang).
- As the matter of the universe flew away from the explosion, the forces of gravity and other laws of science joined some of the matter into stars and, about 5 billion years ago, the solar system was formed.
- The combination of gases on the Earth's surface produced primitive life forms, like amoeba.
- The genetic structure of these life forms produces changes (mutations).
- Any change that is better suited to living in the environment will survive and reproduce.
- Over millions of years new life forms were produced leading to vegetation, then invertebrate animals, then vertebrates and finally, about 2.5 million years ago, humans evolved.

Evidence for the Big Bang

The main evidence for the Big Bang theory is called the Red Shift Effect (shown below) where the red shift in light from other

galaxies is evidence that the universe is expanding.

Evidence for evolution

The evidence for the theory of evolution is the fossil record (the evidence from fossils of life developing from simple to complex), and the similarities between life forms being discovered through genetic research (about 50 per cent of human DNA is the same as that of a cabbage).

How the scientific explanation of the world may lead to agnosticism or atheism

Science can explain where the world came from and where humans came from without any reference to God. This may lead some people to be **agnostic**, that is they are unsure whether there is a God or not. The argument that you need God to explain why we are here is no longer valid for them.

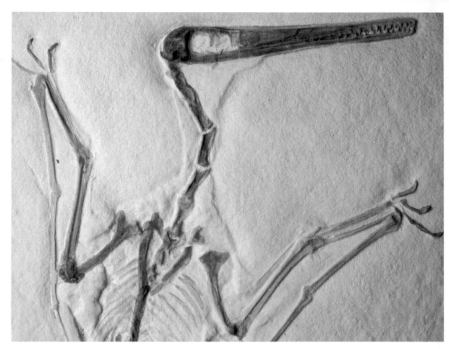

This Pterodactylus dinosaur fossil is from the Late Jurassic era (over 145.5 million years ago).

Other people may be led to become **atheists** and be sure there is no God because they believe that, if God exists, he must have made the world and he must be the only explanation of the world. The scientific explanation of the world and humans without any reference to God is proof to such people that God does not exist.

Questions

b Do you think science shows that God did not design the world? Give two reasons for your point of view. **4**

c Explain why the scientific explanation of the world leads some people to become atheists or agnostics. **8**

d 'Science proves that God did not create the universe.'
  i Do you agree? Give reasons for your opinion. **3**
  ii Give reasons why some people may disagree with you. **3**

Exam Tip

d Use the answering evaluation questions advice from page 9. The arguments for the statement are in this topic, the arguments against are in Topic 3.1.6.

SUMMARY

Science says that matter is eternal and that the universe began when this matter exploded. The solar system came out of the explosion, and the nature of the Earth allowed life to develop through evolution.

Topic 3.1.6 How Catholics respond to scientific explanations of the world

There are two main Catholic responses to scientific explanations of the world.

Response 1

Many Catholics believe that the scientific explanations are true. However, they believe that the scientific explanation does not mean that everyone should be agnostic or atheist. They believe that the scientific explanation proves that God created the universe because of such reasons as:

- The Big Bang had to be at exactly the right micro second. If it had been too soon it would have been too small to form stars; if it had been too late, everything would have flown away too fast for stars to form.
- There had to be scientific laws such as gravity for the matter of the universe to form solar systems, and only God could have made the laws on which the universe is based.
- Life on Earth requires carbon to be able to bond with four other atoms and water molecules. This could not have happened by chance, so God must have ensured it happened.

Can you explain how the solar ▶ system works without using the laws of gravity and motion created by God?

Response 2

Some Catholics believe that both the scientific explanations and the Bible are correct. They claim that the main points of the Bible story fit with science. One of God's days could be millions or billions of years. They claim that Genesis 1:3 'God said, "Let there be light"', is a direct reference to the Big Bang and that the order in which God creates life as described in Genesis – plants, trees, fish, birds, animals, humans – is the same order as described in the theory of evolution for the development of species.

Can we know how God created the world?

The Vatican observatory is one of the most specialised in the world and the Pontifical Academy of Science conducts leading international research projects. As part of a renewed commitment to the dialogue between faith and science, there has been a recognition that the truth of faith and the truth of science must be respected. As a result, the work of Galileo, previously condemned by the Church, has been recognised.

The question about the origins of the world and of man has been the object of many scientific studies that have splendidly enriched our knowledge of the age and dimensions of the cosmos, the development of life forms and the appearance of man. These discoveries invite us to even greater admiration for the greatness of the Creator.
Catechism of the Catholic Church 283

Questions
b Do you think the scientific explanation of the universe shows that God exists? Give two reasons for your point of view. **4**
c Explain how Catholics respond to scientific explanations of the world. **8**
d 'Science needs God to explain the universe.'
  i Do you agree? Give reasons for your opinion. **3**
  ii Give reasons why some people may disagree with you. **3**

Exam Tip
c 'Explain how' means explaining the responses of Catholics to the scientific explanation. You should take two responses and explain each in detail. For tips on Quality of Written Communication, look at page 3.

SUMMARY
Many Catholics accept the scientific explananations but believe they show that God created the universe through the Big Bang.

Some Catholics believe that both science and the Bible are true because one of God's days could be billions of years.

Topic 3.1.7 Why unanswered prayers may lead to agnosticism or atheism

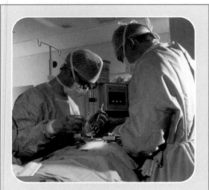

Prayer appears to have no effect on patients undergoing heart surgery, a new study has found. Researchers at Duke University Medical Center in North Carolina followed the progress of 750 patients, half of whom were prayed for by a team of Christians, Jews, Buddhists and Muslims. Those who were prayed for fared no better than those who were not.

The Times, 18 October 2003

If God exists, shouldn't those who are prayed for have better results than those who are not?

As can be seen in Topic 3.1.2 How religious experience may lead to belief in God (pages 4–7), one reason for people believing in God is that when they pray, they feel the presence of God and/or their prayers seem to be answered by God. However, prayer can also lead people to become agnostics or atheists.

Not feeling God's presence when praying

Prayer can be defined as 'an attempt to contact God, usually through words'. So when people pray, they are attempting to contact God. Many religious people claim that when they pray, they feel that God is there listening to their prayers.

However, other people say their prayers in church and at home, but never feel the presence of God when they pray. This is likely to make them feel that something is wrong: either they are not praying correctly, or there is no God listening to them. They may ask for advice from people they respect within the religion and try even harder in their praying. But if, despite all their efforts, they still have no feeling of the presence of God when they pray, then they may begin to question whether God is there at all. In other words the feeling that no one is listening to their prayers may lead them to agnosticism, or even atheism.

Prayers not being answered

Even more likely to make people reject belief in God are unanswered prayers. Christians believe that God is their loving heavenly father who will answer their prayers. In some churches, they are likely to be told of people whose prayers have been answered by God. For example, many Catholic Christians believe that St Jude is the patron saint for those who have no other hope of help and many Catholics believe that St Jude has helped them after they prayed to him. This is one example from a Catholic Christian.

Example of an answered prayer

I spent five years with a boyfriend who would not commit himself to marriage. I was severely depressed and prayed to St Jude for help. With St Jude's intervention, my prayers were finally answered, and at last I am happily married.
Thank you St Jude, I promise to let your good deeds be known to all.

However, if another person prays, and their prayer is not answered, they may begin to wonder about a God who answers some people's prayers, but not others.

If parents have a child suffering from leukaemia, for example, and they pray to God for help, yet the child still dies, this may make them question or reject the existence of God. If there was a God who helped Jairus' daughter recover from a life-threatening disease, surely he would have helped their child recover. As their child did not recover, they may begin to think that God does not exist.

If prayers continue to be unanswered, especially if the person believes they are praying for good things like the end of wars, or the end of a terrible drought in a developing country, then the unanswered prayers become evidence that God does not exist. In this way, unanswered prayers can lead a person to become an agnostic or an atheist.

A young missionary couple asked the members of their church to pray that they would have a safe journey to their new posting in Nepal. However, the plane crashed killing them and their three young children.

Quoted in *If I were God I'd Say Sorry*

Why do you think the church's prayers were unanswered?

Questions

b Do you think unanswered prayers prove that God does not exist? Give two reasons for your point of view. **4**

c Explain why unanswered prayers may lead some people to become atheists. **8**

d 'God always answers prayers.'
  i Do you agree? Give reasons for your opinion. **3**
  ii Give reasons why some people may disagree with you. **3**

Exam Tip

d Use the answering evaluation questions advice from page 9. Evidence for God answering prayers is in Topic 3.1.8. Evidence against God answering prayers is in this topic.

SUMMARY

If people do not feel God's presence when they pray, or if people pray for good things, but their prayers are not answered, this might make some people doubt God's existence. If God does not answer prayers, how do you know he exists?

Topic 3.1.8 How Catholics respond to unanswered prayers

> *Do not be troubled if you do not immediately receive from God what you ask him; for he desires to do something even greater for you, while you cling to him in prayer.*
>
> **Catechism of the Catholic Church 2737**

> *Gracious Lord, oh bomb the Germans*
> *Spare their women for Thy Sake,*
> *And if that is not too easy*
> *We will pardon Thy Mistake,*
> *But, gracious Lord, whate'er shall be,*
> *Don't let anyone bomb me.*
>
> *In Westminster Abbey*, John Betjeman
>
> **Why do you think God might not have answered this prayer supposedly made by an Englishwoman during the Second World War?**

> *Some even stop paraying because they think their petition is not heard. Here two questions should be asked: Why do we think our petition has not been heard? How is our prayer heard, how is it efficacious?*
>
> **Catechism of the Catholic Church 2734**

Most Catholics believe that God answers all prayers and that what seem to be unanswered prayers can be explained in many different ways.

- If what you pray for is selfish, for example, 'Please God, help me to pass this exam', it would be wrong of God to allow you to pass the exam if you had not revised for it. So God is answering your prayer by encouraging you to work hard for what you want to achieve.
- If what you pray for is personal, for example, 'Please cure my Grandad from his cancer', your prayer may not be answered in the way you expect because God has different plans and may be wanting your Grandad to enter **heaven**.
- Human parents do not always give their children what they ask for, but they do give them what they need. In the same way God may be answering our prayer by giving us what we need rather than what we have asked for.
- Catholics believe that God loves people and they trust God's love to do what is best for them. They believe that God's **omnipotence** and **benevolence** mean that he knows them better than they know themselves, therefore they trust God to answer their prayers in the best possible way, even though it does not look like a direct answer.
- Jesus said that his followers must have faith to have their prayers answered. Modern Catholics have faith that God will answer all prayers in a way designed for the long-term good of the person praying, or the people prayed for, even though God's way might be a different way from the expected one.

Why do you think people pray ▶ in times of stress and danger?

Why do you think people pray after a disaster has struck them?

Questions

b Do you think prayer is a waste of time? Give two reasons
for your point of view. **4**

c Explain how Catholics respond to unanswered prayers. **8**

d 'Unanswered prayers prove that God does not exist.'

    i Do you agree? Give reasons for your opinion. **3**

    ii Give reasons why some people may disagree with you. **3**

Exam Tip

d You should already have thought about this, and you just have to
give two reasons for your opinion. For example, if you think prayer
is not a waste of time, you could use these two reasons:

- For people who believe in God, prayer is the best way to
improve their relationship with God.
- If God answers your prayers, for example, by helping you pass
an exam, you are not going to think prayer is waste of time.

SUMMARY

Catholics believe that God
cannot answer selfish prayers.
But, he answers all other
prayers, though not always in
the way people expect, because
his answers have to fit in with
his overall plans.

Topic 3.1.9 Evil and suffering

Evil and suffering can take two forms:

1. Moral evil

This is evil that is caused by humans misusing their **free will** (the human faculty of making choices). It is always possible to choose to do something good or something evil. Humans choosing to do evil makes a **moral evil**.

War is a good example of moral evil. Wars cause large amounts of suffering. Not only are military personnel on both sides made to suffer, but modern warfare also involves the use of weapons that kill and maim large numbers of innocent civilians. All wars are caused by the actions of humans who could have chosen to act differently. Suicide bombers actively choose to cause suffering to innocent people, who are likely to include babies and children, in order to draw attention to their cause.

Rape, murder and burglary are clear examples of moral evil. Less clear would be such suffering as famines where humans making wrong choices may have caused the suffering, for example, landowners growing **cash crops** like cotton instead of food in order to make more money. However, the famine could have been caused by something out of the control of humans, such as a lack of rain.

Christians often call acts of moral evil **sins** because they are against what God wants humans to do (as revealed to them, for example, in the **Ten Commandments**).

You shall not murder.
You shall not commit **adultery.**
You shall not steal.
You shall not give false testimony ...
You shall not covet ...
The last five of the *Ten Commandments*, **Exodus 20:13–17**

Would breaking these lead to moral evil?

Burglaries cause much suffering ▶ by the actions of humans.

2. Natural evil

Natural evil is suffering that has not been caused by humans. Earthquakes, floods, volcanoes, drought, tsunamis, hurricanes, tornadoes, cancers and so on are not actually caused by humans, but they result in massive amounts of human suffering. However, the destruction of the natural environment by humans does lead to the balance of nature being upset and more disasters happening.

A mother crying after her home has been destroyed by an earthquake. Would a good omnipotent God cause so much suffering?

The aftermath of the tsunami of December 2004 in Southeast Asia. This event caused many people to ask how God could let something like that happen.

21

How evil and suffering cause people to question or reject belief in God

Some people cannot believe that a good God would have designed a world with natural evils in it. If they had been God, they would not have created a world with floods, earthquakes, volcanoes, cancers, etc.; and, as they believe God must be better than them, they cannot believe that God would have done so. They find it easier to believe that these features are a result of the Earth evolving by accident from the Big Bang and so they question or reject God's existence.

When British and ▶ American troops liberated concentration camps in 1945 it made many of the soldiers doubt God's existence. Why do you think this was?

Some people cannot believe in a God who allows humans to cause so much evil and suffering when he could stop it if he wanted to. If God exists, he must have known what Adolf Hitler would do, so why did he not give Hitler a heart attack before all the suffering caused by the Second World War and the Holocaust? As the suffering was not stopped, this may mean that God does not exist.

Philosophers express the problem in this way:
- If God is **omnipotent** (all-powerful), he must be able to remove evil and suffering from the world.
- If God is **omni-benevolent** (all-good), he must want to remove evil and suffering from the world because they cause so much unhappiness.
- It follows that, if God exists, there should be no evil or suffering in the world.
- As there is evil and suffering in the world, either God is not omnipotent, or God is not omni-benevolent, or God does not exist.

This is often connected with God's omniscience, because if God knows everything that is going to happen, he must have known all the evil and suffering that would come from creating the universe in the way he did. Therefore he should have created the universe in a different way to avoid evil and suffering.

Most religious believers (especially Christians, Jews and Muslims) believe that God is omnipotent, omni-benevolent and **omniscient**. So the existence of evil and suffering challenges their beliefs about God, and as these beliefs come from their **holy** books, it challenges the whole of their religion.

For many religious believers evil and suffering become a problem when they come into contact with it. So, if they experience the suffering caused by a natural disaster like an earthquake, or if their child dies from a disease, the problem can sometimes change them into an atheist or agnostic.

El Salvador's highest volcano Llamatepec erupted in October 2005 making tens of thousands of people homeless.

Questions

b Do you think evil and suffering show that God does not exist? Give two reasons for your point of view. **4**

c Explain how the existence of evil and suffering may lead some people to deny God's existence. **8**

d 'A loving God would not let us suffer.'
  i Do you agree? Give reasons for your opinion. **3**
  ii Give reasons why some people may disagree with you. **3**

Exam Tip

c Look at the problems caused to people's lives by evil and suffering and explain why these may stop them believing in God – remember to include the philosophers' explanation. For tips on Quality of Written Communication, look at page 3.

SUMMARY

Some people do not believe in God because they think that there would be no evil and suffering in a world created by a good and powerful God. A good God should not want such things to happen, and a powerful God ought to be able to get rid of them but does not.

Topic 3.1.10 How Catholics respond to the problem of evil and suffering

> *Then the righteous will answer him, 'Lord, when did we see you hungry and feed you, or thirsty and give you something to drink? When did we see you a stranger and invite you in, or needing clothes and clothe you? When did we see you sick or in prison and go to visit you?' The King will reply, 'I tell you the truth, whatever you did for one of the least of these brothers of mine, you did for me.'*
>
> **Matthew 25:37–40**

There are several Catholic responses to the problem of evil and suffering, and most Catholics would combine at least two to explain why evil and suffering is compatible with God's omni-benevolence and omnipotence. However, almost all Catholics would begin with response one.

Response One

Catholics believe that God wants them to help those who suffer. The **New Testament** teaches Catholics that Jesus regarded evil and suffering as something to be fought against. Jesus healed the sick, fed the hungry, challenged those who were evil, and even raised the dead.

Catholics feel that they should follow the example of Jesus and fight against evil and suffering by:

- praying for those who suffer. This is called intercessionary prayer and all Christian services include prayers of **intercession** asking God to help those who suffer from poverty, sickness, famine, war, and so on. Catholics believe that prayer is a powerful way of dealing with a problem.
- helping those who suffer. Many Catholics become doctors, nurses, social workers, for example, so that they can help to reduce the amount of suffering in the world. Catholics have also founded charities to help to eliminate suffering, such as the St Vincent de Paul Society to help the poor and homeless, and CAFOD to help to ease the suffering of those in less economically developed countries (**LEDCs**).

Christ's actions were focused on those who were suffering. Four of his beatitudes are addressed to people who are afflicted. He suffered fatigue, homelessness, misunderstanding, hostility, torture and death on the cross. Catholics also pray to Mary as the mother of those in sorrow because she saw her own son suffer.

Response Two

Many Catholics respond by claiming that evil and suffering are not God's fault. According to Genesis 1, God created humans in his image, which means he created them with free will. They claim that God wanted people to be free to decide whether to believe in God or not. To be free means to be free to do either good or evil, and so God could not have created people who always did the good. So evil and suffering are a problem caused by humans, and are not God's fault.

A CAFOD (Catholic Agency for Overseas Development) partner with armed child soldiers. Do you think Christian workers feel compelled to do this kind of work by the words of Jesus in Matthew 25?

Response Three

Often connected with the free will response is the Christian belief that the evil and suffering in this life are not a problem because they are part of a plan in which those who suffer will be rewarded by eternal paradise after they die.

Most Catholics claim that this life is a preparation for paradise. If people are to improve their souls they need to face evil and suffering in order to become good, kind and loving. They claim that the evil and suffering of this life is something God cannot remove if he is going to give people the chance to become good people. But, in the end, he will show his omni-benevolence and omnipotence by rewarding them in heaven.

Catholics often connect this to the belief that good can come out of evil. For example, in the evil of the Holocaust, Maximilian Kolbe, a Franciscan friar, was arrested and sent to Auschwitz. Here he continued his priestly ministry discreetly, hearing many confessions and smuggling in bread and wine for Mass. When a married man with children was to be executed, Maximilian offered to take his place. He was **canonised** in 1982, when the man whose life he saved was still living, and able to attend the ceremony in Rome.

Response Four

Many Catholics believe that there is no point in worrying about the problem because humans cannot understand God's reasons for doing things. God must have a reason for allowing evil and suffering, but humans cannot know what it is because they are not God. However, Catholics know from the life of Jesus that even God's own Son had to suffer, and that Jesus commanded his followers to respond to suffering by helping those who suffer. They believe that Catholics should respond to the problem by helping those who suffer and trusting in God for the answer to the problem.

SUMMARY

Catholics respond to the problem of evil and suffering by:

- praying for and helping those who suffer
- claiming that evil and suffering are the fault of humans misusing their free will
- claiming that evil and suffering are part of a test to prepare people for heaven.

Some Catholics believe that God has a reason for allowing evil and suffering, but humans are too limited to understand it.

Questions

b Do you think God allows us to suffer? Give two reasons for your point of view. **4**

c Explain how Catholics respond to the problem of evil and suffering. **8**

d 'Evil and suffering in the world prove that God does not exist.'
  i Do you agree? Give reasons for your opinion. **3**
  ii Give reasons why some people may disagree with you. **3**

Topic 3.1.11 How two programmes about religion may affect a person's attitude to belief in God

A *Seaside Parish* was a fly-on-the-wall documentary about the work of a divorced, re-married woman priest, Reverend Christine Musser, as the new vicar of Boscastle, an insular coastal village in Cornwall with a thriving pagan as well as Christian community. It proved surprisingly popular and is now into its third series.

You have to study two programmes about religion in depth and assess how they could affect a person's attitude to belief in God.

The programmes do not have to be factual programmes about religion (for example, a worship programme like *Songs of Praise*, a reality show like *The Convent*, or *A Seaside Parish*, a documentary like *The Miracles of Jesus*, or a discussion programme like *The Sunday Edition*). The crucial thing about the programmes is that they should be about belief in God, so programmes like *The Simpsons* and *The Vicar of Dibley* could be used as long as they have sufficient content about belief in God. Your programme does not have to be on television, it could be a radio programme or a film.

When you have chosen your two programmes, you need to make notes on the following for each of them:

1. Write a summary of the programme.

2. Decide which parts of the programme might have encouraged belief in God in some people and write down four reasons (using evidence from the programme) for this.

3. Decide which parts of the programme might have encouraged some people not to believe in God and write down four reasons (using evidence from the programme) for this.

4. Decide what effect the programme had on your own attitude to belief in God and write down four reasons for this.

Sample programme – *Songs of Praise*

On Sunday 3 February 2008, *Songs of Praise* came from St Wilfred's, Harrogate. Although the interviews at the Royal Pump Room Museum and at St Wilfred's Church might have had little effect on people's attitude to belief in God, two other interviews, and the hymns might have because they enabled people to have a religious experience.

Mark Pallant, Head of Music at St Aidan's Church of England High School, talked about his own faith, and how he feels that music can put people in touch with God, the creator of the universe. If you had watched this programme, you would need to note the points Mark made and decide whether they would encourage you to believe in God. If not, you would need to write

Where have we come from?

Why are we here?

How should we live?

BBC Religion exists to ask the big questions that underlie all human life and explore the different ways in which people try to answer them, whether through worship, prayer, or simply giving food for thought.

The aim of Religious Broadcasting by the BBC

down reasons why they did not affect your beliefs. Then you would need to note down reasons why some people might disagree with you.

Phil Willis, the MP for Harrogate, talked about how he changed from an agnostic to a Christian through someone he used to teach with. You would need to note the points Phil made and decide whether they would encourage you to believe in God. If not, you would need to write down reasons why they did not affect your beliefs. Then you would need to note down reasons why some people might disagree with you.

You would need to watch the singing of the hymns, listen to the music and think about the words to gain evidence about whether or not they would influence attitudes to belief in God. Remember you need evidence for your point of view and why some people might disagree with you.

Phil Willis, the Liberal Democrat MP for Harrogate.

Sample programme – *The Sunday Edition*

On 27 December 2006, *The Sunday Edition*, which is an ITV politics programme, broadcast an edition on the nature of religion. The programme featured a discussion between Tony Benn, a Christian agnostic and ex-Labour minister, and Richard Dawkins, an outspoken atheist, Professor of Biology and author of *The God Delusion*.

If you watched this programme, you would need to note what things were said that might make people disbelieve in God, and what things were said that might make people believe in God. You would then need to decide what you thought about the programme and why.

Questions

b Do you think programmes about religion can affect your belief in God? Give two reasons for your point of view. **4**

c Choose one programme about religion and explain how it might affect someone's belief about God. **8**

d 'Religious programmes on television or the radio encourage you to believe in God.'
  i Do you agree? Give reasons for your opinion. **3**
  ii Give reasons why some people may disagree with you. **3**

Exam Tip

d Use the answering evaluation questions advice from page 9. Evidence for your own opinion will come from your notes about how the programme affected your attitude to belief in God. Evidence for why some people might disagree with you will come from your notes on the programme either on how it encouraged or how it discouraged belief in God.

SUMMARY

You need to study two programmes or films about religion. For each of them, you will need to know:

- an outline of its contents
- how it might have encouraged some people to believe in God
- how it might have encouraged some people not to believe in God
- whether it affected your beliefs about God.

How to answer exam questions

Question A What is atheism?   2 marks

Atheism is believing that there is no God.

Question B Do you think God is the cause of the universe?
Give two reasons for your point of view.   4 marks

Yes I do think that God is the cause of the universe because everything needs a cause and God is the only thing that could have created something as big as the universe. Also I am a Christian and it is one of the beliefs of Christianity that God created the universe. In fact it says so in the creed.

Question C Explain how a religious upbringing can lead to, or support, belief in God.   8 marks

Christians usually teach their children to pray to God. This will make the children believe that God exists because otherwise their parents would not want them to pray to him. If God did not exist, they and their parents would not waste their time praying to nothing. Also they may feel God's presence when they pray. So because they've been brought up to pray, they believe that God must exist.

Another feature of a Christian upbringing is going to church. When children go to church they see lots of people praying to God and worshipping God and this is bound to make them think that God must exist because all these people believe he does.

Many Christian parents also send their children to a Church school. Here they will have RE lessons which teach them that God exists and the children are likely to believe it because their teachers tell them it is true.

Question D 'Considering the evidence, everyone should be an agnostic.'

 i Do you agree? Give reasons for your opinion.   3 marks

 ii Give reasons why some people may disagree with you.   3 marks

i I do not agree because I am a Catholic and I believe there is evidence for believing in God. The universe must have been caused by someone or something because every effect has a cause. The only possible cause of the universe is God so he must exist. Then there is the evidence of the laws of science which keep the universe in being. They must have been designed and their only possible designer is God. Finally, there is the evidence of my own experience, when I go to Mass, I feel God's presence. So the evidence leads to belief in God, not agnosticism.

ii I can see why some people would disagree with me because evidence such as design can be used both for and against God's existence. The Design Argument seems to prove God's existence, but the Big Bang seems to disprove it. In the same way the First Cause argument seems to prove God's existence, but then there is the question of what caused God. Then the religious evidence to prove God's existence such as miracles, holy books etc., can be explained in non-religious ways. So, it seems logical to say there is not enough evidence either way, so they are agnostics.

QUESTION A
High marks because it is a correct definition.

QUESTION B
A high mark answer because an opinion is backed up by two developed reasons.

QUESTION C
A high mark answer because it begins with a developed reason on how being taught to pray leads to belief in God. This is backed up by two further reasons – going to worship and going to a Church school. It is written in a formal style of English in sentences and paragraphs. The spelling is good and it uses specialist vocabulary such as prayer, worship, church, God's presence.

QUESTION D
A high mark answer because it states the candidate's own opinion and backs it up with three clear reasons for thinking that the evidence for God's existence is greater than the evidence for agnosticism. It then gives three reasons for people disagreeing and believing that the evidence shows that everyone should be agnostic.

Section 3.2 **Matters of life and death**

Introduction

This section of the examination specification requires you to look at issues surrounding life after death, abortion, euthanasia, the media and matters of life and death, and Catholicism and world poverty.

Life after death
You will need to understand the effects of, and give reasons for your own opinion about:
- why Catholics believe in life after death and how this belief affects their lives
- non-religious reasons for believing in life after death (near-death experiences, ghosts, mediums and evidence of reincarnation)
- why some people do not believe in life after death.

Abortion
You will need to understand the effects of, and give reasons for your own opinion about:
- the nature of abortion, including current British legislation, and why abortion is a controversial issue
- different Christian attitudes to abortion and the reasons for them.

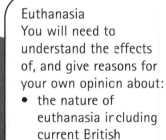

Euthanasia
You will need to understand the effects of, and give reasons for your own opinion about:
- the nature of euthanasia including current British legislation, and why euthanasia is a controversial issue
- different Christian attitudes to euthanasia and the reasons for them.

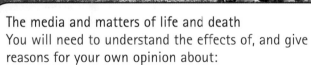

The media and matters of life and death
You will need to understand the effects of, and give reasons for your own opinion about:
- arguments over whether the media should or should not be free to criticise religious attitudes to matters of life and death
- how an issue from matters of life and death has been presented in one form of the media, including whether the treatment was fair to religious beliefs and religious people.

World poverty
You will need to understand the effects of, and give reasons for your own opinion about:
- the causes of world poverty
- how and why CAFOD is trying to end world poverty.

Topic 3.2.1 Why Catholics believe in life after death and how this affects their lives

For what I received I passed on to you as of first importance: that Christ died for our sins according to the Scriptures, that he was buried, that he was raised on the third day according to the Scriptures, and that he appeared to Peter, and then to the Twelve ... But if it is preached that Christ has been raised from the dead, how can some of you say that there is no resurrection of the dead ... For as in Adam all die, so in Christ all will be made alive.

1 Corinthians 15: 3–5, 12, 22

Why Catholics believe in life after death

Catholics believe that this life is not all there is. They believe God will reward the good and punish the bad in some form of life after death. Catholics believe in life after death because:

- The main Catholic belief is that Jesus rose from the dead. All four **Gospels** record that Jesus was crucified and buried in a stone tomb. They also record that, on the Sunday morning, some of his women disciples went to the tomb and found it empty. Different Gospels then record different 'resurrection appearances' of Jesus. The rest of the New Testament is full of references to the **resurrection** of Jesus. Clearly, if Jesus rose from the dead, then there is life after death.
- St Paul teaches in 1 Corinthians 15 that people will have a resurrection like that of Jesus, and will have a spiritual resurrection body given to them by God.
- The major **creeds** of the Church teach that Jesus rose from the dead and that there will be life after death. Catholics follow the teaching in the creeds about life after death.
- Most Catholics believe in the **immortality of the soul**. They believe that when the body dies, the soul leaves the body to live with God.
- The Catholic Church teaches that there is life after death. The Catechism is very clear there is life after death. The Catechism represents the teaching of the **Magisterium**, which all Catholics should believe, and so Catholics should believe in life after death.
- Many Catholics believe in life after death because it gives their lives meaning and purpose. They feel that for life to end at death does not make sense. A life after death, in which people will be judged on how they live this life with the good rewarded and the evil punished, makes sense of this life.

How beliefs about life after death affect the lives of Catholics

1. Many Catholics believe that they will be judged by God after death and that only if they have lived a good Catholic life will they be allowed into heaven. This means that Catholics will try to live a good Catholic life following the teachings of the Bible and the Church so that they go to heaven and not **purgatory** or **hell** when they die.

2. Living a good Catholic life means following scripture, tradition and the teaching authority of the church. The teachings of Jesus taught that the two greatest commandments are to love God and to love your neighbour as yourself. So Catholics' lives will be affected as

I believe in ... the resurrection of the body and the life everlasting.

Apostles' Creed

◀ No one knows what heaven is like, some Christians believe it will be approached through the tunnel of light seen in near-death experiences.

they try to love God by praying and by worshipping God as well as attending Mass every Sunday.

3. Trying to love your neighbour as yourself is bound to affect a Catholic's life. In the Parable of the Sheep and Goats, Jesus said that only those who fed the hungry, clothed the naked, befriended strangers, visited the sick and those in prison, would be allowed into heaven. This is a similar teaching to the Good Samaritan where Jesus taught that loving your neighbour means helping anyone in need. These teachings are bound to affect Catholics' lives and explains why Catholic charities like CAFOD are so involved in helping those in need.

4. Catholics believe that sin prevents people from going to heaven. The Catholic Church teaches that those who die with unforgiven sins will go to purgatory to be purified before they can reach heaven. Clearly these teachings mean that Catholics will try to avoid committing sins in their lives so that they will go to heaven.

5. Catholic beliefs about life after death give their lives meaning and purpose. Living your life with a purpose and believing that this life has meaning, both affect the way you live. It may be why in surveys Christians suffer less from depression and are less likely to commit suicide than atheists and agnostics.

> *Jesus links faith in the resurrection to his own person: 'I am the Resurrection and the life'. It is Jesus himself who on the Last Day will raise up those who have believed in him.*
>
> **Catechism of the Catholic Church 994**

> *Every action of yours, every thought, should be those of one who expects to die before the day is out. Death would have no terrors for you if you had a quiet conscience.*
>
> *The Imitation of Christ* **by Thomas à Kempis (a medieval saint)**

Questions

b Do you think Catholics are right to believe in life after death? Give two reasons for your point of view. **4**

c Explain why Catholics believe in life after death. **8**

d 'Catholics only believe in life after death because they're scared of dying.'
  i Do you agree? Give reasons for your opinion. **3**
  ii Give reasons why some people may disagree with you. **3**

Exam Tip

c 'Explain' means give reasons. To answer this question you should give four reasons why Catholics believe in life after death and make each of them into a short paragraph. For tips on Quality of Written Communication, look at page 3.

SUMMARY

Catholics believe in life after death because:

- Jesus rose from the dead
- The Bible and the creeds say there is life after death
- The Church teaches that there is life after death
- The soul is something that can never die.

Their beliefs about life after death affect their lives because Catholics will try to love God and love their neighbour so that they go to heaven and not purgatory or hell.

Topic 3.2.2 Non-religious reasons for believing in life after death

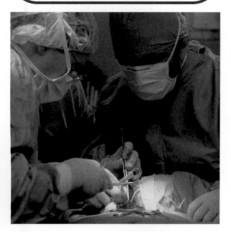

Some people have near-death experiences during heart surgery.

This research is very good work, which is needed to understand the near-death experience, but it proves absolutely nothing about the soul. All claims about this being evidence for consciousness existing without a brain are unfounded, baseless rubbish.

Dr Sue Blackmore

Non-religious reasons for believing in life after death are connected to evidence for the **paranormal**. This can refer to a wide range of things from ghosts to telekinesis (moving objects without touching them). However, there are three main parts of the paranormal that provide reasons for believing in life after death:

1. Near-death experiences

This is a fairly recent phenomenon and happens when people are clinically dead for a period of time and then come back to life. In his research, Dr Sam Parnia of Southampton General Hospital found that four out of 63 patients who had survived a heart attack had **near-death experiences**. Similar research in Holland by Dr Pim van Lommel, in the USA by Dr Raymond Moody and elsewhere in Britain by Dr Peter Fenwick and Dr Sue Blackmore produced similar results.

Frequently quoted in near-death experiences are: feelings of peace and joy; feelings of floating above the body; seeing a bright light; entering another world; meeting dead relatives; coming to a point of no return.

Example of evidence of a near-death experience

Jeanette Mitchell-Meadows had such an experience when she was undergoing major spinal surgery. She felt herself leaving her body and following a bright light to what she thought was heaven. It was very peaceful, she heard music more clear and tuneful than anything on Earth and then she felt she met Jesus. She met her grandparents and her daughter, who had been killed in an accident about six months earlier. She did not want to leave, but was told God had things for her to do on Earth. When she returned to her body she felt great pain.

Clearly, if near-death experiences are true then there is a heaven and there is life after death, but this is not the same as resurrection, as described in the Gospels.

2. Evidence for a spirit world

Ghosts and ouija boards appear to give evidence of the spirits or souls of the dead surviving death, but the clearest evidence seems to come from mediums.

A medium is a person who claims to have the gift of communicating between the material world in which we live and the spirit world inhabited by those who have died. They are sometimes called psychics, clairvoyants or spirit guides.

Mediums exist in all countries and all religions, though they have become more publicised recently. Living TV regularly features mediums in programmes such as: *Street Psychic, Beyond with James van Praagh*, and *Crossing Over with John Edward*.

There are many TV shows featuring mediums. Two of the most famous are Craig and Jane Hamilton-Parker, who claim they met through Craig contacting the spirit of Jane's dead grandmother.

Example of evidence for the spirit world

The medium Stephen O'Brien told Marion Jones that he could see a peasant grandmother figure sitting on a rickety chair outside a wooden shack. She was nodding and looking very happy. Then she told Stephen that she was thanking Marion for helping her grandson and she was speaking the word Cruz. Stephen thought perhaps there was a South American connection. Marion realised that Cruz was the surname of a 10-year-old Mexican boy whose education and health she was sponsoring. She was sure that Stephen O'Brien had contacted the boy's grandmother in the spirit world and had information he could not possibly have known.

If mediums can contact the dead in a spirit world, then there must be a life after death.

3. The evidence of reincarnation

Hindus, Sikhs and Buddhists believe that life after death involves souls being reborn into another body (**reincarnation**). There are many stories of this in India, one of the most famous being reported in July 2002 at the National Conference of Forensic Science in India.

Example of reincarnation

In 1996, Taranjit Singh was born to a poor peasant family and received no education. From the age of two he claimed he had a previous life and had been killed by a motor scooter on 10 September 1992. His present parents took him to the village he said he came from and the village teacher confirmed the accident had happened and introduced him to his original parents whom he recognised. The forensic scientist, Vikram Chauhan, checked the first boy's education and asked Taranjit to write the English and Punjabi alphabets (even though Taranjit had never been taught them). Not only could he write them, but when Vikram tested his handwriting against that of the dead boy, he found they were identical.

We know that memories are extremely fallible. We are quite good at knowing that something happened, but we are very poor at knowing when it happened. It is quite possible that these experiences happened during the recovery or just before the cardiac arrest. To say that they happened when the brain was shut down, I think there is little evidence for that at all.

Dr Chris Freeman, Consultant Psychiatrist

Robert Thouless (President of the Society for Psychical Research) made an encrypted message before he died that would allow mediums to prove that they had contacted him after his death. At least 100 mediums submitted keys to the cypher, but not were correct, whereas a computer program solved it easily. A simple explanation is that Thouless had not survived death and so could not be contacted by mediums.

Adapted from *The Case Against Immortality* by Keith Augustine

---

The theory that mediums communicate with discarnate intelligences becomes even more suspect in the light of experiments in which mediumistic contact has been made with living or demonstrably fictional characters.

From *Paranormal Experiences and Survival of Death* by C. Becker

Example of reincarnation

Crowds are flocking to Indian temples to see a Muslim baby with a tail who is believed to be the reincarnation of a Hindu god. The 11-month-old boy has been named Balaji, another name for monkey-faced Lord Hanuman. He is reported to have a four-inch tail caused by genetic mutations during the development of the foetus. Iqbal Qureshi, the child's maternal grandfather, is taking Balaji from temple to temple where people offer money to see the boy. Mr Qureshi says the baby has nine spots on his body like Lord Hanuman and has shown them to journalists.

Source: The Tribune of India, 2003

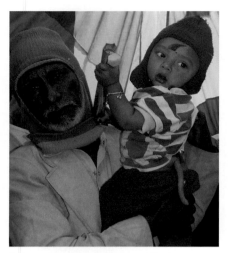

Baby with tail who some Hindus believe to be a reincarnation of a Hindu god.

In only eleven of the approximately 1,111 rebirth cases had there been no contact between the two families before an investigation was begun. Of these, seven were seriously flawed in some respect ... The rebirth cases are anecdotal evidence of the weakest sort.

From *Immortality* **by Paul Edwards**

If these examples are true, then it would be evidence for reincarnation, and so life after death.

The Catholic Response

The Catholic Church rejects the evidence of mediums, ghosts, and so on, as superstitions: 'All forms of divination are to be rejected ... Consulting horoscopes, astrology, palm reading ... the phenomena of clairvoyance and recourse to mediums all ... contradict the honour, respect and loving fear that we owe to God alone' (Catechism of the Catholic Church 2116). The Church also rejects reincarnation: 'It is appointed for men to die once. There is no reincarnation after death' (Catechism of the Catholic Church 1013).

SUMMARY

Some people believe in life after death for non-religious reasons such as:

• near-death experiences when people see things during heart attacks, operations, etc.

• evidence of the spirit world, ghosts, mediums, etc.

• evidence of reincarnation, such as people remembering previous lives.

Questions

b Do you think that some people see ghosts? Give two reasons for your point of view. **4**

c Explain why some people believe that the paranormal proves there is life after death. **8**

d 'The paranormal proves that there is life after death.'
  i Do you agree? Give reasons for your opinion. **3**
  ii Give reasons why some people may disagree with you. **3**

Exam Tip

d Use the answering evaluation questions advice from page 9. The arguments for can be found in this topic. The arguments against could be the quotes in the margin from Sue Blackmore, Chris Freeman, Keith Augustine and Paul Edwards. You could also use some of the arguments from Topic 3.2.3.

Topic 3.2.3 Why some people do not believe in life after death

Not all people believe in life after death. Many people who do not believe in God believe this life is all there is, and, just like animals and plants, humans cease to exist when they die.

They believe this because:

- If there is no God, there is nothing non-material. There is no heaven to go to after death.
- The different religions have different ideas about life after death, whereas, if it were true, they would all say the same things about it. This is especially true of the difference between the reincarnation ideas of Hinduism, Buddhism and Sikhism and the one life leading to **judgement** and heaven and hell of Judaism, Christianity and Islam.
- The evidence for life after death is either based on holy books, and there is no way for a non-believer to decide which holy book should be believed, or the paranormal, which has been criticised by scientists.
- Most beliefs in life after death assume that the mind or soul can survive without the body. But the evidence of science is that the human mind developed as the brain grew more complex, and so the mind cannot exist without the brain (for example, people who are brain dead on a life-support machine).
- There is nowhere for life after death to take place. Space exploration has shown there is no heaven above the sky and physics has shown there is no non-material world on Earth. Where, then, could life after death take place?
- We can only recognise people by their bodies, so how would we recognise souls without bodies? If souls survive death, then they would be alone with no way of contacting other souls, which would not really be life after death.
- Some people have been brought up not to believe in life after death either because their parents are not religious, or because their parents' experience of the death of loved ones is that there is nothing after death.

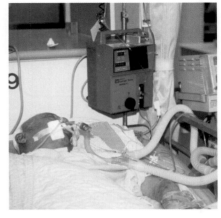

Does a person whose brainstem is dead still have a mind or soul?

Exam Tip

c 'Explain' means give reasons. To answer this question you should use four reasons from this topic, and make each of them into a short paragraph. For tips on Quality of Written Communication, look at page 3.

Questions

b Do you believe there can be a life after death? Give two reasons for your point of view. **4**

c Explain why some people do not believe in life after death. **8**

d 'When you're dead, you're dead and that's the end of you.'

   i Do you agree? Give reasons for your opinion. **3**

   ii Give reasons why some people may disagree with you. **3**

SUMMARY

Some people do not believe in life after death because:

- they do not believe in God
- there is no scientific evidence
- they do not see where life after death could take place.

Topic 3.2.4 The nature of abortion

KEY WORD

Abortion – the removal of a foetus from the womb before it can survive.

Statistics

Number of abortions carried out in England and Wales

1971	94,570
1995	154,315
1999	173,701
2001	176,364
2006	193,700

(89 per cent carried out at under 13 weeks' gestation)

Source: Office of National Statistics

Pro-choice is the name ▶ given to those who support a woman's right to abortion. They do not want women to risk their lives by having operations carried out by non-doctors in bad conditions.

United Kingdom law on abortion

The 1967 Act states that an **abortion** can be carried out if two doctors agree that:

- the mother's life is at risk
- there is a risk of injury to the mother's physical or mental health
- there is a risk that another child would put at risk the mental or physical health of existing children
- there is a substantial risk that the baby might be born seriously handicapped.

The 1990 Act states that abortions cannot take place after 24 weeks of pregnancy, unless the mother's life is gravely at risk or the foetus is likely to be born with severe mental or physical abnormalities, because advances in medical techniques mean that such foetuses have a chance of survival.

Why abortion is a controversial issue

Abortion is a controversial issue because there are so many different issues about abortion itself:

- Many religions, and anti-abortion groups (many of which are religious), believe that life begins at the moment of conception when the male sperm and the female ovum combine. Therefore abortion is wrong because it is taking a human life.
- Many people believe that a baby cannot be considered as a separate life until it is capable of living outside the mother. Therefore abortions before a certain length of pregnancy are not taking life.

- Many non-religious people believe that a woman should have the right to do what she wants with her own body in the same way that men do. They would argue that an unwanted pregnancy is no different from an unwanted tumour. The problems caused to a woman by having an unwanted baby justify her having an abortion.
- Many religious people believe that the unborn child's rights are equivalent to those of the mother and that both the father and the child have claims on the mother's body.
- Some people argue that because foetuses born at 22–24 weeks can now survive, the time limit for abortions should be reduced to 18 or 20 weeks.
- There are also arguments about whether medical staff should have to carry out abortions. Some people argue that they should not be made to act against their conscience; others argue that abortion is just a medical procedure like any other.

Pro-life is the name given to those who support the foetus' right to life and want abortion banned because it denies the foetus' right to life.

If carrying out a particular procedure or giving advice about it conflicts with your religious or moral beliefs, and this conflict might affect the treatment or advice you provide, you must explain this to the patient and tell them they have the right to see another doctor. You must be satisfied that the patient has sufficient information to enable them to exercise that right. If it is not practical for a patient to arrange to see another doctor, you must ensure that arrangements are made for another suitably qualified colleague to take over your role. You must not express to your patients your personal beliefs, including political, religious or moral beliefs, in ways that exploit their vulnerability or that are likely to cause them distress.

Advice to doctors from *Personal Beliefs and Medical Practice* **published by the General Medical Council 2008**

Questions

b Do you agree with abortion? Give two reasons for your point of view. **4**

c Explain why abortion is a controversial issue. **8**

d 'Abortion is always wrong.'
  i Do you agree? Give reasons for your opinion. **3**
  ii Give reasons why some people may disagree with you. **3**

Exam Tip

b You should already have thought about this, and you just have to give two reasons for your opinion. For example, if you do not agree with abortion you could use the first and fourth bullet points from 'Why abortion is a controversial issue' or two Catholic reasons against abortion from Topic 3.2.5. If you agree with abortion you could use the arguments such as of the woman's rights over her body and the foetus not being a human life until it can survive outside the womb from this topic.

SUMMARY

Abortion is allowed in the United Kingdom if two doctors agree that there is medical reason for it.

Abortion is a controversial issue because:

- people disagree about when life begins
- people disagree about whether abortion is murder
- people disagree about whether a woman has the right to choose.

Topic 3.2.5 Different Christian attitudes to abortion

KEY WORD

Sanctity of life – the belief that life is holy and belongs to God.

Christians have two differing attitudes to abortion:

1 The Catholic attitude

The Catholic Church teaches that all direct abortion is wrong whatever the circumstances and so can never be permitted. This teaching is based on scripture, **Apostolic Tradition** and the **Magisterium**. The Church teaches that life begins at the moment of conception. This means that a woman does not have the right to do what she wants with her body after she has become pregnant because the new life has rights. The Church also teaches that because abortion is wrong, all medical staff should have the right to refuse to be involved in abortions. They believe abortion is wrong because:

- Life is holy and belongs to God, therefore only God has the right to end a pregnancy.
- Life begins at conception. Human life begins when an ovum is fertilised and, as there is no break from conception to birth, abortion is therefore taking life.
- The Ten Commandments teach that it is wrong to take life, therefore abortion is wrong.
- Every person has a natural 'right to life'. A foetus is a human being and abortion destroys its right to life, so it follows that abortion is wrong.
- The Church points to evidence that women who have abortions can suffer from traumas leading to guilt complexes and sometimes mental illness.
- They also believe that adoption is always a better solution to unwanted pregnancy than abortion as it preserves life and brings joy to a new family.

Human life must be respected and protected absolutely from the moment of conception. From the first moment of his existence, a human being must be recognised as having the rights of a person – among which is the inviolable right of every innocent being to life ... Abortion and infanticide are abominable crimes ... The law must provide appropriate penal sanctions for every deliberate violation of the child's rights.

Catechism of the Catholic Church 2270–71, 2273

Catholics accept there are difficult issues surrounding abortion, for example if doctors discover that a pregnant mother has cancer and chemotherapy would kill the foetus. In this situation Catholic moral philosophers use the doctrine of double effect – the first effect is to save the mother's life, the second (double) effect is to end the life of the foetus. As the death of the foetus is secondary, and so not intended, an abortion has not occurred.

Before I formed you in the womb I knew you, before you were born I set you apart; I appointed you as a prophet to the nations.

Jeremiah 1:5

Another difficult situation is if a woman becomes pregnant as a result of rape. The Church teaches that one sinful act should not provoke another. With counselling, help and adoption, good can come out of evil in the form of a new life. The **Bishops** of England and Wales issued a statement saying that a rape victim may be given **contraception** to prevent implantation of the rapist's sperm as long as it could be established that conception had not taken place.

The Catholic Church recognises that the decision to have an abortion is often complex and painful: the mother can be under severe psychological pressure from family and friends. Efforts should be made by individuals and politicians to come to the help of families, mothers and children so as to prevent abortion occurring for socio-economic reasons such as poverty etc.

Evangelical Protestant Christians have exactly the same attitude to abortion as Catholics.

2 The Liberal Protestant attitude

Other Christians (mainly **Liberal Protestants**) believe that abortion is wrong, but it must be permitted in certain circumstances such as if the mother has been raped, if the mother's life is at risk or if the foetus is so handicapped that it would have no **quality of life**. Some of these Christians would also allow abortion for social reasons such as poverty and the effects on the rest of the family. These Christians believe that abortion can be permitted in certain circumstances because:

- Jesus told Christians to love their neighbour as themselves, and abortion may be the most loving thing to do.
- They believe life does not begin at conception.
- The **sanctity of life** can be broken in such things as a **just war**, so why not in a just abortion (e.g. when the mother's life is at risk)?
- Christians should accept technological advances in medicine, therefore if doctors have developed amniocentesis tests to detect disease and suffering in a foetus, parents should be allowed abortions on the basis of such tests.
- Christianity is concerned with **justice** and if abortions were banned, an unjust situation would arise. Rich women would pay for abortions in another country, but the poor would use '**back-street**' **abortionists**.

Life is an organisation dedicated to protecting the rights of unborn children. Why do you think Life is supported by Catholics?

Methodists would strongly prefer that through advances in medical science and social welfare, all abortions should become unnecessary. But termination as early as possible in the course of pregnancy may be the lesser of evils. If abortion were made a criminal offence again, the result would be 'one law for the rich and another for the poor', with increased risks of ill-health and death as a result of botched 'back-street' abortions.

Statement by the Methodist Church of England and Wales in *What the Churches Say*

Questions

b Do you think abortion is murder? Give two reasons for your point of view. **4**

c Explain why some Christians allow abortion, but some do not. **8**

d 'No Christian should ever have an abortion.'
  i Do you agree? Give reasons for your opinion. **3**
  ii Give reasons why some people may disagree with you. **3**

Exam Tip

c 'Explain why' means give four brief, or two developed, reasons why some Christians do not allow abortion (Catholics and Evangelical Protestants); and four brief, or two developed, reasons why some Christians allow abortion in certain circumstances (Liberal Protestants). For tips on Quality of Written Communication, look at page 3

SUMMARY

Christians have different attitudes to abortion:

- Some Christians believe that abortion is always wrong because it is murder and against God's will.
- Some Christians believe that abortion is wrong but must be allowed in some circumstances as the lesser of two evils.

Topic 3.2.6 The nature of euthanasia

KEY WORDS

Assisted suicide – providing a seriously ill person with the means to commit suicide.

Euthanasia – the painless killing of someone dying from a painful disease.

Non-voluntary euthanasia – ending someone's life painlessly when they are unable to ask, but you have good reason for thinking they would want you to do so.

Quality of life – the idea that life must have some benefits for it to be worth living.

Voluntary euthanasia – ending life painlessly when someone in great pain asks for death.

A dictionary definition of **euthanasia** is that it provides a gentle and easy death to someone suffering from a painful, terminal disease who has little **quality of life**. This can be done by: **assisted suicide, voluntary euthanasia, non-voluntary euthanasia**.

British law says that all these methods of euthanasia can lead to a charge of murder. However, the law now agrees that withdrawing artificial nutrition and hydration is not murder. In the same way, withholding treatment from patients with little or no chance of survival and ensuring a peaceful death for them is not murder. These two types of euthanasia (the withdrawal or withholding of treatment) are often called passive euthanasia, in contrast to positive euthanasia which is actually bringing someone's life to an end.

Why euthanasia is a controversial issue

1. Many people want euthanasia to remain illegal because:
   - There is always likely to be doubt as to whether it is what the person really wants. If there is money involved, unscrupulous relatives might request euthanasia for a rich relative to gain from their will.
   - There is also the problem as to whether the disease is terminal. A cure might be found for the disease, or the patient may go into remission. Also people thought of being in irreversible comas have recovered after many years.
   - Doctors would also face a big problem if they started to kill patients, even though the patient requested it. It is the role of doctors to save lives, not end them. Would patients trust their doctors if they weren't sure about their dedication to saving life?
   - People might change their mind about wanting euthanasia, but then it would be too late.
   - Who would decide to allow the euthanasia to take place? What safeguards could there be that they were only killing people who really wanted and needed euthanasia?

2. Many people want euthanasia to be made legal because they argue that:
   - Advances in medicine have led to people being kept alive who would previously have died, but they judge their quality of life as poor. It is claimed that doctors and relatives should have the right to give such patients a painless death.

◄ Nancy Crick was assisted to commit suicide by right-to-die campaigners because she had terminal cancer. After her death it was discovered that she was in remission. Her relatives and the campaigners still believe it was right. Her son said, 'It makes little difference whether she had cancer or not. Our main concern is that our mother is at peace.'

- The development of life-support machines has already brought in a form of euthanasia as doctors and relatives can agree to switch off such machines if there is no chance of the patient regaining consciousness because they are said to be brain-stem dead. It is claimed that the National Health Service cannot afford to keep people alive for years on a life-support machine that could be used to save the life of someone who has a chance of recovery.
- Just as doctors can now switch off life-support machines, so judges have said that doctors can stop treatment.
- Many people feel that it is a basic human right to have control about ending your life. If people have the right to commit suicide, then they have the right to ask a doctor to assist their suicide if they are too weak to do it themselves.

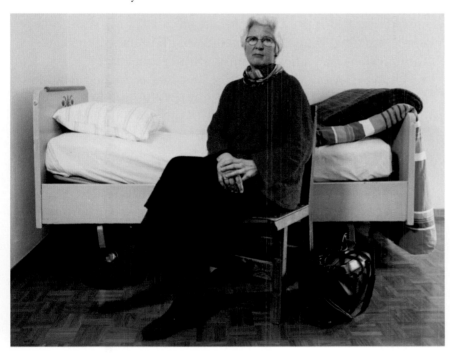

◀ This suicide room in Zurich is owned by Dignitas, a charity that provides assisted suicide for those whose illnesses are unbearable.

SUMMARY

There are various types of euthanasia that are all aimed at giving an easy death to those suffering intolerably. British law says that euthanasia is a crime, but withholding treatment from dying patients is not.

Euthanasia is a controversial issue because:

- Medicine can keep people alive with little quality of life.
- Suicide is no longer a crime.
- We give euthanasia to suffering animals.
- The role of doctors is to save life, not kill.
- Can you ever be sure that euthanasia is what someone wants?

Questions

b Do you agree with euthanasia? Give two reasons for your point of view. **4**

c Explain why euthanasia is a controversial issue. **8**

d 'The law on euthanasia should be changed.'
  i Do you agree? Give reasons for your opinion. **3**
  ii Give reasons why some people may disagree with you. **3**

Exam Tip

b You should already have thought about this, and you just have to give two reasons for your opinion. For example, if you don't agree with euthanasia, you could use the reasons of unscrupulous relatives and doctors having a duty to save lives, not kill.

Topic 3.2.7 Christian attitudes to euthanasia

> *The use of painkillers to alleviate the suffering of the dying, even at the risk of shortening their days, can be morally in conformity with human dignity if death is not willed either as an end or a means, but only foreseen and tolerated as inevitable.*
>
> **Catechism of the Catholic Church 2279**

> *If we live, we live to the Lord; and if we die, we die to the Lord. So, whether we live or die, we belong to the Lord.*
>
> **Romans 14:8**

> *Discontinuing medical procedures that are burdensome, dangerous, extraordinary, or disproportionate to the expected outcome can be legitimate; it is the refusal of 'over-zealous' treatment.*
>
> **Catechism of the Catholic Church 2278**

Although all Christians believe that euthanasia is basically wrong, there are slightly different attitudes to the complex issues.

1. Catholics believe that assisted suicide, voluntary euthanasia and non-voluntary euthanasia are all wrong. However, they accept that modern medicine has introduced new issues. The Catechism defines euthanasia as 'an act or omission which, of itself or by intention, causes death' (Catechism of the Catholic Church 2277). They believe that the switching off of life-support machines is not euthanasia if brain death has been established by medical experts. They also believe that it is not wrong to allow death to occur by not giving extraordinary treatment (treatment that could cause distress to the patient and family and is only likely to put off death for a short time), nor is it wrong to give dying people painkillers which may shorten their life. They have this attitude because:

   * They believe in the sanctity of life. Life is created by God and so it is sacred to God. It is up to God, not humans, when people die. Euthanasia is to put oneself on a par with God, which is condemned in the Bible.
   * They regard any form of euthanasia as a form of murder, and murder is forbidden in the Ten Commandments.
   * They believe that it is up to medical experts to determine when death has occurred. If doctors say someone is **brain-dead**, then they have already died, so switching off the machine is accepting what God has already decided and it is not euthanasia.
   * They believe painkillers may be given to a dying person in great pain. This might shorten the person's life but the painkillers are given to remove the pain. That is the intention, rather than to hasten the person's death. This is called the doctrine of double effect. There must not be a direct link between painkillers and the death of the patient.
   * Not giving extraordinary treatment is permitted by the Catechism – see Catechism 2278 quote on the left.

Most non-Catholic Christians have very similar attitudes to euthanasia as Catholics.

2. Some Christians believe any form of euthanasia is wrong and they do not allow the switching off of life-support machines, the refusal of extraordinary treatment, or the giving of large doses of painkillers. They have this attitude because:

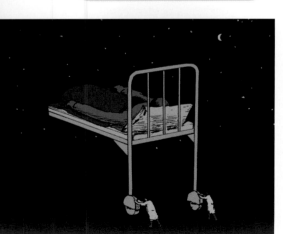

◄ 'Patient being pushed into eternity.' Is this a doctor's right? Or are Christians right in believing that only God should do this?

- They take the Bible teachings literally and the Bible bans suicide. Both assisted suicide and voluntary euthanasia are forms of suicide, so they are wrong.
- They regard switching off a life-support machine, the refusal of extraordinary treatment, or giving a large dose of painkillers, as euthanasia. Life is being ended by humans, not God, and this is wrong.
- They regard any form of euthanasia as murder, and murder is banned by God in the Ten Commandments.
- They believe in the sanctity of life. Life is created by God and so it is sacred to God. It is up to God, not humans, when people die. Euthanasia is to put oneself on a par with God, which is condemned in the Bible.

3. A few Christians accept a limited use of euthanasia. They agree with living wills in which people state what sort of treatment they wish to receive and how they want to die if they have a terminal illness. They believe this because:
   - Modern medical science means that we can no longer be sure what God's wishes about someone's death actually are.
   - The teaching of Jesus on loving your neighbour and helping people in trouble could be used to justify assisting suicide.
   - Living wills give people a chance to be in control of what doctors are doing to them, which is a basic human right.

The common experience of Christians throughout the ages has been that the grace of God sustains heart and mind to the end. To many, the end of life is clouded by pain and impaired judgement, and whilst we believe that it is right to use all and any medical treatment to control pain, experience denies the rightness of legalising the termination of life by a doctor, authorised by a statement signed by the patient whilst in health. Such euthanasia threatens to debase the function of doctors and impairs the confidence of their patients.

Statement by the Salvation Army in *What the Churches Say on Moral Issues*

◀ Many Christians help in the running of hospices to ease the suffering and pain of the terminally ill. The Catholic Church has been a great supporter of the hospice movement.

Questions

b Do you think switching off a life-support machine is euthanasia? Give two reasons for your point of view. **4**

c Explain two different Christian attitudes to euthanasia. **8**

d 'Life belongs to God and should only be taken by God.'
  i Do you agree? Give reasons for your opinion. **3**
  ii Give reasons why some people may disagree with you. **3**

Exam Tip

d Use the answering evaluation questions advice from page 9. The arguments for could come from the Christian arguments against euthanasia. The arguments against could be from Topic 3.2.6 on reasons for allowing euthanasia.

SUMMARY

All Christians are against euthanasia because they believe life is sacred and belongs to God.

However, there are some different attitudes among Christians about switching off life-support machines, withdrawing treatment, and so on, because some think these are not euthanasia.

Topic 3.2.8 The media and matters of life and death

Different forms of communication.

The media are all forms of communication, whether written, spoken or printed. In this specification, it refers to newspapers, television, radio, films and the internet. Note that the word is plural, in the singular it would be medium.

Religion makes many statements in the media about such matters of life and death as abortion, euthanasia, transplants, genetic engineering, cloning and fertility treatments. What you need to know to answer questions on this topic are:

1 arguments which say that the media should not be free to criticise what religion says about these issues

2 arguments which say that the media must be allowed to criticise what religion says about these issues.

1. Arguments that the media should not be free to criticise what religions say about matters of life and death

- Some people would argue that criticising what religions say about issues like abortion and genetic engineering is a way of stirring up religious hatred, which is banned by the Racial and Religious Hatred Act of 2007. For example, the Catholic Church told Catholics to withdraw their support from Amnesty International because Amnesty had decided in 2007 to back abortion as a human right for women who had been raped. When the media reported this, they quoted examples that were bound to show the Catholic position in a bad light. One of the examples used related to the Christian women of Darfur who were gang-raped by Sudanese soldiers and were expected to have the babies and bring them up, even though their husbands and families rejected them.

- Many religious believers would argue that there should be some restrictions on the freedom of the media because criticism of religious attitudes can cause serious offence to believers. For example, when the Danish newspaper *Jyllands-Posten* published cartoons of the Prophet Muhammad, thousands of Muslims around the world were very offended and there were riots in some countries (see photo, page 45).

- Some religious believers, but not the Catholic Church itself, would argue that criticising what religious leaders such as the **Pope** or the Archbishop of Canterbury say about matters of life and death is close to the crime of blasphemy. Essentially, if the media criticise the Pope's teachings on a topic like abortion or euthanasia, they are condemning the Catholic Church. The

In 2006 a Danish newspaper printed cartoons of the Prophet Muhammad, which caused worldwide protest by Muslims who believe the prophet should not be pictured. This picture shows Pakistanis at a protest rally. Do you think that there should be total freedom of speech, or that where offence can be caused the media should exercise restraint?

last trial on the blasphemy law was in 1977, when the trial judge said blasphemous libel was committed if a publication about God, Christ, the Christian religion or the Bible used words that were scurrilous, abusive or offensive, which vilified Christianity and might lead to a breach of the peace.

- Some religious believers might feel that because their attitude is based on what God says, it should not be criticised because God is beyond human criticism.

2. Arguments that the media should be free to criticise what religions say about matters of life and death

- All societies with democratic forms of government claim to believe in freedom of expression (it is Article 10 of the European Convention on Human Rights). In order for democracy to work, the electorate has to be able to make informed choices before they vote. For this they need a free media so that they can know what is going on in the world and in their own country and they can then work out which political party will deal best with the problems of the country and the world. If the media have freedom of expression, then they must be free to criticise religious attitudes to matters of life and death.

It is deeply misguided to propose a law by which it would be legal for the terminally ill to be killed or assisted in suicide by those caring for them, even if there are safeguards to ensure it is only the terminally ill who would qualify. To take this step would fundamentally undermine the basis of law and medicine and undermine the duty of the state to care for vulnerable people ... As a result many who are ill or dying would feel a burden to others. The right to die would become the duty to die.

Part of a joint submission by all the Church of England and Catholic bishops to the House of Lords Select Committee on the Assisted Dying for the Terminally Ill Bill. Should the media have a right to criticise such statements?

SUMMARY

Some people think that what religions say about matters of life and death should not be criticised by the media because:

- They might stir up religious hatred.
- They might be offensive to religious believers.

Other people think the media should be free to criticise religious attitudes because:

- A free media is a key part of democracy.
- If religions want to be free to say what they want, then the media must also be free to criticise religion.

- Many religious leaders use the media to criticise government policies on matters of life and death, for example the use of human embryos for stem cell research. If religions wish to have the right to criticise the attitudes of other people on issues of life and death, they must be prepared to have their attitudes criticised.

- In a multi-faith society such as the United Kingdom, there must be freedom of religious belief and expression (as guaranteed by Article 9 of the European Convention on Human Rights). This means that the media must have the right to question and even criticise not only religious beliefs, but also what religions say about controversial issues such as abortion, euthanasia and genetic engineering.

- Life and death issues are of such importance to everyone that people want to know what is the right thing to do about them. Society cannot find the truth by allowing religions to put forward opinions that no one can criticise. A free media gives religious people a chance to put forward their ideas whilst at the same time allowing non-religious people (or people from a different religion) the chance to put forward their ideas.

- Sir Karl Popper, one of the greatest twentieth-century philosophers, argued that freedom of expression is essential for human societies to make progress. He claimed that it is no accident that the most advanced societies also have the greatest freedoms for their citizens. According to Popper, progress is made by subjecting all ideas, policies and so on to scrutiny, discovering what is false in them and then putting forward a new form without the false elements. This can only happen if government policies and religious attitudes can be scrutinised by a free media.

Questions

b Do you think the media should be free to criticise religion? Give two reasons for your point of view. **4**

c Explain why people argue about the way the media treat religion. **8**

d 'The media should not criticise religious attitudes to abortion.'
   i Do you agree? Give reasons for your opinion. **3**
   ii Give reasons why some people may disagree with you. **3**

Exam Tip

d Use the answering evaluation questions advice from page 9. The arguments for could be three of the reasons from point 1 of this topic. Arguments against could be three of the reasons from point 2 of this topic.

Topic 3.2.9 How an issue from matters of life and death has been presented in one form of the media

You have to study how **one** issue from matters of life and death has been presented in one form of the media.

Your issue could be connected with:
- life after death
- abortion
- euthanasia
- world poverty.

You can choose the media but it should only be one of the following:
- a soap opera
- a film
- a television drama
- a television documentary
- a radio programme
- a newspaper article in two different types of newspaper, for example *The Times* and the *Sun*.

◀ If you study a TV drama such as *Law and Order SVU* where, in a 2007 episode, Melissa Joan Hart starred as a Catholic who had an abortion after getting pregnant as a result of rape, you must concentrate on whether the way it presented the issue was fair to Catholic people and Catholic beliefs.

Is the presentation of life after death in *Torchwood* fair to Catholics and Catholic beliefs?

You must choose both the issue and the type of media carefully to be able to answer questions on:
- why the issue is important
- how it was presented
- whether the presentation was fair to religious beliefs
- whether the presentation was fair to religious people.

To do this you must:

1. Select an issue and a form of media. It is very important that you select only one issue. Some films have several issues running through them. If you choose more than one issue, your answers are likely to be confused.

2. Decide why the issue is important (you may need to look at the views of different members of the particular religion and of the impact of the issue on society as a whole) and why you think the producers of the media decided to focus on this issue.

3. Write an outline of how the issue was presented, listing the main events and the way the events explored the issue.

4. Look closely at the way religious beliefs are treated in the presentation of the issue. Use this information to decide whether you think the presentation was fair to religious beliefs.

5. Look closely at the way religious people are treated in the presentation of the issue. Use this information to decide whether you think the presentation was fair to religious people.

SUMMARY

When studying the presentation of an issue from matters of life and death in the media, you must be able to explain why the issue was chosen, how it was presented, whether the presentation treated religious people fairly and whether the presentation treated religious beliefs fairly.

Questions

b Do you think the media presented an issue from matters of life and death fairly? Give two reasons for your point of view. **4**

c Choose an issue from matters of life and death presented in one form of the media and explain whether the presentation was fair to religious people. **8**

d You are unlikely to be asked an evaluation question on this section as you only have to study one issue in one form of the media.

Exam Tip

c Briefly summarise the presentation, then explain why some religious people would think the presentation was fair (with reasons) and others would think it was unfair (with reasons) then decide what you think.

Topic 3.2.10 The causes of world poverty

World poverty is a very complex issue. The countries of the West (such as the USA, United Kingdom, France and Australia) are regarded as rich. The countries of the East (such as Bangladesh and India) are regarded as poor. However, things are constantly changing as countries move from being poor to rich, for example Dubai, Kuwait and Singapore; or from poor to less poor (not poverty stricken, but not rich), for example Mexico and Malaysia; or from less poor to poor, for example Zimbabwe.

It is common for countries to be classified as:
- **MEDC** – more economically developed countries or First World, for example, USA
- **EDC** – economically developing countries or Second World, for example, Mexico
- **LEDC** – less economically developed countries or Third World, for example, Bangladesh.

There are many causes of world poverty and reasons for a country being less economically developed.

Natural disasters

Many LEDCs are situated in areas of the world where natural disasters (earthquakes, floods, droughts, etc.) are more frequent and more severe than anywhere else. An earthquake or a flood, for example, can destroy many thousands of homes and the farmland on which the inhabitants depend. If rain does not fall, crops will not grow unless people have the wealth to sink wells, install pumps and organise an irrigation system.

Debt

Most LEDCs have to borrow money from the banks of developed countries to survive and begin to develop. However, these banks charge interest, so a less developed country can find itself paying more in interest than it earns in foreign currency. African countries have paid back $550bn in interest on $540bn in loans between 1970 and 2002 but still owe$295bn. In 2003, developing countries paid out $23.6bn in interest to the banks of rich countries, but still owed the same amount of money.

Because unpaid interest is added to the original debt, since 1990 the amount of money poor countries have had to pay in interest to rich countries has risen from £7.4 billion to £10.3 billion.

> *I am Tonganhe. I live in Mozambique. When the floods came, I got separated from my family. But Save the Children helped me find them again. I was so happy they were still alive. We had lost all our crops in the floods, but then Save the Children gave us food and seeds to grow new crops.*
>
> **Letter from an African boy to Save the Children Fund from SCF publication *Welcome to Our World***

> *Researchers estimate that 10.8 per cent of all South Africans over two years old were living with HIV in 2005. Among those aged 25–49 years, the rise was 169 per cent in a nine-year period.*
>
> **Statistics South Africa**

The Burj al Arab hotel in Dubai is the first ▶ seven-star hotel in the world, showing how Dubai has moved from LEDC to MEDC.

Wars

Many LEDCs have been badly affected by wars. In Africa, many civil wars (wars fought between people from the same country) have been caused by European empire-building in the nineteenth century. Countries such as Ethiopia and Somalia were constructed, expanded or reduced by Europeans without any thought given to ethnic links, language, or even traditional grazing rights. So different ethnic groups of people were sometimes artificially put together in one country. When these countries achieved independence, they were still artificial countries and civil war often ensued as various ethnic groups fought for control. Something similar happened in Europe in the 1990s when the various parts of Yugoslavia (artificially formed after the Second World War) fought bitter wars of independence.

LEDCs can also suffer from wars between countries, for example Ethiopia and Somalia, and from wars caused by corruption and political differences, for example Mozambique, Angola and Guatemala.

Wars destroy crops, homes, schools, hospitals, and so on, causing even more poverty. They also force many people to leave their homes and become refugees in other safer countries. These neighbouring countries may have been developing, but a sudden influx of refugees with no money or food can make that country poor again.

Unfair trade

World trade is dominated by the rich countries of the world. It is often the rich countries that determine the prices paid for products from LEDCs.

Most people in poor countries work in agriculture and one way for them to become richer would be for them to grow surplus crops and export their surplus to earn money from MEDCs. However, the rich countries are using their wealth to protect their farmers. They pay subsidies to their farmers to grow crops, and put high tariffs (import taxes) on crops from poor countries so that their products are more expensive. Then, if the MEDC farmers produce more crops than are needed, they export them at lower prices than the LEDCs can produce them for.

> *The leader of the International Monetary Fund last week said hundreds of thousands of people were at risk of starvation because of food shortages.*
>
> *Prices have risen sharply in recent months, driven by increased demand, poor weather in some countries that has ruined crops, and reduced production areas thanks to an increase in the use of land to grow crops for transport fuels ... The sharp rises have led to protests and unrest in many countries, including Egypt, Ivory Coast, Ethiopia, the Philippines and Indonesia.*
>
> *In Haiti, protests last week turned violent, leading to the deaths of five people and the fall of the government.*
>
> *'We have to put our money where our mouth is now so that we can put food into hungry mouths,' Mr Zoellick said. 'It's as stark as that.'*
>
> BBC News, 14 April 2008

Refugees from the Darfur conflict are causing major problems for neighbouring countries as well as for aid agencies.

Sugar costs £319 per tonne to grow in the EU. European farmers are guaranteed £415 per tonne and are protected against non-EU imports by a 140 per cent tariff. Farmers in LEDCs produce sugar cane rather than sugar beet and this only costs £183 per tonne to produce. EU farmers overproduce and the surplus of seven million tonnes is dumped onto the world market. This has depressed the world market price to £121 per tonne so that, although LEDC farmers produce sugar at roughly a third of the MEDC cost, they still cannot make a profit.

Poor countries are also being kept poor by the trade policies of rich countries. The rich nations pay $350 billion in subsidies to their farmers and $57 billion in aid to poor countries. The World Bank estimates that if the subsidies and tariffs were halved, it would increase the economies of poor countries by $150 billion a year.

To overcome the problem, many LEDCs grow cash crops such as cotton, coffee, tea and tobacco, which they can sell to the developed world. Many people in LEDCs are starving because land is used to grow cash crops instead of food, and the prices for the cash crops go down because too many countries are growing them.

HIV/AIDS

This disease is sweeping LEDCs, especially in Southern Africa. The loss of so many earners and the presence of so many children who will not be able to have an education is causing many African countries to become poorer. This effect is going to get worse, and only the rich countries can help.

Other factors

There are other factors contributing to world poverty. Lack of education means that young people in LEDCs do not have the skills needed to work in industries that might improve the country. Lack of clean fresh water leads to disease and children dying at a young age; such low life expectancy leads families to have a large number of children so that a sufficient number will survive to look after their parents in their old age. Relying on one export (such as copper or oil) can lead to poverty because, if the value of the product goes down in the world market, the country will be making a loss instead of a profit. This can change a country from rich to poor almost overnight.

The price of coffee has fallen by 70 per cent since 1996, costing poor countries $8 billion.

Exam Tip

d Use the answering evaluation questions advice from page 9. The arguments for could come from such reasons as debt, unfair trade, war. The arguments against could be from natural disasters, HIV/AIDS war.

Questions

b Do you think world poverty can be ended? Give two reasons for your point of view. **4**

c Explain why some countries in the world are very poor. **8**

d 'World poverty is caused by the greed of rich countries.'

  i Do you agree? Give reasons for your opinion. **3**

  ii Give reasons why some people may disagree with you. **3**

SUMMARY

The main causes of world poverty are:

- natural disasters
- wars
- debt
- unfair trade
- lack of education
- HIV/AIDS.

Topic 3.2.11

How and why CAFOD is trying to remove world poverty

Following the example given in the parable of the Good Samaritan, Christian charity is first of all the simple response to immediate needs and specific situations: feeding the hungry, clothing the naked, caring for and healing the sick, visiting those in prison, etc. The Church's charitable organisations, beginning with those of Caritas (at diocesan, national and international levels), ought to do everything in their power to provide the resources and above all the personnel needed for this work. Individuals who care for those in need must first be professionally competent: they should be properly trained in what to do and how to do it, and committed to continuing care ... In addition to their necessary professional training, these charity workers need a 'formation of the heart': ... As a result, love of neighbour will no longer be for them a commandment imposed, so to speak, from without, but a consequence deriving from their faith, a faith which becomes active through love.

Deus Caritas Est, Encyclical of Pope Benedict XVI 2006

The major Catholic agency working for world development and supported by the Catholics of England and Wales is CAFOD (Catholic Fund for Overseas Development). It was established by the Catholic Bishops of England and Wales in 1962. It is the English and Welsh arm of Caritas International (a worldwide network of Catholic relief and development organisations) supporting 1000 development projects in over 60 countries.

How CAFOD is trying to end world poverty

1. Development Programmes

CAFOD promotes long-term development so that LEDCs can become self-supporting and have the opportunities to become MEDCs. Some examples of CAFOD's development aid are:

- The area around Hola in south eastern Kenya is arid and poor. Its 12,000 people make a subsistence living as nomadic farmers moving around with their cattle. These people have no access to state health care. Since 1985 CAFOD has been helping the Hola Catholic Mission health programme. During this time three clinics have been opened and 40 health workers (chosen by the local community and working for no pay) have been trained to provide basic medical care and advice on hygiene, nutrition and child health.

- In Brazil, the richest 10 per cent of the 150 million people receive 53.2 per cent of the wealth whilst the poorest 10 per cent receive 0.6 per cent. This has led to about 6 million homeless children living on the streets. CAFOD is helping the parish of Piexnhos in Olinda (part of Helder Camara's old **diocese**) to run a scheme known as 'The Community Taking Responsibility for its Children'. Street educators give the children literacy classes and training in skills so that they can earn a living.

- In Bangladesh, floods in the district of Khulna often wipe out poor farmers' entire rice crops. CAFOD is helping the Organisation of Peasant Farmers which sets up savings schemes to help them when crops fail and which is starting up different farming projects such as duck-rearing units.

2. Disasters and emergencies

CAFOD has a disaster fund to deal with natural disasters and refugees, which often have to take priority over long-term aid. CAFOD's emergency aid has included: sending food, antibiotics and shelters to victims of the tsunami and sending blankets and food to war refugees in Bosnia, Kosovo and Rwanda.

3. Raising awareness

About 5 per cent of CAFOD's budget is spent on educating the people and churches of England and Wales about the need for development and the ways in which Catholics can help less developed countries. It publishes a newspaper called 'Friday' and many educational materials. These give information not only about what CAFOD is doing, but also about world development.

4. Speaking out on behalf of poor communities to bring social justice

CAFOD was heavily involved in the Make Poverty History campaign of 2005, the biggest ever global mobilisation to end poverty. It is now involved in the Trade Justice Campaign to change the rules and practices of international trade to help developing countries work themselves out of poverty. CAFOD is also campaigning to cancel the debt owed by some of the world's poorest countries. Many developing countries spend twice as much on debt repayments to rich creditors than they do on healthcare and education. CAFOD also promotes Fairtrade products to bring better prices, decent working conditions, local sustainability, and fair terms of trade for farmers and workers in the developing world.

Why CAFOD is trying to end world poverty

- According to the New Testament, riches must be used for the help of others, especially the poor.
- Jesus told the Parable of the Sheep and the Goats where he said, 'When I was hungry, you fed me. When I was thirsty, you gave me drink. When I was naked, you clothed me. When I was sick or in prison, you visited me.' The good people wanted to know when they had ever done this and Jesus said, 'When you did it for the least of my brothers, you did it for me.' Catholics want to help Jesus and so they help the poor and suffering.
- The parable also teaches that the way to heaven is helping those less fortunate than you, and Catholics want to get to heaven.
- In the **Sermon on the Mount** (Matthew 5–7), Jesus taught that Christians should share their time and possessions to help those in need. So Catholics should try to end world poverty.
- The Catholic Church teaches that Christians have a duty to help the poor and suffering. Pope Benedict's first **encyclical** reminded Catholics of their duty to try to end poverty.
- The **Golden Rule** for Christians is to treat other people in the way you would like to be treated. CAFOD believes that they would want rich Christians to try to end world poverty if they were suffering from it.

Questions

b Do you think all Catholics should help CAFOD? Give two reasons for your point of view. **4**

c Explain how CAFOD is trying to end world poverty. **8**

d 'If everyone was Catholic, there would be no world poverty.'

  i Do you agree? Give reasons for your opinion. **3**

  ii Give reasons why some people may disagree with you. **3**

Exam Tip

c 'Explain how' means outline four CAFOD activities and explain how each is trying to end world poverty. For tips on Quality of Written Communication, look at page 3.

SUMMARY

CAFOD works for world development by:

- promoting long-term development schemes
- responding to emergencies
- raising public awareness of the causes of poverty
- speaking out on behalf of poor communities.

It works to end world poverty because:

- Jesus taught that Christians should help the poor.
- The Catholic Church teaches that Catholics should help the poor.
- They believe it is the way to follow the Golden Rule.

How to answer exam questions

Question A What is non-voluntary euthanasia?   **2 marks**

Ending someone's life painlessly when they are unable to ask, but you have good reason for thinking they would want you to do so.

Question B Do you agree with abortion?
Give two reasons for your point of view.   **4 marks**

No I do not agree with abortion because life is holy and belongs to God, so only God has the right to end a pregnancy.
I also believe that life begins at conception. Abortion is therefore taking life, which is banned in the Ten Commandments.

Question C Explain why Catholic agencies work to end world poverty.   **8 marks**

Catholic agencies work to end world poverty because Jesus taught in the Sermon on the Mount that Christians should share their time and possessions to help those in need. So Catholics should try to end world poverty.

Also the Catholic Church teaches that Christians have a duty to help the poor and suffering. Pope Benedict's first encyclical reminded Catholics of their duty to try to end poverty.

The Golden Rule for Christians is to treat other people in the way you would like to be treated. CAFOD believes rich Christians would want to try to end world poverty if they were suffering from it.

Finally, Jesus told the Parable of the Sheep and the Goats about the good and bad people being sorted out at the end of the world. He said helping the poor and those who are starving was like helping him. Clearly this means that Catholics should help to relieve world poverty.

Question D 'Your soul will never die.'

  i Do you agree? Give reasons for your opinion.   **3 marks**

  ii Give reasons why some people may disagree with you.   **3 marks**

In your answer, you should refer to Catholic Christianity.

i *As a Catholic, I agree with this because I believe there is life after death because Jesus rose from the dead. Also it is part of the creeds to believe in the life everlasting, which means the soul cannot die. Also Jesus said to one of the robbers crucified with him, 'This day you will be with me in paradise.' I think this means that the robber's soul would not die at the crucifixion but live on in heaven.*

ii *I can see why some people might disagree. They might not believe in God's existence and if there is no God, there can be no life after death. They might not see how the soul can live on after the death of the brain. Also they might think there is nowhere for life after death to take place as space exploration has shown there is no heaven above the sky.*

QUESTION A
A high mark answer because it is a correct definition of the key word.

QUESTION B
A high mark answer because an opinion is backed up by two developed reasons.

QUESTION C
A high mark answer because four reasons for Catholic agencies working to end world poverty are given. A formal style of English is used and there is good use of specialist vocabulary such as Jesus, Sermon on the Mount, Pope Benedict, encyclical, Golden Rule, Parable of the Sheep and Goats.

QUESTION D
A high mark answer because it states the candidate's own opinion and backs it up with three clear Catholic reasons for thinking that the soul will never die. It then gives three reasons for people disagreeing and believing that the soul dies at the death of the body.

Section 3.3 **Marriage and the family**

Introduction

This section of the examination specification requires you to look at issues surrounding sex and marriage, divorce, family life, homosexuality and contraception.

Sex and marriage
You will need to understand the effects of, and give reasons for your own opinion about:
- changing attitudes to marriage, divorce, family life and homosexuality in the UK
- Christian attitudes to sex outside marriage
- the purposes of marriage in Catholic Christianity and how this is shown in the wedding ceremony.

Family life
You will need to understand the effects of, and give reasons for your own opinion about:
- Catholic teachings on family life and its importance
- how Catholic parishes help with the upbringing of children
- how Catholic parishes help to keep the family together.

Divorce
You will need to understand the effects of, and give reasons for your own opinion about different Christian attitudes to divorce and the reasons for them.

The media and marriage and family life
You will need to understand the effects of, and give reasons for your own opinion about:
- how an issue from marriage and the family has been presented in one form of the media
- whether the treatment of the issue in the media was fair to religious beliefs and religious people.

Homosexuality
You will need to understand the effects of, and give reasons for your own opinion about Christian attitudes to homosexuality and the reasons for them.

Contraception
You will need to understand the effects of, and give reasons for your own opinion about:
- different methods of contraception and the reasons for them
- different Christian attitudes to contraception and the reasons for them.

Topic 3.3.1 Changing attitudes to marriage, divorce, family life and homosexuality in the UK

KEY WORDS

Civil partnership – a legal ceremony giving a homosexual couple the same legal rights as a husband and wife.

Cohabitation – living together without being married.

Contraception – intentionally preventing pregnancy from occurring.

Homosexuality – sexual attraction to the same sex.

Nuclear family – mother, father and children living as a unit.

Re-constituted family – where two sets of children (stepbrothers and stepsisters) become one family when their divorced parents marry each other.

Re-marriage – marrying again after being divorced from a previous marriage.

In the United Kingdom in the 1960s, it was expected that: young people would not have sex until they were married; most people would be married in church by the age of 25; most **marriages** would last for life; most families would consist of husband, wife and their children (**nuclear family**); homosexuals would not be seen in public because homosexual sex between adult males was a criminal offence.

How attitudes have changed

- Most people now have sex before they get married.
- It is now socially quite acceptable for couples to live together (**cohabit**) rather than marry and a greater percentage are doing so. Most people who marry are now living with their partner first.
- The average age for marrying has increased enormously (31.8 for men and 29.7 for women in 2006).
- Only a minority of marriages now take place in church (60 per cent in 1970, 34 per cent in 2006).
- Divorce is accepted as a normal part of life, and no one is looked down on for being divorced. There has been a great increase in the number of divorces.
- The **extended family** is becoming more popular as more mothers are in paid employment and use retired grandparents to look after the children.
- Single-parent families have increased considerably as more couples divorce.
- There are far more families where the children are being brought up by cohabiting parents (11 per cent of all families in 2006).
- **Re-constituted families** are increasing rapidly as more people divorce and re-marry.
- Homosexual sex in private between two consenting adults (over 21) was made legal in 1967 and subsequent reforms have led to society treating homosexual sex the same way as heterosexual sex.
- The Civil Partnerships Act 2004 created a new legal relationship of **civil partnership**. This is where two people of the same sex can form a union or partnership by signing a registration document. It provides same-sex couples with the same rights and treatment as opposite-sex couples who enter into a civil marriage.

Reasons for the changes

Cohabitation and marriage

- The increased availability of effective **contraception** (especially the contraceptive pill) made it safer to have sex without becoming pregnant.
- Christianity lost its influence as fewer people went to church and so were not encouraged to refrain from sex until they married.
- There was increased media publicity of celebrities, which made cohabitation appear respectable and led to it becoming more popular.
- The presentation on television and in films of sexual relationships outside marriage as the norm led to more people regarding sex outside marriage as acceptable.

Do you think this nuclear family would be any different if the parents were cohabiting rather than married?

Most cohabiting couples think that they have the same rights about financial support, property, children, and so on, as they would if they were married, but this is not the case. 'The law that currently applies to such couples (cohabiting couples) on separation is unclear and complicated, and it can produce unfair outcomes. This causes serious hardship not only to cohabitants themselves, but also to their children.'

Statement from the Law Commission about proposals to give legal rights to cohabiting couples that were shelved in March 2008

Divorce

- In 1969, new laws made divorce much cheaper and easier to obtain for ordinary people. This led to a huge increase in the number of divorces.
- Expectations of what marriage should be like have changed greatly. Increased **equality** for women means that women are no longer prepared to accept unequal treatment from men. Women expect to have as good a life as their husbands and if their husbands treat them badly, they will divorce them.
- Before the equal rights legislation (see Topic 3.4.1), married women were often dependent on their husbands for financial support. Nowadays, many women are financially independent and can afford to live after a divorce.
- Demographic changes – there has also been a great change in how long people are likely to be married. A hundred years ago, many men could expect to have more than one wife because so many women died in childbirth. Most divorces occur after ten years of marriage, which was the average length of a marriage 100 years ago.

In 2005, the government and the Church of England agreed to the marriage of Prince Charles to Camilla Parker Bowles, even though both had been divorced.

◀ Elton John and David Furnish on the day they formed their civil partnership. Do you think civil partnerships are a good idea?

Family life

- The increase in the number of cohabiting couples means that there are now many more families where the parents are not married.
- The increase in divorce has led to an increase in **re-marriage** (most people who divorce before the age of 50 re-marry). This means that there are now many more re-constituted families.
- The extended family is becoming more popular as more mothers are in paid employment and use retired grandparents or non-working close relatives to look after the children.
- The increase in the number of divorces plus the acceptance by society of unmarried mothers has led to an increase in the number of single-parent families.

Homosexuality

- The various changes in the laws on **homosexuality** have made it easier to be openly homosexual and made society more aware and accepting of homosexuality.
- Medical research has shown that homosexuality is most probably genetic. As society began to realise that at least five per cent of the population is homosexual, so people began to accept equal status and rights for homosexual couples.
- The increased openness of gay celebrities has led to a greater acceptance of all gay people.
- The work of such organisations as Stonewall changed many people's attitudes and led to a greater acceptance of equal rights for homosexuals.

SUMMARY

Fifty years ago, most people only had sex in marriage, and they married in church. Now, people have sex before they marry, cohabiting is socially acceptable and most marriages are not in church. This could be caused by safer contraception and fewer people being influenced by religion.

Divorce and re-marriage used to be rare but are accepted today, and two in five marriages end in divorce. The changes may have been caused by cheaper divorce and women having more equality.

Family life has changed so that, although most children are still brought up by a mother and a father, the parents may not be married or they may have been married more than once. These changes are probably caused by the changing attitudes to sex, marriage and divorce.

Homosexuality used to be illegal, but now homosexuals have the same rights to sexual activity as heterosexuals including civil partnerships. These changes are probably due to discoveries showing homosexuality is natural and changes to the law.

Questions

b Do you think homosexuals should be allowed to marry? Give two reasons for your point of view. **4**

c Explain why attitudes to marriage and divorce have changed. **8**

d 'There's no difference between living with a partner and being married to them.'
  i Do you agree? Give reasons for your opinion. **3**
  ii Give reasons why some people may disagree with you. **3**

Exam Tip

c 'Explain' means give reasons. To answer this question you should use two reasons from cohabitation and marriage and two from divorce, and make each of them into a short paragraph. For tips on Quality of Written Communication, look at page 3.

Topic 3.3.2 Christian attitudes to sex outside marriage

Christianity teaches that sex should only take place between a man and woman married to each other. Therefore most Christians believe that sex outside marriage is wrong because:

- Christianity teaches that sex was given to humans by God for the joy, pleasure and bond of a married couple and for the **procreation** of children, and children should be brought up in a Christian family so sex should only take place within marriage.
- The Bible says that fornication (a word used in religion for both **pre-marital sex** and **promiscuity**) is sinful and Christians should follow the teachings of the Bible.
- The Catechism of the Catholic Church teaches that pre-marital sex is wrong and Catholics are encouraged to follow the teachings of the Church.
- All Christians are against **adultery** because it breaks the wedding vows to be faithful to each other.
- They are also against adultery because it is condemned in the Ten Commandments, which all Christians should follow.
- Adultery is condemned by Jesus in the Gospels and all Christians should follow the teachings of Jesus.

Some Christians accept that couples may live together before marriage, but they would expect them to marry when starting a family and would only accept a sexual relationship between two people committed to a long-term relationship.

KEY WORDS

Adultery – a sexual act between a married person and someone other than their marriage partner.

Pre-marital sex – sex before marriage.

Procreation – making a new life.

Promiscuity – having sex with a number of partners without commitment.

The sexual act must always take place exclusively within marriage ... Human love does not tolerate 'trial marriages'. It demands a total and definitive gift of persons to one another.
Catechism of the Catholic Church 2390–91

Cohabiting couples should be welcomed and supported by the Church, 'recognising that for many this is a step along the way to the fuller commitment of marriage'.
Something to Celebrate
A report published by the Church of England's Board of Responsibility in 1995

You shall not commit adultery.
Exodus 20:14

SUMMARY

- All Christians believe adultery is wrong as it breaks one of the Ten Commandments.
- Most Christians believe that sex before marriage is wrong because the Church and the Bible teach this.

Questions

b Do you think Christians should be allowed to have sex before marriage? Give two reasons for your point of view. **4**

c Explain why most Christians are against sex outside marriage. **8**

d 'Christians should never have sex outside marriage.'
 i Do you agree? Give reasons for your opinion. **3**
 ii Give reasons why some people may disagree with you. **3**

Exam Tip

c 'Explain' means give reasons. To answer this question you should use two reasons against pre-marital sex and two reasons against adultery, and make each of them into a short paragraph. For tips on Quality of Written Communication, look at page 3.

Topic 3.3.3 The purposes of marriage in Catholic Christianity

The Catholic Church teaches that God created man and woman for each other in the **sacrament** of marriage. The purposes of Catholic marriage are:

- so that a couple can have a life-long relationship of love and **faithfulness**
- so that a couple can have the support and comfort of each other
- for the procreation of children
- for the bringing up of a Christian family.

Marriage is one of the seven sacraments of the Church and as such it is a sign of grace, instituted by Christ himself and, through the Church, imparting God's grace and strength. As a sacrament, Catholic marriage involves not only the bride and groom, but also God himself. It can be argued its sacramental nature is a further purpose of marriage in Catholic Christianity.

The matrimonial covenant, by which a man and a woman establish between themselves a partnership of the whole of life, is by its nature ordered toward the good of the spouses and the procreation and education of offspring; this covenant between baptised persons has been raised by Christ the Lord to the dignity of a sacrament.

Catechism of the Catholic Church 1601

How the purposes of marriage are shown in the wedding ceremony

The life-long relationship of love and faithfulness is shown in:
- the exchange of vows committing the partners to lifetime marriage and restricting sex to each other
- the exchange of rings symbolising the unending nature of marriage
- the **priest's** introduction to the service which emphasises the fact that marriage is a special sacrament which cannot be broken by the husband or wife
- readings from the Bible and a sermon or **homily** given by the priest or **deacon** on the nature of Christian marriage as a life-long relationship of love and faithfulness.

The couple having the support and comfort of each other is shown in:
- a preparation course which the couple must take before the wedding ceremony. This is religious counselling between the bride, the groom and a priest or deacon (sometimes assisted by a relationship counsellor) before the wedding ceremony takes place. This helps the couple to understand the nature of Catholic marriage and how to provide support and comfort for each other

The exchange of vows and the signing of the register make a Catholic wedding legal according to UK law.

- the priest asking the couple if they will honour and love one another as husband and wife for the rest of their lives. He asks this before the marriage vows, and they must agree to this promise of love and support for the ceremony to continue
- the marriage vows and exchange of rings (see margin)
- the readings and homily are also likely to refer to the need for support and comfort
- the prayers and Nuptial Mass (if this is part of the ceremony) give the couple God's grace and strength to support and comfort each other.

The procreation of children is shown in:
- the priest asking the couple if they will accept children from God lovingly and bring them up according to the law of Christ and his Church. He asks this before the marriage vows and the couple must agree to this for the wedding ceremony to continue
- the readings, homily and prayers all refer to the acceptance of children as an essential feature of Catholic marriage.

The bringing up of a Christian family is shown in:
- the preparation course, which will involve discussion about how the couple should bring up their children, with reference to baptism, First Confession, Communion and Confirmation, and the Catholic schools connected with the parish
- the priest asking the couple if they will accept children from God lovingly and bring them up according to the law of Christ and his Church. He does this before the marriage vows.

Bringing children up in this way (and the couple living in a marriage of love and faithfulness) is what makes a Christian family.

The Vows

Priest: 'Do you take ___ as your lawful wife/husband, to have and to hold, from this day forward, for better or for worse, for richer or for poorer, in sickness and in health, to love and cherish until death do you part?'

Bride/Groom: 'I do.'

The exchange of rings

Bride/Groom: 'I take this ring as a sign of my love and faithfulness in the name of the Father, the Son and the Holy Spirit.'

Priest: 'Are you ready; freely and without reservation to give yourselves to each other in marriage? Are you ready to love and honour each other as man and wife for the rest of your lives? Are you ready to accept children lovingly from God, and bring them up according to the law of Christ and his Church?'

Source: Catholic Rite of Marriage During Mass

Questions

b Do you think the Catholic wedding ceremony helps a Catholic marriage to work? Give two reasons for your point of view. **4**

c Explain the purposes of Christian marriage that are shown in a Catholic wedding ceremony. **8**

d 'The main purpose of a Catholic marriage is to have children.'
  i Do you agree? Give reasons for your opinion. **3**
  ii Give reasons why some people may disagree with you. **3**

Exam Tip

b You should already have thought about this, and you just have to give two reasons for your opinion. For example, if you agree you could explain how the exchange of vows and exchange of rings might help.

SUMMARY

Catholic marriage is for a life-long relationship of love and faithfulness and bringing up a Catholic family. These purposes can be seen in the marriage ceremony where the pre-Cana discussions, exchange of vows and rings, Bible readings, homily and prayers all emphasise them.

Topic 3.3.4 Christian attitudes to divorce

There are different attitudes to divorce in Christianity:

1. The Catholic attitude

The Catholic Church does not allow religious divorce or re-marriage. Catholic marriage is a sacrament and the exchange of vows means that the only way a marriage between baptised Catholics can be dissolved (religiously) is by the death of one of the partners or if the marriage is annulled.

However, the Catholic Church does allow for the legal separation of spouses if they find it impossible to live together, and even civil divorce (an ending of the marriage according to the laws of the country but not the Church) if that will ensure the proper care of the children and the safety and security of the married partner. Neither of these routes, however, has ended the marriage: the couple are still married in the eyes of God and the Church and so cannot re-marry. Catholics have this attitude because:

- Jesus taught that divorce is wrong in Mark's Gospel and Christians should follow the teachings of Jesus.
- The couple have made a **covenant** with God in the sacrament of marriage and that covenant cannot be broken by any earthly power.
- The Church teaches very clearly in the Catechism that a marriage cannot be dissolved and so religious divorce is impossible. Catholics should follow the teachings of the Church and so should not divorce.
- As there can be no religious divorce, there can be no re-marriage because that would be the same as **bigamy** and adultery, both of which are very serious sins.

However, the Catholic Church does allow **annulment** if it can be proved that the marriage was never consummated or that it was not a true Christian marriage.

> *Thus the marriage bond has been established by God himself in such a way that a marriage concluded and consummated between baptised persons can never be dissolved.*
>
> **Catechism of the Catholic Church 1640**

> *The re-marriage of persons divorced from a living, lawful spouse contravenes the plan and law of God as taught by Christ.*
>
> **Catechism of the Catholic Church 1665**

> *When they were in the house again, the disciples asked Jesus about this. He answered 'Anyone who divorces his wife and marries another woman commits adultery against her. And if she divorces her husband and marries another man, she commits adultery.'*
>
> **Mark 10:10–12**

Why do you think divorce is ▶ sometimes considered the lesser of two evils?

2. The attitude of non-Catholic Christians

Most non-Catholic Churches think that divorce is wrong, but allow it if the marriage has broken down. Most of these Churches allow divorced people to re-marry, but they usually require them to talk to the priest/minister about why their first marriages failed. They are sometimes asked to show **repentance** for the failure and required to promise that this time their marriage will be for life.

Non-Catholic Churches allow divorce because:

* Jesus allowed divorce in Matthew 19:9 for a partner's adultery, therefore Jesus showed that divorce can happen if the reasons for it are sufficiently severe.
* They believe that there are certain situations where Christians must choose 'the lesser of two evils'. If a marriage has really broken down then the effects of the couple not divorcing would be a greater evil than the evil of divorce itself.
* Christians are allowed **forgiveness** and a new chance if they confess their sins and are truly repentant. This belief in forgiveness should apply to divorce and re-marriage as much as anything else. So a couple should have another chance at marriage as long as they are determined to make it work the second time.
* It is the teaching of these Churches that it is better to divorce than live in hatred and quarrel all the time.

What type of Christian do you think might have drawn this cartoon?

> For those who have taken their vows before God as Christians, there is no divorce. But most **Baptists** would acknowledge that human beings can make mistakes, and what appeared as a life-long relationship may eventually break down.
>
> **Statement by the Baptist Church in *What the Churches Say on Moral Issues***

> I tell you that anyone who divorces his wife, except for marital unfaithfulness, and marries another woman commits adultery.
>
> **Matthew 19:9**

Questions

b Do you think divorce is better than an unhappy marriage? Give two reasons for your point of view. **4**

c Explain why some Christians allow divorce and some do not. **8**

d 'No Christian should ever get divorced.'
  i Do you agree? Give reasons for your opinion. **3**
  ii Give reasons why some people may disagree with you. **3**

Exam Tip

b You should already have thought about this, and you just have to give two reasons for your opinion. For example, if you agree with divorce you could use two reasons for non-Catholic Churches agreeing with divorce.

SUMMARY

* Catholics do not allow religious divorce and re-marriage because they believe the marriage vows cannot be broken.
* Other Christians disapprove of divorce, but allow religious divorce and re-marriage if the marriage has broken down, because Christianity teaches forgiveness.

Topic 3.3.5 Why family life is important for Catholics

> The family is the original cell of social life ... The family is the community in which, from childhood, one can learn moral values, begin to honour God and make good use of freedom. Family life is an initiation into life in society.
>
> **Catechism of the Catholic Church 2207**

> Children, obey your parents in the Lord, for this is right. 'Honour your father and mother' – which is the first commandment with a promise – 'that it may go well with you and that you may enjoy long life on the earth.'
>
> Fathers, do not exasperate your children; instead, bring them up in the training and instruction of the Lord.
>
> **Ephesians 6:1–4**

Family life is important for Catholics because:

- One of the main purposes of Catholic marriage is to have children and bring them up in a secure and loving Catholic environment so that they will love God and follow Jesus.
- Catholicism teaches that the family was created by God as the basic unit of society and as the only place in which children should be brought up. Therefore it is the most important part of society and without the family society would collapse.
- Catholic teaching on divorce makes it clear that Catholic parents should stay together wherever possible and bring up their children together because the family is so important.
- The family is the place where children learn the difference between right and wrong, so without the family there would be much more evil in the world.
- The family is the place where children are introduced to the faith through baptism and then through being taken to church for Mass, **First Communion** and so on. This means that the family is very important for Christianity to continue and grow.
- Having a family is an expected outcome of Catholic marriage.
- Christian children are expected to care for their parents when they are no longer capable of caring for themselves. This is based on the fourth commandment and the teachings of Jesus.

However, there is a strong Catholic tradition dating back to Jesus, which says that the Christian family is more important than the human family. Priests, nuns and monks leave their families to serve God. Jesus himself never married.

Questions

b Do you think families need a mother and father who are married? Give two reasons for your point of view. **4**

c Explain why family life is important for Catholics. **8**

d 'Family life is more important for Catholics than for non-religious people.'

  i Do you agree? Give reasons for your opinion. **3**

  ii Give reasons why some people may disagree with you. **3**

Exam Tip

d Use the answering evaluation questions advice from page 9. Arguments for the statement would be the reasons why family life is important for Catholics. Arguments against would have to come from your class discussion or your own ideas. For example, if your own family is not religious, you could give examples of how important your family is to you and your parents.

SUMMARY

Catholics believe that the family is important because: it is taught in the Bible; Catholic marriage services refer to bringing up a family as the main purpose of marriage; Catholics believe that the family was created by God.

Topic 3.3.6 How Catholic parishes help with the upbringing of children

- Most **parishes** have a local Catholic primary and secondary school connected to them. These provide Catholic education and worship in addition to the standard education. (The school buildings are provided and maintained by the Church. The teachers and equipment are paid for by the state). This education helps parents because it teaches children right from wrong and helps parents to fulfil their marriage and baptism promises to bring their children up as Catholics.
- Parishes run classes to prepare children for First Confession, Communion and Confirmation. These help parents with the Catholic upbringing of their children as they bring children into full membership of the Church.
- Some parishes run children's liturgies to help young children understand the Church and the Mass, and to allow parents to be at Sunday worship. This helps parents to bring their children up as good Catholics and gives parents and their children the spiritual strength of the Mass.
- Some parishes also run youth clubs and youth activities so that children are kept off the streets and away from bad influences. Again this helps parents to bring up their children as good Catholics.

The Church has an important role to play in the upbringing of Catholic children. This photo shows a children's liturgy.

> *Education in the faith by the parents should begin in the child's earliest years ... The parish is the Eucharistic heart of the liturgical life of Christian families; it is a privileged place for the catechesis of children and parents.*
>
> **Catechism of the Catholic Church 2226**

Questions

b Do you think Catholic children should go to a Catholic school? Give two reasons for your point of view. **4**

c Explain how parishes support parents in the Catholic upbringing of their children. **8**

d 'You can't be a good Catholic if you don't go to a Catholic school.'
  i Do you agree? Give reasons for your opinion. **3**
  ii Give reasons why some people may disagree with you. **3**

Exam Tip

c 'Explain' means give reasons. To answer this question you should use four of the ways outlined above, and make each of them into a short paragraph explaining how each helps Catholic parents in the upbringing of their children. For tips on Quality of Written Communication, look at page 3.

SUMMARY

Catholic parishes help parents with the upbringing of their children by:
- supporting the local Catholic schools
- running classes for First Communion and Confirmation
- running children's liturgies
- running youth clubs and youth activities.

Topic 3.3.7 How Catholic parishes help to keep families together

Lord, by this sacrament you make us one family in Christ your Son, one in the sharing of his body and blood, one in the communion of his Spirit. Help us to grow in love for one another and come to the full maturity of the **Body of Christ.**

Prayer from the Baptismal Mass

Because family life is so important, Catholic parishes offer lots of help to keep families together:

- During Mass the priest may remind parents of the vows they made in their marriage ceremony and also of other reasons not to divorce.
- The parish priest is always available to give help and advice to couples having family problems.
- *Celebrating Family: Blessed, Broken, Living Love* is the national programme of support for marriage and family life within the Catholic community in England and Wales. The Marriage and Family Life Project Office provides support, resources and advice to parishes as they respond to families' expressed needs.
- The Church has provided a package 'Everybody's Welcome? Helping Your Parish to Become More Friendly for Families of All Kinds' to help parishes explore new ways to be more family friendly. Parishes try to be family friendly so that family life can be strengthened by families celebrating Mass together.
- The Church has produced a series of leaflets – 'What is Life Like?' – to help parishes understand and meet the needs of families facing specific challenges: divorce and re-marriage, bereavement, disability, mental ill-health, living without a shared faith in God, belonging to two Christian communities, and dealing with gay or lesbian family members.
- Many parishes also provide financial support if, for example, the family wage-earner is ill or made redundant, and have links to national Catholic charities to help family life, for example: Catholic Marriage Care, the National Catholic Child Welfare Council.

This photo shows a Catholic family celebrating Mass together.

SUMMARY

Catholic parishes help to keep families together by:

- welcoming families to worship together
- the priest offering help and advice for family problems
- homilies at Mass encouraging and strengthening family values
- providing leaflets on how to deal with family problems
- providing financial support and links to Catholic family charities.

Questions

b Do you think parishes provide enough support for family life? Give two reasons for your point of view. **4**

c Explain how parishes support Catholic family life. **8**

d 'Catholic parishes spend too much time helping families.'
  i Do you agree? Give reasons for your opinion. **3**
  ii Give reasons why some people may disagree with you. **3**

Exam Tip

d Use the answering evaluation questions advice from page 9. Arguments for the statement could be the things parishes are doing to help families. Arguments against could be from the importance of family life in Topic 3.3.5, showing that family life is so important that it needs a lot of time spending on it.

Topic 3.3.8 Christian attitudes to homosexuality

There are several attitudes to homosexuality in Christianity. The main ones are:

1. The Catholic attitude

The Catholic attitude towards homosexuality is that being a homosexual is not a sin but that homosexual sexual relationships are a sin. The Catholic Church asks homosexuals to live without any sexual activity (i.e. be celibate). They believe that the sacraments of the Church will help them do this. The Catholic Church condemns all forms of **homophobia**. It believes it is sinful to harass homosexuals or attack their behaviour. Catholics have this attitude because:

- The Bible condemns homosexual sexual activity.
- It is the tradition of the Church that sexual activity should be creative as well as unitive (see page 72), and it is not possible for homosexuals to have procreative sex.
- It is the teaching of the Magisterium found in the Catechism of the Catholic Church, which Catholics should believe.
- The Church teaches that people cannot help their sexual orientation (but they can control their sexual activity). Therefore discriminating against people because of their sexual orientation is wrong.
- The Bible teaches that everyone has human dignity because they are made in the image of God.
- The Church does not refer to 'heterosexual' or 'homosexual' alone, but speaks about homosexual persons whose identity is as a child of God.

Christians, Jews and Muslims joined forces to campaign against the Gay Rights Bill in January 2007. Here a group of Christian protestors sing hymns.

> It is necessary to distinguish between sexual orientation or inclination and indulging in sexual (genital) activity, homosexual or heterosexual. Neither a homosexual nor a heterosexual orientation leads inevitably to sexual activity. Furthermore, an individual's sexual orientation can be unclear, even complex. Also, it may vary over the years. Being a homosexual person is, then, neither morally good nor morally bad: it is homosexual genital acts that are morally wrong ... The Church does not consider the whole personality and character of the individual to be thereby disordered. Homosexual people, as well as heterosexual people, can, and often do, give a fine example of friendship and the art of chaste loving.
>
> *A Note on the teaching of the Catholic Church concerning Homosexual People*, Cardinal Hume 1995

> The Church utterly condemns all forms of unjust discrimination, violence, harassment or abuse directed against people who are homosexual. Consequently, the Church teaches that homosexual people 'must be accepted with respect, compassion, and sensitivity.'
>
> *Cherishing Life*, Catholic Bishops' Conference of England and Wales 2004

2. The Evangelical Protestant attitude

Many Evangelical Protestants believe that homosexuality is a sin. They believe that there should be no homosexual Christians and hold special prayer meetings to give homosexuals the power of the Spirit to change their sexual preference (orientation). The reasons for this attitude are:

- They believe that the Bible is the direct word of God and as the Bible condemns homosexuality in some passages of both the Old and New Testaments, it must be wrong.
- They believe that the **salvation** of Christ can remove all sins, including homosexuality.
- They believe it because all the Churches have taught it, even though some now say homosexuality is acceptable.

However, the Evangelical Alliance has recently made this statement: 'At the same time we utterly repudiate homophobia and call upon Churches to welcome those of a homosexual orientation as they would welcome any other person.'

The issue of homosexuality has caused major divisions in the Anglican Church (Churches in communion with the Church of England) since the Episcopal Church of the USA appointed an openly gay priest, Gene Robinson, as Bishop of New Hampshire. The Lambeth Conference declared in 1998 that homosexuals in a relationship should not be ordained as priests, and in 2004 called on the US Episcopal Church to repent for consecrating an openly gay bishop.

Compiled from news stories

If all the gay people stayed away from church on a given Sunday, the Church of England would be close to shut down, between its organists, its clergy, its wardens ... it seems less than humble not to admit that.

Right Reverend Gene Robinson interviewed in London, July 2007

The Right Reverend Gene Robinson, who is the ninth bishop of New Hampshire in the Episcopal Church in the USA. He became the first openly gay bishop inside the wider Anglican Church in 2003. Should an openly gay man be appointed bishop?

3. The Liberal Protestant attitude

Many **Liberal Protestants** have the attitude that lifelong homosexual relationships are acceptable and homosexuals are welcomed into the Church, but homosexual relationships cannot be equal to Christian marriage. It is accepted that ministers/priests may have a homosexual orientation but they must not take part in homosexual sex. Some Liberal Protestants provide blessings for civil partnerships. The reasons for this attitude are:

- They believe that the teachings of the Bible need re-interpreting in the light of modern knowledge and that the anti-homosexual texts in the Bible are a reflection of the Jewish culture at the time rather than the word of God.
- They feel that the major Christian belief in love and acceptance means that homosexuals must be accepted.
- Many believe that inspiration comes from the Holy Spirit as well as the Bible and if Christians feel the Spirit approves of their homosexuality, it cannot be denied.
- They believe that Christians should be open and honest and refusing rights to gay Christians encourages them to be dishonest and hypocritical about their nature and life.

◀ Some Christian ministers and priests will give a church blessing for a civil partnership. Is this a good idea?

Questions

b Do you think homosexuals should have equal rights? Give two reasons for your point of view. **4**

c Explain why some Christians accept homosexuality and some do not. **8**

d 'No Christian should be homosexual.'
  i Do you agree? Give reasons for your opinion. **3**
  ii Give reasons why some people may disagree with you. **3**

Exam Tip

d Use the answering evaluation questions advice from page 9. Arguments for the statement would be the reasons for the Evangelical Protestant view. Arguments against would be the reasons for the Liberal Protestant view.

SUMMARY

- Catholics believe there is nothing wrong with friendships between homosexuals or relationships as long as there is no sexual activity because this is the teaching of the Church.
- Evangelical Protestants believe that homosexuality is sinful because it is condemned in the Bible.
- Liberal Protestants believe that homosexuality is acceptable because it is natural and Christians should love and accept everyone.

Topic 3.3.9 Different methods of contraception

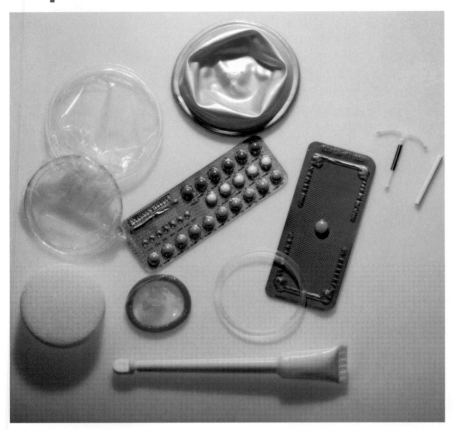

There are many types of artificial contraceptives.

Throughout history people have tried to control the number of children that they have had for a number of reasons:

- for the health of the mother
- to provide more food for the family unit
- to provide a better standard of living for the family unit.

Contraception is something that allows sex to happen without conception occurring, so allowing a couple to control the number of children they have. The use of contraception in the West has become very popular (it is now estimated that 90 per cent of the sexually active population of childbearing age in the UK use some form of contraception).

There are two fundamentally different types of contraception:

1. Natural methods of contraception

The most common form of natural contraception is known as natural family planning (NFP), or fertility awareness. It involves reducing the chance of becoming pregnant by planning sex around the most infertile times during the woman's monthly cycle. To be as effective as possible, it should be taught by an experienced NFP teacher.

Another method uses a device to measure hormone levels in the urine. If used according to the instructions, these methods can be 94 per cent effective.

Natural methods require a couple to be in a loving, stable relationship as they require planning and sufficient love and **concern** for the partner to give up sex at certain times of the month. As they are natural they do not involve any drugs or any risk of promoting an early abortion. Natural methods do not prevent sexually transmitted diseases, but these will not affect a couple who only have sex with each other as required in Catholic marriage.

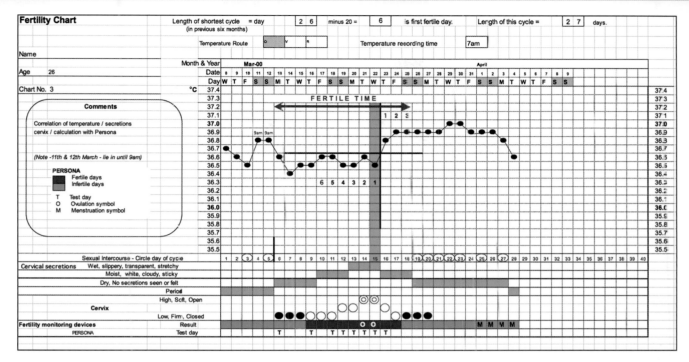

A completed fertility chart combining several indicators or signs of fertility.

2. Artificial methods of contraception

There are several types of artificial contraception. Barrier methods such as condoms prevent the sperm from reaching the egg. Hormonal drugs (the pill) stop a woman from producing eggs. There are also methods such as the coil (IUD) and the morning-after pill, which prevent a fertilised egg from attaching itself to the womb wall (these methods are sometimes called abortifacients).

Artificial methods can be used without any planning, and in any form of sexual relationship, however casual. They involve either changes to a woman's body or interfering with the normal sexual process. Condoms are also effective in preventing the transmission of sexually transmitted diseases (especially AIDS).

Questions

b Do you think contraception should be used? Give two reasons for your point of view. **4**

c Explain the main differences between natural and artificial methods of contraception. **8**

d 'It doesn't matter what type of contraceptive you use.'
   i Do you agree? Give reasons for your opinion. **3**
   ii Give reasons why some people may disagree with you. **3**

Exam Tip

c 'Explain' means give reasons. To answer this question you should refer to the last paragraph of natural methods and the last paragraph of artificial methods, clearly indicating the differences. For tips on Quality of Written Communication, look at page 3.

SUMMARY

Natural methods of contraception require planning, love and commitment by avoiding having sex in a woman's fertile period.

Artificial methods of contraception either prevent the sperm from meeting the egg, stop a woman producing eggs, or stop the fertilised egg from staying in the womb. They can be used in any type of sexual relationship.

Topic 3.3.10 Different Christian attitudes to contraception

> Contraception is seen as a gift from medical science under God's sovereignty. Choosing not to have or space families is morally defensible, considering the needs of the world, population size and family responsibility. However, those contraceptives that have an abortifacient function (for example, IUD and various pills) are considered to take human life and should be avoided.
>
> **Statement by the Baptist Church in *What the Churches Say***

> In July 1987, at a conference on responsible procreation, Pope John Paul II reminded Christians attending that Humanae Vitae *affirms the Church's consistent and historical teaching that there is an 'inseparable connection, willed by God and unable to be broken by man on his own initiative, between the two meanings of the conjugal act (married sexual act); the unitive and the procreative.'*

There are two main attitudes to contraception among Christians.

1. The Catholic attitude

The Catholic Church has always taught responsible parenthood. The Church teaches that sexual intercourse is a gift from God as a source of joy and pleasure to married couples (the unitive purpose) as well as a means of creating a family (the creative purpose). Responsible parenthood involves deciding on the number of children to have and when to have them. However, the Catholic way to achieve this is through using natural family planning (see page 70). The Church in its documents always refers to natural and artificial methods of birth regulation, but the exam specification uses the word contraception. The Church teaches that using artificial methods of contraception is going against God's intentions. Catholics believe this because:

- In *Casti Connubii*, published in 1930, Pope Pius XI condemned all forms of artificial contraception.
- In 1951, Pope Pius XII declared that Catholics could use natural methods of contraception as these are natural and so part of God's creation.
- In 1968, Pope Paul VI's encyclical *Humanae Vitae* affirmed the teaching of previous Popes that the only allowable forms of contraception are natural methods. This teaching has been confirmed in the Catechism of the Catholic Church.
- Artificial methods of birth control separate the unitive and creative aspects of sex, which is not what God intended.
- Some contraceptives have abortifacient effects (they bring about a very early abortion) and so are against the teaching of the Church.
- The Catholic Church regards contraception as a major cause of sexual promiscuity, broken families, the rise in the divorce rate and sexually transmitted diseases.

2. The attitude of non-Catholic Christians

Almost all non-Catholic Christians believe that all forms of contraception are permissible as long as they are used to restrict the size of the family and not simply to stop having children altogether. They have this attitude because:

- Christianity is about love and justice, and contraception improves women's health and raises the standard of living of children as families are smaller.
- God created sex for enjoyment and to cement the bonds of marriage. Within marriage, contraception allows the role of sex to be separated from making children and this is not against God's will.
- There is nothing in the Bible that forbids the use of contraception.
- In 1930, the Lambeth Conference of the worldwide Anglican Communion (Church of England) declared it was legitimate for Christians to use contraception to limit family size. This has been followed by the major Protestant Churches and the **Orthodox Churches**.
- They believe that it is better to combat HIV/AIDS by using condoms than by expecting everyone to follow Christian rules about sex and marriage.

> *The methods of birth regulation based on self-observation and the use of infertile periods ... respect the bodies of the spouses, encourage tenderness between them ... In contrast, 'every action which, whether in anticipation of the conjugal act, or in its accomplishment, or in the development of its natural consequences, proposes, whether as an end or as a means, to render procreation impossible' is intrinsically evil.*
>
> **Catechism of the Catholic Church 2370**

Questions

b Do you think it is wrong for Christians to use artificial methods of contraception? Give two reasons for your point of view. **4**

c Explain why some Christians allow artificial methods of contraception and some do not. **8**

d 'Christians should never use contraceptives.'
  i Do you agree? Give reasons for your opinion. **3**
  ii Give reasons why some people may disagree with you. **3**

Exam Tip

b You should already have thought about this, and you just have to give two reasons for your opinion. For example, if you agree you could use two reasons for the Catholic Church disagreeing with artificial methods of contraception.

SUMMARY

The Catholic Church teaches that using artificial methods of contraception to stop a baby being conceived is wrong. God gave sex in order to create children as well as strengthening the marriage. Natural methods of contraception are acceptable. Other Christians allow the use of contraception because they believe God gave sex to strengthen a married relationship.

Topic 3.3.11 How an issue from marriage and the family has been presented in one form of the media

You have to study how **one** issue from marriage and the family has been presented in one form of the media.

Your issue could be connected with:

- sex outside marriage
- adultery
- divorce
- re-marriage
- family life
- homosexuality
- contraception.

You can choose the media but it should only be one of the following:

- a soap opera
- a film
- a television drama
- a television documentary
- a radio programme
- a newspaper article in two different types of newspaper, for example *The Times* and the *Sun*.

If you study a film such as *Keeping Mum*, where ▶ Rowan Atkinson starred as a Church of England vicar whose preoccupation with the Church led his wife to adultery and his daughter to promiscuity, you need to investigate whether the way the film presented the issue was fair to religious people and religious beliefs.

You must choose both the issue and the type of media carefully to be able to answer questions on:

- why the issue is important
- how it was presented
- whether the presentation was fair to religious beliefs
- whether the presentation was fair to religious people.

To do this you must:

1. Select an issue and a form of media. It is very important that you select only one issue. Some films have several issues running through them. If you choose more than one issue, your answers are likely to be confused.

2. Decide why the issue is important (you may need to look at the views of different members of the particular religion and of the impact of the issue on society as a whole) and why you think the producers of the media decided to focus on this issue.

3. Write an outline of how the issue was presented, listing the main events and the way the events explored the issue.

4. Look closely at the way religious beliefs are treated in the presentation of the issue. Use this information to decide whether you think the presentation was fair to religious beliefs.

5. Look closely at the way religious people are treated in the presentation of the issue. Use this information to decide whether you think the presentation was fair to religious people.

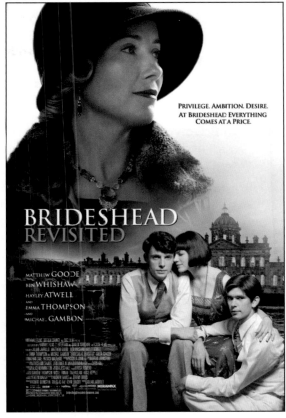

If you study a film such as *Brideshead Revisited*, you need to investigate whether the treatment of Catholic beliefs and people in regard to homosexuality is fair.

Questions

b Do you think the media presented an issue from marriage and the family fairly? Give two reasons for your point of view. **4**

c Choose an issue from marriage and the family presented in one form of the media and explain whether the presentation was fair to religious people. **8**

d You are unlikely to be asked an evaluation question on this section as you only have to study one issue in one form of the media.

Exam Tip

c Briefly summarise the presentation, then explain why some religious people would think the presentation was fair (with reasons) and others would think it was unfair (with reasons) then decide what you think.

SUMMARY

When studying the presentation of an issue from marriage and the family in the media, you must be able to explain why the issue was chosen, how it was presented, whether the presentation treated religious people fairly and whether the presentation treated religious beliefs fairly.

How to answer exam questions

Question A What is a re-constituted family?   **2 marks**

Where two sets of children (step-brothers and sisters) become one family when their divorced parents marry each other.

Question B Do you think it is wrong for Christians to use artificial methods of contraception?

Give two reasons for your point of view.   **4 marks**

Yes I do because the Catholic Church teaches that artificial methods are against the will of God. Also I believe they are wrong because they encourage people to have casual sex, and even to have sex with other people than their husband/wife, which is breaking one of the Ten Commandments.

Question C Explain why family life is important in Catholic Christianity.   **8 marks**

Family life is important for Catholics because the marriage service and baptism service teach it is the way given by God for the upbringing of children, and if it is given by God it must be important. It is important because the Bible teaches in Genesis and Ephesians that the family is a part of God's plan; and Catholics believe the Bible is the word of God.

The family is also important for Catholics because the Catholic Church teaches that it is the duty of parents to care for their children and bring them up in the Christian faith. As Catholics should follow the teachings of the Church, this makes family life important for them. Finally the family is the place where children learn about the faith. If it were not for the family, there would be fewer new Christians and so this makes the family very important for Catholics.

Question D 'A religious wedding ceremony helps to make a marriage work.'

  i Do you agree? Give reasons for your opinion.   **3 marks**

  ii Give reasons why some people may disagree with you.   **3 marks**

In your answer, you should refer to Catholic Christianity.

i I agree because I am a Catholic and I believe that a Catholic wedding ceremony helps to make a marriage work because the couple make promises to God to stay together and breaking that promise would be like lying to God. Also at the ceremony prayers are said by a priest asking God's blessing and so God will be helping to make the marriage work. Finally they get advice at the ceremony from the Bible and the priest about how to make the marriage work.

ii Some people do not agree because they believe that love is what makes a marriage work. They may think that just as many people who have a religious wedding ceremony get divorced as those who do not have a religious wedding ceremony. They may also think that if you make a promise to stay with someone you love, you will not break that promise whether you make it to God as well or not. Finally they may believe that people who have affairs do not seem to think, 'God will punish me for this'. So the religious ceremony has not helped.

QUESTION A
A high mark answer because it gives a correct definition.

QUESTION B
A high mark answer because an opinion is backed up by two developed reasons.

QUESTION C
A high mark answer because four reasons for family life being important in Catholic Christianity are developed. A formal style of English is used and there is good use of specialist vocabulary such as baptism, Bible, Ephesians, Genesis, the Church, Christian faith.

QUESTION D
A high mark answer because it states the candidate's own opinion and backs it up with three clear reasons for thinking that a religious ceremony helps to make a marriage work. It then gives three reasons for some people disagreeing and believing that a religious ceremony does not help to make a marriage work.

Section 3.4 Religion and community cohesion

Introduction

This section of the examination specification requires you to look at issues surrounding the roles of men and women, racial harmony, religious harmony and the media and community cohesion.

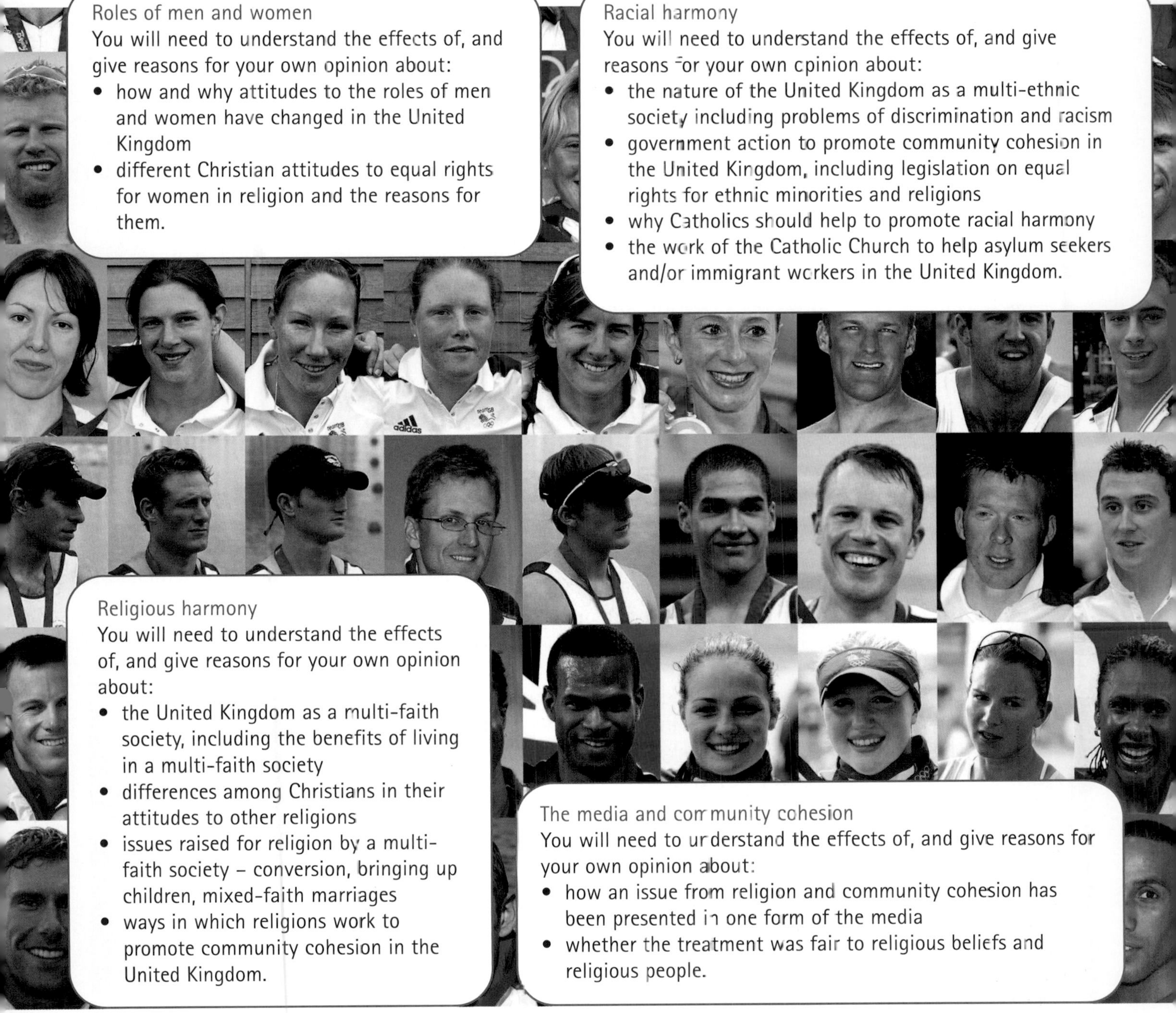

Roles of men and women

You will need to understand the effects of, and give reasons for your own opinion about:

- how and why attitudes to the roles of men and women have changed in the United Kingdom
- different Christian attitudes to equal rights for women in religion and the reasons for them.

Racial harmony

You will need to understand the effects of, and give reasons for your own opinion about:

- the nature of the United Kingdom as a multi-ethnic society including problems of discrimination and racism
- government action to promote community cohesion in the United Kingdom, including legislation on equal rights for ethnic minorities and religions
- why Catholics should help to promote racial harmony
- the work of the Catholic Church to help asylum seekers and/or immigrant workers in the United Kingdom.

Religious harmony

You will need to understand the effects of, and give reasons for your own opinion about:

- the United Kingdom as a multi-faith society, including the benefits of living in a multi-faith society
- differences among Christians in their attitudes to other religions
- issues raised for religion by a multi-faith society – conversion, bringing up children, mixed-faith marriages
- ways in which religions work to promote community cohesion in the United Kingdom.

The media and community cohesion

You will need to understand the effects of, and give reasons for your own opinion about:

- how an issue from religion and community cohesion has been presented in one form of the media
- whether the treatment was fair to religious beliefs and religious people.

77

Topic 3.4.1 How and why attitudes to the roles of men and women have changed in the United Kingdom

Women make up 84 per cent of employees in personal services (care assistants, child minders, hairdressers, etc).

Men make up 66 per cent of managers, senior officials, professionals.

Source: Census 2001

Statistics

The gender pay gap (the difference between men's and women's median hourly pay) is narrowing:

1986	26%
2002	19%
2007	12.6%

Average minutes spent per day

Activity	Men	Women
Cooking	27	54
Cleaning	13	47
Laundry	4	18
Caring for children	22	42

Source: National Statistics

How attitudes have changed

Women in the UK have always had the right to own property and earn their own living, but in the past they did not have the same rights as men and, when women married, their husbands had the right to use their property. During the second half of the nineteenth century, it became the accepted view that married women should stay at home and look after the children (in 1850 about 50 per cent of married women had been in employment, but by 1900 this was down to about 15 per cent).

During the late nineteenth and early twentieth centuries, women began to campaign to be treated as the equals of men. The growth of equal rights for women began with the Married Women's Property Act 1882, which allowed married women to keep their property separate from their husband's. In 1892, the Local Government Act gave women the right to stand as councillors. In 1918, the Representation of the People Act allowed women over 30 to vote in parliamentary elections (men could vote at 21). However, it was not until 1928 that the Electoral Reform Act gave equal voting rights to women, and allowed women to stand as MPs.

Equal rights in employment did not arrive until the Equal Pay Act of 1970, which required employers to give women the same pay as men – equal pay for like work regardless of the employee's sex. Then, in 1975, the Sex Discrimination Act made it illegal to discriminate in employment on grounds of gender or whether someone is married (though religion was given an opt-out). These Acts gave women the right to take employers to court if they treated them differently.

Although women achieved equal rights in law, attitudes to the roles of men and women have been even slower to change.

Men's attitudes to the roles of men and women have changed considerably – in 1989, 32 per cent of men agreed that, 'a man's

A female technician. How does this ▶ image show changing attitudes to the role of women?

job is to earn money, a woman's job is to look after the home and family' whereas in 2008 only 17 per cent of men agreed with the statement. However, there has been less progress in who actually does the work around the home. Sixty-eight per cent of women say they do all the housework, though only 54 per cent of men agree.

Why attitudes have changed

- During the First and Second World Wars, women had to take on many of the jobs previously done by men and proved they could do them just as well.
- The development of equal rights for women in other countries (New Zealand was the first country to give women equal political rights) made it difficult to claim it was not needed.
- The success of women as councillors and the important contribution of women to developments in health and social care showed that women were the equals of men in these areas.
- The work of the suffragette movement to gain equal voting and political rights for women showed the men in authority that women were no longer prepared to be treated as second class citizens.
- Social and industrial developments in the 1950s and 1960s led to the need for more women workers and for married women to provide a second income.
- The UN Declaration of Human Rights and the development of the Feminist Movement put forward a case for equal rights that could not be contradicted.
- The Labour Governments of 1964–70 and 1974–79 were dedicated to the equal rights campaign and passed the Equal Pay Act and the Sex Discrimination Act.

Why might this have surprised people in 1943?

> *Everyone is entitled to all the rights and freedoms set forth in this Declaration, without distinction of any kind, such as race, colour, sex, language, religion, political or other opinion, national or social origin, property, birth or other status. Furthermore, no distinction shall be made on the basis of the political, jurisdictional or international status of the country or territory to which a person belongs, whether it be independent, trust, non-self-governing or under any other limitation of sovereignty.*
>
> **Article 2 of the UN Declaration of Human Rights**

Questions

b Do you think men should share housework with women? Give two reasons for your point of view. **4**

c Explain how attitudes to the roles of men and women have changed. **8**

d 'Men and women should have equal roles in life.'
  i Do you agree? Give reasons for your opinion. **3**
  ii Give reasons why some people may disagree with you. **3**

Exam Tip

c 'Explain' means give reasons. To answer this question you should use four changes from this topic, beginning with what the attitude used to be and explaining how it has changed. Your answer should be four short paragraphs. For tips on Quality of Written Communication, look at page 3.

SUMMARY

Attitudes to the roles of men and women have changed greatly. Women now have equal rights and men and women are expected to share roles in the home. Attitudes have changed because of the Feminist Movement, social and industrial changes and the effects of the World Wars.

Topic 3.4.2 Different Christian attitudes to equal rights for women in religion

> A wife is to submit graciously to the servant leadership of her husband even as the Church willingly submits to the leadership of Christ ... she, being in the image of God, as is her husband and thus equal to him, has the God-given responsibility to respect her husband and to serve as his helper.

Statement by the Southern Baptist Convention of the USA, June 1998

> The Lord Jesus chose men to form the college of the twelve apostles, and the apostles did the same when they chose collaborators to succeed them in their ministry ... for this reason, the **ordination** of women is impossible.

Catechism of the Catholic Church 1577

Traditional Protestant Christians believe women should grow their hair long and keep their heads covered as instructed in 1 Corinthians 11:3–10.

1. Catholic attitudes

The Catholic Church teaches that men and women should have equal roles in life and equal rights in society. As far as ministry is concerned, women are able to study and teach in **theological colleges**. Women can also be **extraordinary ministers** of Holy Communion (people who give out the bread and wine which has been consecrated by a priest), visit the sick, take funerals in certain circumstances, and so on. Indeed it is estimated that over 80 per cent of religious teachers and **pastoral** visitors in the USA Catholic Church are women. Over half of the **lectors** and extraordinary ministers in the British Catholic Church are women.

However, the Catholic Church teaches that only men can be ordained priests. It teaches that this does not affect the equal status of women. It is because of the special function of the priest representing Jesus at the Mass. This teaching is based on:

- Genesis 1:27 which teaches that God created men and women at the same time and both in the image of God. So the Church teaches that men and women have equal status in the sight of God.
- The teaching of the Catholic Catechism that men and women are equal, and should have equal rights in life and society, and Catholics should follow the teachings of the Catechism.
- The 1971 report, 'Justice in the World', in which the Third World Synod of Bishops called for women to 'participate in, and share responsibility for, the life of society and of the Church'.
- The teaching of the Catechism that only men can be priests because the **apostles** were all men, and priests and bishops are successors of the apostles.
- The teaching of the Catechism that only men can be priests because Jesus was a man and the priest represents Jesus in the Mass.

2. The traditional attitude of Protestant Christianity

Many Evangelical Protestants teach that men and women have separate and different roles and so cannot have equal rights in religion. It is the role of women to bring up children and run a Christian home. Women should not speak in church and must submit to their husbands. It is the role of men to provide for the family and to lead the family in religion. Men must love their wives as themselves, but only men can be church leaders and teachers.

They have this attitude because:

- It is the teaching of the New Testament, which they believe is the final word of God. St Paul teaches that women should not teach or speak in church.

- St Paul also uses the story of Adam and Eve in Genesis to show that men have been given more rights by God because Adam was created first and it was the woman who was led astray by Satan and then led man astray.
- Although Jesus had women followers, he chose only men as his twelve apostles.
- It has been the tradition of the Church from the beginning that only men should have leadership rights in the Church.

3. The modern attitude of Protestant Christianity

Many Protestant Churches now accept that men and women should have equal rights, and they have women ministers and priests (for example **Church of England**, **Methodist**, United Reformed Church and Baptist). This teaching is based on:

- the creation story in Genesis 1, which says that God created male and female at the same time and of equal status because both were created in the image of God.
- some letters of Paul where he teaches that in Christ there is neither male nor female therefore men and women should have equal rights.
- the evidence from the Gospels that Jesus treated women as his equals. He preached in the Court of Women in the Jerusalem Temple (Matthew 21:23–22:14). He treated a Samaritan woman as his equal (John 4). He had women disciples who stayed with him at the cross (Matthew 27:55, Mark 15:40–41, Luke 23:27, John 19:25–27) unlike the male disciples who ran away. It was to women that Jesus first appeared after the resurrection.
- some evidence that there were women priests in the early Church. The Council of Laodicea banned women priests in the fourth century and it would not have banned something that did not exist.

Should women be allowed to become bishops?

Questions

b Do you think women should have equal rights in religion? Give two reasons for your point of view. **4**

c Explain why some Christians give equal roles to women in religion and some do not. **8**

d 'Women should have equal roles in Christianity.'
   i Do you agree? Give reasons for your opinion. **3**
   ii Give reasons why some people may disagree with you. **3**

Exam Tip

b You should already have thought about this, and you just have to give two reasons for your opinion. For example, if you agree with equal rights for women in religion except for the priesthood, you could use two reasons for the Catholic attitude.

SUMMARY

- Catholics believe men and women should have equal rights, but only men can become priests because Jesus was a man and the priest is representing him at Mass.
- Traditional Protestants believe only men should be religious leaders because this is what the Bible teaches.
- Liberal Protestants believe men and women have equal rights in religion because Jesus had women disciples.

Topic 3.4.3 The nature of the UK as a multi-ethnic society

KEY WORDS

Discrimination – treating people less favourably because of their ethnicity/gender/colour/sexuality/age/class.

Ethnic minority – a member of an ethnic group (race) which is much smaller than the majority group.

Multi-ethnic society – many different races and cultures living together in one society.

Prejudice – believing some people are inferior or superior without even knowing them.

Racism – the belief that some races are superior to others.

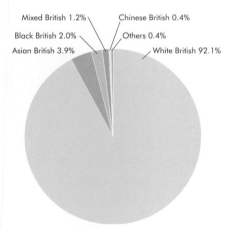

Mixed British 1.2%
Chinese British 0.4%
Black British 2.0%
Others 0.4%
Asian British 3.9%
White British 92.1%

The different ethnicities in the UK, according to the 2001 census.

The United Kingdom has always been a mixed society – Celts, Romans, Angles, Saxons, Jutes, Danes, Vikings and Normans are all ancestors of the British.

The United Kingdom has always believed in human freedom and offered asylum to those suffering persecution; for example, to French Protestants (Huguenots) in the seventeenth century, to Russian Jews in the nineteenth century, to European Jews escaping Hitler in the twentieth century.

In the nineteenth century the United Kingdom built up an empire around the world. In exchange for being ruled by Britain, citizens of the Empire were allowed to settle in the United Kingdom. Slaves who set foot on British soil immediately became free. As a result, small black communities grew up in Bristol, Liverpool and Cardiff.

The Empire became known as the Commonwealth as nations gained their independence from the United Kingdom. In the 1950s there was substantial immigration from the Commonwealth. People came from India, Pakistan, Bangladesh, West Africa and the Caribbean to lessen a labour shortage in the United Kingdom. Many of these workers had fought for the United Kingdom in the Second World War (there were more people in the British armed forces from the Commonwealth than from the United Kingdom itself).

Immigration from the Commonwealth has continued on a smaller scale, but the extension of the EU at the beginning of this century led to a large influx of East Europeans, and wars and racial/religious persecutions have led to an increase of asylum seekers (people wanting to live in the UK because their lives are at risk in their own countries).

Although only 7.9 per cent of the total United Kingdom population is **ethnic minority**, there are big differences in different areas. For example, 29 per cent of London's population is of ethnic minority origin, as opposed to less than 2 per cent of the population of South West England.

Discrimination and racism

Racism is a type of **prejudice** that can cause major problems in a **multi-ethnic society** because of the **discrimination** it leads to. Racist people believe the ethnic group to which they belong to be superior to all other ethnic groups. Therefore they believe that all other races are inferior. Religiously prejudiced people believe

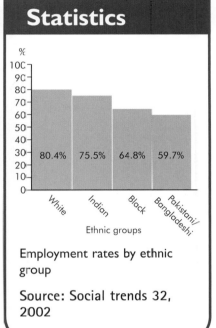

Statistics

Employment rates by ethnic group

Source: Social trends 32, 2002

The Notting Hill Carnival is a celebration of multi-ethnic Britain.

that everyone who does not believe in their religion is wrong.

The problems of discrimination and racism:

- Racially prejudiced employers will not give jobs to certain ethnic groups religiously prejudiced employers will not give jobs to certain religious groups (it is easy, for example, for employers to discriminate against Muslims, Sikhs and Orthodox Jews).
- Prejudiced landlords are likely to refuse accommodation to certain ethnic groups or religions.
- If teachers are prejudiced against certain ethnic minorities or religious groups, they will discriminate against them in their teaching, so that those pupils do not achieve the results (and so gain the jobs) of which they are capable. They could try to get them excluded from school, put them into lower ability groups than their actual ability, etc.
- Prejudiced police officers could potentially discriminate against certain ethnic or religious groups for example by: stopping and searching them if they have no real reason for so doing; not treating evidence from people against whom they are prejudiced in the same way that they treat evidence from people against whom they are not prejudiced.

Skilled immigrants from Eastern Europe, far from posing a threat, will help to raise wages in Britain and boost exports, economists predict ... Eastern European countries have plenty of skilled people with post-school education and training.

The Times, 5 April 2004

The effects of discrimination and racism

The effects of discrimination and racism can be quite devastating for a multi-ethnic society:

- If certain groups feel that they are being treated unfairly by society, then they will begin to feel alienated by society and so work against that society.
- Some politicians believe that young black people turn to crime because they feel they will not be able to get good well-paid jobs because of racism and discrimination and so they might as well earn good money from crime. If true, this might lead to an increase in crime.
- Some politicians believe that some young people have been turning to extremist Islamic groups because they feel they have no chance of success in a prejudiced British society that discriminates against their religion. This can then lead them to commit terrorist acts.
- Racism and discrimination can lead to the rise of groups like the BNP (British National Party), which stir up hatred of different ethnic groups leading to violence and communal warfare.

◀ The BNP (British National Party) campaigned in the London Mayor elections of 2008 to have a mayor who would treat London's ethnic and religious minorities differently from white English Christians. Their candidate gained 2.89 per cent of the first choice votes and 6.42 per cent of the second choice votes.

If a multi-ethnic society is to function well, it must treat all it members fairly, and give equal opportunities to all its members to produce their best.

The benefits of living in a multi-ethnic society

Multi-ethnic societies bring far more benefits than problems:

- There is likely to be less chance of war because people of different ethnic groups and nationalities will get to know and like each other, and probably intermarry.

- More progress will be made in a multi-ethnic society because new people will bring in new ideas and new ways of doing things. Societies that are cut off and do not mix with other cultures tend to be less progressive, for example, the Amazonian Indians.
- Life is more interesting with a much greater variety of food, music, fashion and entertainment.
- A multi-ethnic society helps people to see that different ethnic groups are all part of the human race and we have more in common than we have differences. This is vital in a world of multi-national companies and economic interdependence between all nations.

Why do you think President Barack Obama is seen by many as a sign that the USA now has equal rights?

Barack Hussein Obama was elected the 44th president of the United States on Tuesday, sweeping away the last racial barrier in American politics with ease as the country chose him as its first black chief executive ...

Tens of thousands of people turned out to hear Mr. Obama's victory speech in Grant Park Chicago.

"If there is anyone out there who still doubts that America is a place where all things are possible, who still wonders if the dream of our founders is alive in out time, who still questions the power of our democracy, tonight is your answer.

"It's been a long time coming, but tonight, because of what we did on this date in this election at this defining moment, change has come to America."

adapted from *New York Times* November 4th 2008

Questions

b Do you think we need laws against racism? Give two reasons for your point of view. **4**

c Explain why discrimination and racism cause problems in a multi-ethnic society. **8**

d 'Prejudice and discrimination should be banned.'
  i Do you agree? Give reasons for your opinion. **3**
  ii Give reasons why some people may disagree with you. **3**

Exam Tip

c 'Explain' means give reasons. To answer this question you should use four effects of discrimination and racism. Your answer should be four short paragraphs. For tips on Quality of Written Communication look at page 3.

SUMMARY

- Britain has many ethnic minorities and so is a multi-ethnic society.
- Multi-ethnic societies have many benefits, such as advancing more quickly because they have a greater variety of ideas.
- A multi-ethnic society needs equal opportunities and treatment to work, and prejudice and discrimination cause major problems in such a society because they do not treat everyone equally.

Topic 3.4.4 Government action to promote community cohesion in the United Kingdom

In almost every one of the Commonwealth's 53 nations there are schools distinguished by names like King's, Queen's, Bishop's ... We were taught that all traditions could and should play a part in nation building. That we would all have, somehow, to share this space. ... Our planet has never been more in need of that shared set of values and that common sentiment of toleration than today ... (the) Equality and Human Rights Commission has (a duty) to make sure that people who are very different can live together. It is integral to our mandate of reducing inequality, promoting human rights, strengthening good relations.

From a speech by Trevor Phillips, Head of the Equality and Human Rights Commission, January 2008

The United Kingdom believes that a multi-ethnic society needs to promote **community cohesion** in order to overcome the problems of prejudice, discrimination and racism. The British Government promotes community cohesion by:

- financially supporting groups that are working for community cohesion
- making community cohesion part of the national education curriculum. The Education and Inspections Act 2006 introduced a duty on all maintained schools in England to promote community cohesion and on Ofsted to report on the contributions made in this area
- funding research into the best ways of achieving community cohesion
- appointing cabinet ministers, judges, etc., from ethnic minorities
- passing the Race Relations Act, which makes it unlawful to discriminate against anyone because of race, colour, nationality, ethnic or national origin, use threatening or abusive or insulting words in public that could stir up racial hatred; publish anything likely to cause racial hatred
- passing the Crime and Disorder Act, which allows higher maximum penalties where there is evidence of racial or religious motivation or hostility
- passing the Racial and Religious Hatred Act, which makes it an offence to use threatening words or behaviour intended to incite groups of people defined by their religious beliefs or lack of belief
- establishing the Equality and Human Rights Commission, which champions equality and human rights for all
- ensuring that the Labour Party, the Conservative Party and the Liberal Democrat Party oppose racism in any form particularly by encouraging members of ethnic minorities to become MPs.

Why community cohesion is important

Community cohesion is important for all multi-ethnic and **multi-faith societies** because:

- Without community cohesion, different groups in society have different visions of what society should be like and this can lead to violence and civil unrest.
- A lack of community cohesion in Oldham, Burnley and Bradford led to racially/religiously motivated street rioting in

2001. According to the Government Cantle report, the rioting was caused by: different communities living 'parallel lives', ignorance about other communities being exploited by extremists and weak local leadership and policing. Single-faith schools were also criticised for raising the possibility of deeper divisions.

- The 7 July 2007 bombers on the London Underground were British citizens who had lost their sense of allegiance to Britain and, indeed, were prepared to kill, maim and injure their fellow citizens.
- In countries without community cohesion (such as Iraq, Kosovo and Kashmir) violence becomes a way of life.
- Lack of community cohesion leads to different communities leading separate lives, making civilised living impossible.

Community cohesion may have prevented atrocities like the July 7 2007 London bombings.

Community cohesion is therefore about: how to avoid the bad effects of intolerance and harassment that can break down society; how to encourage different groups to work together and treat each other as fellow citizens; how to ensure respect for diversity whilst building up a commitment to common and shared bonds as citizens of the same society.

Questions

b Do you think the government should spend money promoting community cohesion? Give two reasons for your point of view. **4**

c Explain how the government is trying to promote community cohesion. **8**

d 'Promoting community cohesion is the most important thing a government can do in a multi-ethnic society.'
  i Do you agree? Give reasons for your opinion. **3**
  ii Give reasons why some people may disagree with you. **3**

Exam Tip

c 'Explain' means give reasons. To answer this question you should use four government actions from this topic, and for each action explain how it should improve community cohesion. Your answer should be four short paragraphs. For tips on Quality of Written Communication, look at page 3.

SUMMARY

The government is promoting community cohesion in the UK by passing laws against racism and discrimination, and by making community cohesion part of the national curriculum. Community cohesion is important because without it a multi-ethnic society could become violent and divided.

Topic 3.4.5 Why Catholics should help to promote racial harmony

The Catholic Church has members from every country in the world. Almost 30 per cent of the world's population is Catholic and over 70 per cent of Catholics are non-white, non-European.

Catholics should try to promote **racial harmony** because:

- In the Parable of the Good Samaritan (Luke 10:25–37), Jesus taught that Christians should love their neighbours and that neighbour means people of all races. Jews and Samaritans were different races who, according to the Gospels, hated each other. In the parable, Jesus taught that the Good Samaritan treated the Jew who was attacked as his neighbour, so showing that Christians have to treat people of every race as their neighbour who they have to love.
- Scholars point out that Simon of Cyrene, who helped Jesus carry his cross, was a black African.
- Jesus treated a Samaritan woman as his equal (John 4) and healed a Roman centurion's servant (Luke 7).
- St Peter was given a vision by God (Acts 10) in which God sent

'Which of these three do you think, was a neighbour to the man who fell into the hands of robbers?' The expert in the law replied, 'The one who had mercy on him'. Jesus told him, 'Go and do likewise'.

Luke 10:36–37

Then Peter began to speak: 'I now realise how true it is that God does not show favouritism but accepts men from every nation who fear him and do what is right'.

Acts 10:34–35

The Church rejects as foreign to the mind of Christ, any discrimination against men or harassment of them because of their race, colour, condition of life, or religion.

Declaration on the Relationship of the Church to non-Christians

The Good Samaritan by Vincent Van Gogh. How does the Parable of the Good Samaritan encourage Christians to promote racial harmony?

down a sheet filled with all sorts of animals and told Peter to eat from them, but Peter refused because, according to Jewish law, they were unclean. A voice from heaven told him, 'What God has made clean, you have no right to call profane.' Peter believed that God was showing him that God treats all races the same and accepts the worship of anyone who does right whatever their race.

- St Paul taught in Galatians 3:26–29 that everyone is equal in Christ and so there can be no divisions of race among Christians.
- St Paul also taught that as God created all nations from one man, Adam, all nations are therefore equal to each other.
- There are Catholic **cardinals** and bishops of every race and colour of skin, and the Church is dedicated to fighting racism in all its forms.
- Many Christians and Christian groups have worked for racial harmony. A major Catholic organisation working to promote racial harmony in the UK and in the Church is the Catholic Association for Racial Justice (CARJ). You can find details of their work on www.carj.uk. St Martin de Porres (1579-1639) was born of mixed race parents and is the patron saint of inter-racial justice. Blessed Katharine Drexel (1858-1955) founded the Sisters of the Blessed Sacrament to work for racial harmony in the USA. You may have studied the work of Mary Seacole (who was voted the greatest Black Briton in history) during KS3.

Cardinal Francis Arinze of Nigeria, whose senior position is a sign of racial harmony in the Catholic Church.

SUMMARY

Catholics should promote racial harmony because of the teachings of the Bible and Church against racism and because they should follow the example of Jesus.

Questions

b Do you think Catholics should help to promote racial harmony? **4**

c Explain why Catholics should help to promote racial harmony. **8**

d 'If everyone were religious, there would be no racism.'
  i Do you agree? Give reasons for your opinion. **3**
  ii Give reasons why some people may disagree with you. **3**

Exam Tip

b You should already have thought about this, and you just have to give two reasons for your opinion. For example, if you agree with Catholics promoting racial harmony, you could use two reasons from this topic.

It is the way we look at others that must be purified. Harbouring racist thoughts and entertaining racist attitudes is a sin against the specific message of Christ for whom one's 'neighbour' is not only a person from my tribe, my milieu, my religion or my nation: it is every person I meet along the way.

The Church and Racism Article 62, 1998

Respect for the humanity we share with each and every neighbour is the only basis for a peaceful and good society. Any attack on the dignity and human rights of any racial or religious group damages all of us.

From the Churches Together letter to the press, May 1998

Topic 3.4.6 The work of the Catholic Church to help asylum seekers and immigrant workers

> *Globalisation and a more mobile labour market is bringing numbers of people to our parishes. They come with many spiritual and pastoral needs ... The Church has a responsibility to accompany migrants, to create a space where they feel safe, where they can come and talk. This is rooted in scriptural tradition: Jesus was from a migrant family and in the spread of Christianity, migration goes back to the Acts of the Apostles. Advocacy and advice are what the Church can offer today. We can point migrants towards the services available.*
>
> **Bishop Lynch Head of the Bishops' Conference Office for Migrants and Refugee Policy, 12 April 2008**

How the Catholic Church in England and Wales helps asylum seekers and immigrant workers

- It has established The Office for Refugee Policy (ORP) which monitors information and prepares briefs on immigration to enable the bishops to develop policy and respond to debates. The ORP represents the bishops on the immigration issue nationally and internationally and helps ordinary Catholics to become engaged in refugee work.
- In April 2008, the Catholic Bishops' Conference launched 'Mission of the Church to Migrants in England and Wales' putting forward a range of ways in which local parishes can create 'a ministry of welcome' for immigrants worshipping in a local parish. These include:
  - making leaflets on local healthcare, admissions policies of local Catholic schools, etc., available in appropriate languages
  - providing English language classes
  - organising collections of essential equipment to give to migrants to help them set up home.
- Parishes with substantial numbers of immigrants have set up legal advice clinics where lawyers with appropriate language skills help immigrants cope with the legal issues of settling in the UK.
- Some parishes are providing Masses in languages other than English so that immigrant workers can maintain their faith and worship until they learn English.
- Westminster Cathedral has an annual Migrants Mass.
- Parishes are being encouraged to elevate the status of immigrant workers and help British society to see that immigrants are not a drain on Britain's resources, but hard-working dedicated people who have suffered much to reach a haven of peace and opportunity. Newsletters from the ORP point to the vital work being done by immigrant workers in low paid jobs for the NHS.

Campaigning for justice for immigrant ▶ workers in London.

Why the Catholic Church helps asylum seekers and immigrant workers

- The Bible teaches that God is a God of justice who requires his followers to behave justly and seek justice for everyone. This is taught in the Old Testament book of Amos. So Catholics should be seeking justice for immigrants and asylum seekers.
- The Catholic Church teaches that no one should be **oppressed** and that Christians should seek justice for the oppressed.
- Through working for justice for the oppressed, Christians show that they love God and their neighbours.
- Christians should follow the Golden Rule – **service to others** is the way to treat others as you would like to be treated.
- Throughout his life Jesus served others – he came 'not to be served but to serve others' Mark 10:45 and Christians should follow the example of Jesus.
- It is the teaching of Jesus, for example in the Parable of the Good Samaritan (see page 88) and the Parable of the Sheep and the Goats (see page 53).
- Jesus himself was a refugee and asylum seeker when the holy family fled to Egypt to avoid Herod's slaughter of the innocents.

There are so many Polish Catholics living in London who want Mass in Polish that the congregation spills out onto the pavement.

Questions

b Do you think it is important for the Catholic Church to help immigrant workers? Give two reasons for your point of view. **4**

c Explain why Catholics should help immigrant workers and/or asylum seekers. **8**

d 'Catholics should do more to help asylum seekers and immigrant workers.'
  i Do you agree? Give reasons for your opinion. **3**
  ii Give reasons why some people may disagree with you. **3**

Exam Tip

d Use the answering evaluation questions advice from page 9. Arguments for could be the reasons for helping plus any ideas you may have of what more the Church could do. Arguments against would be the work the Catholic Church is doing.

SUMMARY

The Catholic Church helps refugees and immigrant workers though a special office which tells parishes how they can help and which deals with publicity. Parishes offer help with such things as legal problems and English classes.

The Church helps because of the teachings of Jesus such as the parables of the Good Samaritan and the Sheep and the Goats.

Topic 3.4.7 The United Kingdom as a multi-faith society

Statistics

Census facts on religion in England and Wales

Christians
42,558,000 = 72.6%

No religion
8,197,221 = 14%

No answer
4,823,000 = 8.2%

Muslim
1,591,207 = 2.7%

Hindu
558,746 = 0.95%

Sikh
336,040 = 0.57%

Jewish
267,711 = 0.46%

Buddhist
149,237 = 0.25%

Other religions
157,000 = 0.27%

Source: Census 2001 ONS

Many societies were mono-faith (having only one religion) until the twentieth century. In some ways, Great Britain has been a multi-faith society ever since the **Reformation** in the sixteenth century. Although Queen Elizabeth I made the Church of England the state religion, there were other churches: Protestants who were not Church of England (**Nonconformists**), Roman Catholics and, from 1657, Jews. So Britain had to have laws encouraging **religious freedom** (everyone free to follow their chosen religion without discrimination). These were:

- 1688 Nonconformists were given freedom of worship.
- 1828 Nonconformists were given the same political rights as members of the Church of England.
- 1829 Roman Catholics were given the same political rights as members of the Church of England.
- 1858 Jews were given the same political rights as members of the Church of England.

These meant that members of any religion were free to worship in Great Britain and had equal political rights so that it became a **religiously pluralist** society.

However, it was in the twentieth century that Great Britain became truly multi-faith as members of religions other than Christianity and Judaism came to Britain as immigrants (although immigrants from the Caribbean and Africa were mainly Christian).

The Census figures in the margin give the view for the whole of England and Wales, but the percentages of religions can change if you look at certain areas where some religions are more prevalent. For example:

- The London Borough of Tower Hamlets has the highest percentage of Muslims of any UK council area at 36.4 per cent.
- Leicester has the highest percentage of Hindus of any UK council area at 14.3 per cent.
- The London Borough of Barnet has the highest percentage of Jews of any UK council area at 14.8 per cent.
- Slough has highest percentage of Sikhs of any UK council area at 9.1 per cent.
- The London Borough of Westminster has the highest percentage of Buddhists of any UK council area at 1.3 per cent.
- In Birmingham 14.4 per cent of the population are Muslim, 2.9 per cent Sikh, 2 per cent Hindu, 0.3 per cent Buddhist, 0.24 per cent Jewish.
- In Bradford 16 per cent of the population are Muslim, 1.1 per cent Sikh, 0.9 per cent Hindu.

- In the London Borough of Hounslow, there are 110,657 Christians, 16,064 Hindus, 19,378 Muslims and 18,265 Sikhs. However, many non-Christians live in the area of Southall.

The benefits of living in a multi-faith society

A multi-faith society has many benefits:

- People can learn about other religions from their friends and neighbours, and this can help them to see what religions have in common.
- People from different religions may practise their religion more seriously (for example, Muslims praying five times a day) and this may make people think about how they practise their own religion.
- People may come to understand why different religions believe what they do and this may make people think more seriously about their own religion and consider why they believe what they do.
- People are likely to become a lot more understanding about each other's religions and realise that everyone is entitled to their own opinion about religion.
- Religious toleration and understanding will exist in a multi-faith society and this may help to stop religious conflicts such as that between Protestant and Catholic Christians in Northern Ireland or between Hindus, Muslims and Sikhs in India.
- A multi-faith society may even make some people think more about religion as they come across religious ideas they have never thought about before.

> ### Exam Tip
> c 'Explain' means give reasons. To answer this question you should use the census facts and the facts from different local councils and explain how they show the UK to be a multi-faith society. Your answer should be four short paragraphs. For tips on Quality of Written Communication, look at page 3.

These new religious buildings show the multi-faith nature of British society. These pictures show the Shri Swaminarayan Mandir in Neasden, London, and the Tibetan Buddhist Temple of Samye Lings in ◄ Dumfriesshire, Scotland.

Questions

b Do you think it is a good idea to have a lot of different religions in one place? Give two reasons for your point of view. **4**

c Explain why the United Kingdom is often referred to as a multi-faith society. **8**

d 'All societies should be multi-faith societies.'
   i Do you agree? Give reasons for your opinion. **3**
   ii Give reasons why some people may disagree with you. **3**

SUMMARY

Britain is a multi-faith society because several religions are practised here and everyone is free to practise their religion. A multi-faith society has many benefits such as religious freedom and the opportunity to find out about, and think more deeply about, different religions.

Topic 3.4.8 Differences among Christians in their attitudes to other religions

> *Christianity is the one true religion only because God decided so, only because the light of Christ falls on it ... No matter how good and true any other religion might seem, it is false, useless – because the light of Christ has not fallen on it.*
>
> **Karl Barth (Evangelical Protestant theologian)**

> *All nations form but one community. This is so because all stem from the one stock which God created to people the entire Earth, and also because all share a common destiny, namely God ... The Catholic Church recognises in other religions that search for the God who is unknown yet near since he gives life and breath and all things and wants all men to be saved.*
>
> **Catechism of the Catholic Church 842–843**

All Christians believe in religious freedom. That is they believe everyone has the right to follow, or not follow, any religion they wish. However, there are different Christian attitudes to other religions.

1. Catholics and many other Christians believe that non-Christian religions are searching for God and have some truth, but only Christianity has the whole truth (this is often known as **inclusivism**). They believe that other religions should be respected, and that their followers may get to heaven. However, they believe Christians have a duty to try to put across the Gospel message (evangelise) to people of other religions because they have the full truth. They have this attitude because:
   - It is the teaching of the Church in the Catechism and **papal encyclicals**.
   - They believe Jesus is the Son of God who shows the true nature of God.
   - The Bible teaches that Christianity reveals the full truth about God. Only Christians are assured of salvation, depending on future conduct, but other religions such as Judaism can contact God and may have the possibility of eternal life.

2. Some Evangelical Protestant Christians feel that, although members of other religions must be respected and given the freedom to practise their religion, everyone has the right to convert others. They believe Christianity is the only true religion and so they must try to convert everyone to Christianity (this is often called **exclusivism**). They have this attitude because:
   - They believe that sayings of Jesus such as, 'I am the way and the truth and the life. No one comes to the Father except through me' (John 14:6) mean that only Christians will go to heaven.
   - They think the command of Jesus for people to love their neighbour means that if people love their neighbour, they must want their neighbour to go to heaven and so they will want to convert them.

Pope John Paul II meeting the Dalai ▶ Lama in 1982. How does this photo show the Catholic Church teaching that other religions should be respected?

   - They believe that the final words of Jesus to his followers, 'Therefore go and make disciples of all nations' (Matthew 28:19), mean that everyone must be converted to Christianity.

Christian missionaries, like these at a Catholic Mission in Kenya, often proclaim the Gospel by helping people, so showing them God's love.

> Although in ways known only to himself God can lead those who, through no fault of their own, are ignorant of the Gospel, to that faith without which it is impossible to please him, the Church still has the obligation and also the sacred right to evangelise all men.
>
> **Catechism of the Catholic Church 848**

3. Some Liberal Protestant Christians believe that all religions are equal and are just different ways of finding God (this is often called **pluralism**). So they feel that Christians should respect other religions and work with them to make Britain a more spiritual and holy country. They have this attitude because:

- They do not believe the Bible is the word of God.
- They see Muslims, Hindus, Jews, Sikhs and Buddhists living good and holy lives in Britain today.
- They believe God is a force, like gravity, who can be discovered by people in different ways.
- They feel that the words of Jesus such as 'In my Father's house are many rooms' (John 14:2), mean that there is room in heaven for a variety of religions.

> All religions have a common faith in a higher reality which demands brotherhood on Earth ... perhaps one day such names as Christianity, Buddhism, Islam, Hinduism will no longer be used to describe men's religious experience.
>
> **John Hick (Christian philosopher)**

Questions

b Do you think all religions are the same? Give two reasons for your point of view. **4**

c Explain why some Christians believe that all other religions are wrong, and some do not. **8**

d 'All societies should be multi-faith societies.'
  i Do you agree? Give reasons for your opinion. **3**
  ii Give reasons why some people may disagree with you. **3**

Exam Tip

c 'Explain' means give reasons. To answer this question you should use two reasons for exclusivism and two reasons for inclusivism. For tips on Quality of Written Communication, look at page 3.

SUMMARY

All Christians believe in religious freedom, but:

- some Christians believe there is some truth in other religions
- some Christians believe Christianity is the only true religion
- some Christians believe all religions are a path to God.

Topic 3.4.9 Issues raised for religion by a multi-faith society

KEY WORD

Interfaith marriage – marriage where the husband and wife are from different religions.

Tolerance is so important, and never more so for Jews and Muslims. After September 11, the imam of the local mosque came to say a prayer for peace in Arabic, and I went to the mosque to say a prayer for peace in Hebrew.

Dr J. Romaine, rabbi of Maidenhead (quoted in *The Times***, 31 March 2004)**

I'm a minister in the Church with roots in the Sikh faith. The idea that I could be both a Sikh and a Methodist at the same time is a nonsense. The way I would describe myself is as a follower of Jesus Christ with roots in the Sikh faith.

Rev Inderjit Bhogal, former President of the Methodist Conference

He who knows one, knows none.

From *Introduction to the Science of Religion* **by Max Muller 1873**

For a multi-faith society to work, people need to have the same rights regardless of the religion they do or do not belong to. A multi-faith society cannot accept any one religion as being the true one because it would mean that, ideally, that religion should be the only religion and so the society should be mono-faith.

Similarly a multi-faith society must have religious freedom. The people living in the society must be free to choose or reject any or all of the religions practised in the society. If all religions have equal rights, then all people must have the right to pick and choose between religions.

A society that is both religiously pluralist and has religious freedom can raise a number of issues for religion.

Conversion

Conversion is an issue because the teachings of religions and the facts of a multi-faith society conflict with each other.

1. Many religions see it as their right, and even their duty, to convert everyone to their religion because:
   - They believe that their religion is the only true religion and that all other religions are mistaken.
   - They believe that everyone should go to heaven and the only way for the followers of other religions to get to heaven is for them to be converted.
   - Their holy books teach them that they should convert non-believers.

2. Trying to convert other religions in a multi-faith society can cause major problems because:
   - Many people would say that trying to convert followers of other religions when living in a multi-faith society is a type of prejudice and discrimination. Treating people differently because of their religion and trying to convert other religions is discriminating against those who do not have the same faith as you.
   - Many people would say that it is impossible to regard all other religions as wrong unless you have studied all of them and compared them to decide which one is true. No one who is trying to convert others has done this.
   - It can lead to arguments and even violence within a multi-faith society when people are told their religion is wrong.

The Catholic Church, and many other religious groups, differentiate between 'proclamation' and 'proselytisation'. They believe they have a duty to tell people about their faith (proclamation or evangelisation), but not to try to make converts of people from other religions (proselytisation). This ensures religious harmony in a multi-faith society.

Bringing up children

A multi-faith society requires everyone (including children) to have religious freedom. When children reach an age where they can think for themselves about religion they must be able to choose which religion to follow, or to reject religion. It also requires that children should learn about the different religions in the society so that they can respect other religions and respect people's right to be religious or not religious as they wish. However, this causes problems for many religious believers because:

- Most religions encourage parents to ensure that their children are brought up in their religion, and become members of it; consequently many parents do not want their children to learn about other religions or have the chance to choose a different religion, or reject religion.
- Most religions teach that only those who follow their religion will have a good life after death, so religious parents may worry that they will not see their children after death unless they stay in their religion.
- Social and peer pressures compel parents to exert pressure on their children to remain in the faith to preserve family and cultural traditions.
- Children educated in state schools experience the secular nature of British life and are tempted away from religious lifestyles.

Is it easier to keep the faith in a faith school or non-faith school?

The missionary task implies a respectful dialogue with those who do not yet accept the Gospel. Believers can profit from this dialogue by learning to appreciate better those elements of truth and grace which are found among peoples, and which are, as it were, a secret presence of God.

Catechism of the Catholic Church 856

Twelve years ago, Mary and Daniel fell in love with each other. They shared everything – except religion. Mary's parents refused to let her marry a non-Catholic while Daniel's parents were equally adamant that he should not marry outside the Jewish faith. The couple split up. However, although Daniel went away and married someone of his own faith, it proved an unsuccessful match and ended in divorce. He returned to his home town and, to his surprise, found Mary still there. This time they allowed no external factors to impede their togetherness, and they now have two children. Both regard the marriage as blissfully happy, and only regret the twelve years they needlessly spent apart. Their story will be seen in some quarters as the triumph of love over tradition. Others will see it as a religious disaster.

The Times, 7 September 2002

Can it be right to try to convert others when living in a multi-faith society?

Interfaith marriages

In a multi-faith society, young people of different faiths are going to meet, fall in love and want to marry (**interfaith marriage**). This can raise many problems for religious parents and religious leaders because:

- Often there can be no religious wedding ceremony because both couples must be members of the same religion for a religious wedding ceremony to be allowed.
- There is a question of which religion the children of the marriage will be brought up in. Some religions insist on a child being brought up in their religion, but how can a couple decide on this?
- There is also the problem of what will happen after death? Will the couple have to be buried in separate parts of the cemetery according to their religion?
- For the parents and relatives of the couple there is often the feeling that they have betrayed their roots and family by falling in love with someone from a different religion.

Unless these issues are dealt with, then religion itself can work against community cohesion and promote conflict and hatred.

How can you tell this is an interfaith wedding?

SUMMARY

A multi-faith society needs to have laws giving equal rights to all religions and to those who have no religion (religious pluralism). However, a multi-faith society can raise problems for religious people in areas such as:

- conversion attempts by other faiths because it is like discrimination
- bringing up children because they may leave their parents' faith
- interfaith marriages because of having to decide which faith the children should be brought up in.

Questions

b Do you think children should be free to choose their own religion? Give two reasons for your point of view. **4**

c Explain why interfaith marriages may cause problems. **8**

d 'In a multi-faith society, no religion should try to convert other people.'
   i Do you agree? Give reasons for your opinion. **3**
   ii Give reasons why some people may disagree with you. **3**

Exam Tip

b You should already have thought about this, and you just have to give two reasons for your opinion. For example, if you disagree you could use two reasons from the section on bringing up children.

Topic 3.4.10 Ways in which religions work to promote community cohesion in the United Kingdom

The different religions in the United Kingdom are beginning to work to promote community cohesion in the following ways.

1. Different religions are beginning to work with each other to try to discover what is the same in their religions (for example, Judaism, Islam and Christianity believe in the prophets **Abraham** and **Moses**), and from this work out ways of living together without trying to convert each other.

In September 2006, Pope Benedict XVI addressed a meeting with envoys from the Muslim world at the Pope's residence near Rome. 'I would like today to stress my total and profound respect for all Muslims,' the Pope said in the speech, adding that, 'Christians and Muslims alike must reject all forms of violence and respect religious liberty ... The inter-religious and inter-cultural dialogue between Christians and Muslims is, in effect, a vital necessity, on which a large part of our future depends.'

2. Some religious groups are developing ways of helping interfaith marriages.
   - Many Protestant Churches and Liberal/Reform Jewish synagogues have developed special wedding services for mixed faith couples.
   - The Mission and Public Affairs Division of the Archbishops' Council of the Church of England has published *Guidelines for the celebration of interfaith marriages in church*.
   - Some religious leaders who have married partners of another religion have set up the website www.interfaithmarriage.org.uk to offer help and advice to couples from different religions.

> *Catholic schools are always looking for opportunities to improve their contribution to social harmony in the different communities which they serve, whether on the local, national or global level. Oona Stannard, CES Chief Executive and Director of the CES, said: 'If we don't define ourselves, others will do it for us. We have to be transparent about what a Catholic education has to offer the whole community because if we don't make it apparent others will make presumptions. This simple document helps us to share what is good so that we can live up to the goal of learning about one another, learning from one another and learning with one another.'*
>
> **Guidance document on community cohesion 14 February 2008**

> *Religions are different roads converging to the same point. What does it matter which road we take as long as we reach the same goal? In reality, there are as many different religions as there are individuals.*
>
> **Mohandas Gandhi**

◀ Pope Benedict XVI meeting Muslim envoys. Do you think it is possible for Christians and Muslims to accept each other's religion?

> *Let there be no compulsion in religion.*
>
> **Surah 2:256**

> *The lamps are different, but the light is the same.*
>
> **Rumi, a medieval Iranian Sufi, speaking about religions**

3. As far as issues with the upbringing of children are concerned, religions are responding in different ways:
   - Some Protestant Christian Churches and Liberal/Reform Jewish synagogues encourage mixed faith parents to bring up their children in both faiths, leaving it up to the children to choose which faith to follow when they are adults.
   - Leaders from the Church of England, Hindu, Sikh, Catholic, Muslim, Jewish and Buddhist faiths have signed a joint statement to follow the principles for good religious education contained in the non-statutory National Framework on Religious Education so that children in faith schools (schools following a curriculum based on one faith) will now teach the main religions practised in the United Kingdom. In their statement, the faith leaders say religious education 'enables pupils to develop respect for and sensitivity to others, in particular those whose faith and beliefs are different from their own, and promotes discernment and enables pupils to combat prejudice'.
4. The main way in which religions are trying to promote community cohesion is through joining together in special groups to explore ways of helping community cohesion.
   - There are national groups such as the Inter Faith Network for the UK, which was founded in 1987 to promote good relations between people of different faiths in this country. Its member organisations include representative bodies from the Baha'i, Buddhist, Christian, Hindu, Jain, Jewish, Muslim, Sikh and Zoroastrian communities; see www.interfaith.org.uk.

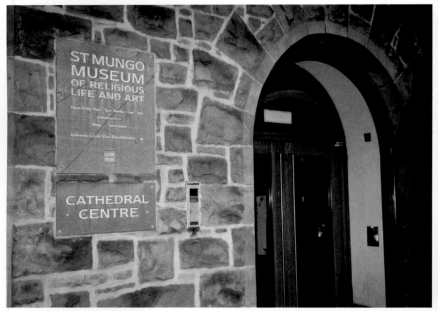

The St Mungo Museum is the only museum in the UK dedicated to promoting community cohesion through religion. It is in the grounds of Glasgow Cathedral.

- There are also groups in most towns and cities that bring together the different religious groups in an area to promote community cohesion between them, for example, Cambridge Inter-faith Group, Concord the Leeds Interfaith Group and the Glasgow Forum of Faiths.

- There are individual places of worship that work together, for example, 'What we are trying to do in Southall is to understand other traditions by living among them and conversing with them on their terms ... Our neighbours next door are Hindus. For the last three years at Diwali, we have gone there for a meal and then gone out into the garden to set off the fireworks.' Father Michael Barnes, parish priest, St Anselm's, Southall.

> All religions should stand side by side and go hand in hand. They are one family ... like windows in an endless tapestry of man's eternal search, they give visions of Truth and Reality. And the real truth of all religion is Harmony.
>
> **His Holiness Pramukh Swami Maharaj (BAPS)**

GLASGOW FORUM OF FAITHS DECLARATION

The current world situation has exposed the fragility of inter-faith relations and the need for an initiative that helps faith communities to listen and build relationships with each other. There is also an urgent need to show the general public that religion should not be a source of strife and that inter-faith activity is worthwhile.

The Forum of Faiths will bring together civic authorities (councillors and council officials) and the leaders of the main faith communities who have subscribed to this Declaration to work together for mutual understanding and the good of the City of Glasgow. We hope the Forum of Faiths will contribute to a better understanding of shared religious values.

The Declaration was signed by the Council leaders, the Strathclyde Police leaders and the Glasgow leaders of the Baha'i faith, the Buddhist faith, the Christian Church of Scotland (like the **URC** in England), the Christian Roman Catholic Church, the Christian Scottish Episcopal Church (like the Church of England), the Hindu faith, the Jewish faith, the Muslim faith and the Sikh faith.

> To recognise the oneness of all humanity is an essential pillar of Sikhism. Some call themselves Hindus, others call themselves Muslims, but humanity worldwide is made up of one race.
>
> **Akal Ustal**

Questions

b Do you think different religions should work together in the United Kingdom? Give the reasons for your point of view. **4**

c Explain how different religions are working together to promote community cohesion in the United Kingdom **8**

d 'It is easy for different religions to work together in the United Kingdom.'
   i Do you agree? Give reasons for your opinion. **3**
   ii Give reasons why some people may disagree with you. **3**

Exam Tip

c 'Explain' means give reasons. To answer this question you should use the facts from this topic, but relate them very clearly to multi-faith society, explaining how the census figures in Topic 3.4.7 show the United Kingdom to be multi-faith, for example.

SUMMARY

Religions are working for community cohesion in the United Kingdom by:

- working to discover what is the same about religions
- helping with mixed-faith marriages
- making sure that all children learn about different faiths
- joining local and national groups to promote community cohesion.

Topic 3.4.11 How an issue from religion and community cohesion has been presented in one form of the media

You have to study how **one** issue from religion and community cohesion has been presented in one form of the media.

Your issue could be connected with:
- equal rights for women in religion
- problems of discrimination and racism
- equal rights for ethnic minorities
- equal rights for religious minorities
- religion and racial harmony
- living in a multi-faith society
- religions working for community cohesion.

You can choose the media but it should only be one of the following:
- a soap opera
- a film
- a television drama
- a television documentary
- a radio programme
- a newspaper article in two different types of newspaper, for example *The Times* and the *Sun*.

If you study a film such as *Bend it like Beckham*, you must concentrate on the way it portrays Sikhs living in a multi-faith environment.

You must choose both the issue and the type of media carefully to be able to answer questions on:

- why the issue is important
- how it was presented
- whether the presentation was fair to religious beliefs
- whether the presentation was fair to religious people.

To do this you must:

1. Select an issue and a form of media. It is very important that you select only one issue. Some films have several issues running through them. If you choose more than one issue, your answers are likely to be confused.

2. Decide why the issue is important (you may need to look at the views of different members of the particular religion and of the impact of the issue on society as a whole) and why you think the producers of the media decided to focus on this issue.

Is the *Vicar of Dibley*'s presentation of equal rights for women in religion fair to religious people?

3. Write an outline of how the issue was presented, listing the main events and the way the events explored the issue.

4. Look closely at the way religious beliefs are treated in the presentation of the issue. Use this information to decide whether you think the presentation was fair to religious beliefs.

5. Look closely at the way religious people are treated in the presentation of the issue. Use this information to decide whether you think the presentation was fair to religious people.

Questions

b Do you think the media present religious people fairly? Give two reasons for your point of view. **4**

c Choose an issue from religion and community cohesion presented in one form of the media and explain whether the presentation was fair to religious people. **8**

d You are unlikely to be asked an evaluation question on this section as you only have to study one issue in one form of the media.

Exam Tip

c Briefly summarise the presentation, then explain why some religious people would think the presentation was fair (with reasons) and others would think it was unfair (with reasons) then decide what you think.

SUMMARY

When studying the presentation of an issue from religion and community cohesion in the media, you must be able to explain why the issue was chosen, how it was presented, whether the presentation treated religious people fairly and whether the presentation treated religious beliefs fairly.

How to answer exam questions

Question A What is racism?   2 marks

The belief that some races are superior to others.

Question B Do people from a different religion have the right to try to convert you?
Give two reasons for your point of view.   4 marks

No I do not think they do because trying to convert followers of other religions when living in a multi-faith society is a type of prejudice and discrimination. Trying to convert other religions is discriminating against those who do not have the same faith as you.

Also trying to convert others can lead to arguments and even violence within a multi-faith society when people are told their religion is wrong.

Question C Explain why Catholics should help to promote racial harmony.   8 marks

Catholics should help to promote racial harmony because this is the teaching of Jesus especially in the Parable of the Good Samaritan. Jesus was asked what loving your neighbour meant and he told the parable as a reply. As Samaritans and Jews hated each other and the Samaritan endangered himself to help a Jew, Jesus was clearly showing that no Christian should be racist.

Also St Peter received a vision in which God showed him that all races are equal and must be treated equally.

Finally the Catholic Church, through the Pope, cardinals and bishops, has made statements in favour of working for racial harmony and Catholics should follow the teachings of the Church.

Question D 'Women should have the same rights as men in religion.'

  i Do you agree? Give reasons for your opinion.   3 marks

  ii Give reasons why some people may disagree with you.   3 marks

i *I think women should have equal rights in religion except for being priests. I believe that women cannot be priests because Jesus only appointed men as his apostles so only men can be priests. Also the priest represents Jesus at Mass and as Jesus was a man, only male priests can celebrate Mass. However, in the rest of religion women should have equal rights because this is the teaching of the Church.*

ii *I think most Protestant Christians would disagree with me because they believe that men and women were created totally equal by God. It says in Genesis 1 that God created male and female equally. Also Jesus treated women as his equals and had women disciples showing that women should have equal rights. They believe that Jesus would have appointed women as apostles if it had been the culture of the time and they do not believe the priest represents Jesus in their worship.*

Section 10.1 **Beliefs and values**

Introduction

This section of the examination specification requires you to look at the meaning and importance of Christian beliefs and values.

Beliefs about God

You will need to understand the meaning and importance for Christians of, and give reasons for your own opinion about:
- believing in God as Unity and Trinity
- believing in God as the Father
- believing in God as the Creator
- believing that Jesus is the Son of God
- believing in the Holy Spirit.

Christian beliefs

You will need to understand the meaning and importance of, and give reasons for your own opinion about:
- Christian beliefs about salvation from sin
- Christian beliefs about loving God and how love of God affects Christians' lives
- Christian teachings on the love of others (Mark 12:29–31, Luke 10:25–37, Matthew 25:31–46).

Religious groups

You will need to understand the effects of, and give reasons for your own opinion about:
- how love of God is expressed in the life of a religious community
- how love of others is expressed in the life of a religious community
- how a Christian church shows love of God and love of others in the local area.

Topic 10.1.1 The meaning, and importance for Christians, of believing in God as Unity and Trinity

KEY WORDS

Catechism – official teaching of the Roman Catholic Church

Creeds – statements of Christian belief.

Monotheism – belief in one God.

Salvation – the act of delivering from sin, or saving from evil.

Trinity – the belief that God is three in one.

Unity – God's way of being one.

I am the Lord your God, who brought you out of Egypt, out of the land of slavery. You shall have no other gods before me.

Exodus 20:2–3

'The most important one,' answered Jesus, 'is this': "Hear, O Israel, the Lord our God, the Lord is one."'

Mark 12:29

We believe in one God.

The beginning of the Nicene Creed

The meaning of believing in God as Unity and Trinity

Christian beliefs are that there is only one God (God's **Unity**) who reveals himself to the world in three persons (the Holy Trinity). Believing in one God is called **monotheism**. Christians believe that God is One because the nature of the universe God has made shows oneness. It is a universe (uni meaning one) not a multiverse (multi meaning many). Everything in the universe has a pattern (such as the whorls in the centre of flowers or finger prints), indicating it was made by one God.

Most Christians believe that although God is one, he is experienced in the world as a **Trinity** – the Father, the Son and the Holy Spirit. This is a complex idea which the Church tries to explain by using the words 'person' and 'substance'. When Christians speak of God in his Unity, they refer to God's substance. When Christians speak of God at work in the world they refer to the three persons of God:

- The Father who created everything and to whom Christians pray when they say 'Our Father'.
- The Son who revealed God in his life on Earth and who saves people from **sin**.
- The Holy Spirit who inspires Christians and brings the presence of God into their lives.

Christians worship one God. The Trinity is a unity. Although the Church teaches that this is the great mystery, it is sometimes explained by symbols such as the shamrock.

Why it is important for Christians to believe in God's Unity

- The teachings of the **Bible** in both Old and New Testaments show very clearly that there is only one God. As Christians believe the Bible reveals God, God must therefore be a unity.
- The belief that God is a Unity is the first of the **Ten Commandments** which all Christians accept as God's rules about belief and behaviour.
- God's Unity was taught by Jesus as the greatest commandment, and Christians must believe and follow the teachings of Jesus, God's Son.
- God's Unity is the teaching of the Catholic Church (the **Magisterium**), as seen in the **Creeds**, the **Catechism** and the

writings of the **saints**, and Catholic Christians must believe and follow the teachings of the Church.

- Christians believe that God is **omnipotent**, if there were other gods, then they would have some power and so the Christian God would not be all-powerful. Only if God is a Unity can God be all-powerful, which is why it is so important.

Why it is important for Christians to believe in God as the Trinity

- The Trinity helps Christians understand the different ways that God has shown his presence in the world. God the Father helps Christians understand the power and creativity and his care for the world and its peoples. God the Son helps Christians understand the love of God, the sacrifice of God leading to **salvation** from sin and the promise of eternal life. The Holy Spirit helps Christians to understand the presence of God in the world and the strength that it brings to Christians.
- The **baptism** of Jesus as recorded in the **Gospel** descriptions clearly show that God is a trinity – the Father speaks, the Son is baptised and the Spirit descends in the form of a **dove**. If this is how God was revealed at the beginning of Jesus' ministry, it must be important.
- Belief in the Trinity is a part of the **Apostolic Tradition**. The **apostles** such as St Peter and St Paul refer to God as Father, Son and Holy Spirit, and Christians must believe the teachings of the apostles.
- Belief in God as Trinity as well as Unity is the teaching of the Church through the Creeds and the Catechism, and the teaching of the Church should be the basis of a Catholic Christian's life
- The Catechism of the Catholic Church 234 states: *The mystery of the Most Holy Trinity is the central mystery of Christian faith and life.*

> *The Trinity is One. We do not confess three Gods, but one God in three persons.*
>
> **Catechism of the Catholic Church 253**

Exam focus

Quality of Written Communication

Explain questions (part c in the examination) are where your Quality of Written Communication is tested, so you should answer these questions in a formal style of English, be careful with your spelling and try to use some specialist vocabulary (in this topic Trinity, Holy Spirit, salvation, Catechism, Magisterium, omnipotent would all be specialist vocabulary).

SUMMARY

Christians believe in the Unity of God and also that God is a trinity.

God's Unity helps them understand the power and importance of God because there is only one God and Christians should worship him.

God's Trinity helps them to understand God's activity in the world as Father, Son and Holy Spirit

God's Unity and Trinity are important as they are part of the teaching of the Bible and the Church.

Questions

b Do you think all Christians should believe in the Trinity? Give two reasons for your point of view. **4**

c Explain why belief in God's unity is important for Christians. **8**

d 'You can't believe that God is both one and three.'
  i Do you agree? Give reasons for your opinion. **3**
  ii Give reasons why some people may disagree with you. **3**

Exam Tip

c 'Explain' means give reasons. To answer this question you should use four reasons from this topic, and make each of them into a short paragraph. For tips on Quality of Written Communication see opposite.

Topic 10.1.2 The meaning, and importance for Christians, of believing in God as the Father

I believe in God, the Father Almighty.

Apostles' Creed

I will be a Father to you, and you will be my sons and daughters, says the Lord Almighty.

2 Corinthians 6:18

By calling God 'Father', the language of faith indicates two main things: that God is the first origin of everything and transcendent authority; and that he is at the same time goodness and loving care for all his children.

Catechism of the Catholic Church 239

The meaning of believing in God as the Father

- Believing that God is the Father means that the father–child relationship should be the same as a Christian's relationship with God.
- It also shows that God creates human life like a father does. God is not a creator who creates and then leaves his creation to get on with things, he has a relationship of love and care with his creation.
- As their Father, God will provide for his children – in the story of creation it is written that the Earth is given to Adam and Eve and they are told that it will provide food for them.
- In the **Lord's Prayer** or 'Our Father', Christians learn that God will provide their daily bread and protect them from evil precisely because he is 'our Father'.
- Because God is the Father, Christians can turn to God as they would to a human Father when they are in need.

The importance for Christians of believing in God as the Father

- The Bible shows very clearly that Jesus referred to God as his Father. Jesus also told his disciples to call God, Father. The teachings of the Bible and of Jesus are of supreme importance as they are the basis of the **faith**.
- Every time Christians recite the **Apostles' Creed** they say that they believe in God as the Father Almighty, showing how important it is.
- The Catechism teaches Catholics to call God Father, showing how important belief in the fatherhood of God is.
- The importance of God's fatherhood is shown by the fact that without his fatherly care, he would not have sent Jesus to explain how Christians should live and to save people from their sins.
- It allows Christians to have a personal relationship with God because as their father they can talk to God through prayer and the Bible shows that Christians should pray to God as Father.
  - It is a basic Christian belief as shown in the fact that children are taught from a young age that God is their heavenly Father. One of the first prayers they are taught is called the 'Our Father'.

◄ Charles de la Fosse painted God as Father in this way in 1668. Is this the way you think he should be drawn?

This photo shows the Holy Trinity from the Mosol Alterpiece, 1450–70

The Lords Prayer

Our Father, Who art in Heaven, hallowed be Thy Name.

Thy Kingdom come.

Thy Will be done, on Earth, as it is in Heaven.

Give us this day our daily bread and forgive us our trespasses as we forgive those who trespass against us; and lead us not into temptation, but deliver us from evil. Amen.

Luke 11: 2–4

Exam focus

What do you think?

In these questions (part b in the examination) you must decide what you think about the issues and ideas you study. For this topic you need to think about:

- whether it is a good idea to call God Father
- what it means to call God Father
- why calling God Father is important for Christians.

The questions are meant to be quite easy and to get full marks you just need to give two reasons.

Questions

b Do you think Christians should call God Father? Give two reasons for your point of view.   **4**

c Explain why belief in God as Father is important for Christians   **8**

d 'God should not be called Father.'
   i   Do you agree? Give reasons for your opinion.   **3**
   ii Give reasons why some people may disagree with you.   **3**

Exam Tip

b You should already have thought about this, and you just have to give two reasons for your opinion. For example if you think Christians should call God Father, you could use these two reasons:
   - Jesus told his disciples to call God Father so Christians today should do the same.
   - God creates life like a father does so we should call him Father.

SUMMARY

Believing in God as Father means that Christians can have a relationship with God like they can with a human father. It also means that God will love, care and provide for them. This is important for Catholics because it is the teaching of the Bible, Jesus and the Church. It is also important as it gives Christians God's love and salvation.

Topic 10.1.3 The meaning, and importance for Christians, of believing in God as Creator

> *So God created man in his own image, in the image of God he created him; male and female he created them.*
>
> **Genesis 1:27**

The meaning of believing in God as the Creator

- God created the universe and all the things in it. Therefore this life is not an accident. Life has a meaning and purpose given to it by God.
- God created the universe out of nothing (**ex nihilo**), therefore he is all-powerful and is the cause of all life.
- As God has created the universe, and God is good, the universe itself must be good.
- God created human beings in his image, which means humans are a special creation.
- God created human beings last. They were the ultimate creation made after the rest of creation. This shows that they are the most important part, the pinnacle of God's creation.
- God as Creator has given humans the responsibility of caring for and safeguarding his Creation. This is important as it gives Christian life added purpose.

> *God saw all that he had made and it was very good.*
>
> **Genesis 1:31**

> *The heavens declare the glory of God; the skies proclaim the work of his hands. Day after day they pour forth speech; night after night they display knowledge.*
>
> **Psalm 19:1–2**

> *In the creation of the world and of man, God gave the first and universal witness to his almighty love and his wisdom, the first proclamation of the 'plan of his loving goodness', which finds its goal in the new creation in Christ.*
>
> **Catechism of the Catholic Church 315**

This picture of Adam and Eve by Theodore De Bry, 1590, shows how Genesis describes creation. Do you think this is factually correct?

The importance for Christians of believing in God as the Creator

It is important for Christians to believe that God is the creator because it shows:

- God's omnipotence. The Creeds and the Catechism teach that God is the Father Almighty – only an all-powerful God could create the universe.
- that the universe is not an accident. It was created by God who is good for a good purpose. We can find this purpose in the faith and teachings of the Church.
- that life is sacred because God is the creator of it. Those things which God creates must be like him, **holy**, so we need to treat creation carefully and with respect. God as Creator has given humans the responsibility of caring for and safeguarding his Creation.
- God's love for humans. God created the world for humans and gave them their purpose in living.
- that God continues to be the Creator. His work did not stop with the creation of humans, he continues to care for the world and show his love for the world by his creative power in the life, death and resurrection of Jesus, which brought salvation.

Questions

b Do you think it is important to believe in God as Creator? Give two reasons for your point of view. **4**

c Explain what it means for Christians to believe in God as Creator. **8**

d 'It does not matter whether or not God created the universe.'
   i   Do you agree? Give reasons for your opinion. **3**
   ii Give reasons why some people may disagree with you **3**

Exam Tip

d Use the evaluation technique from this page.
   Arguments for the statement could be the reasons why it is important in this topic. Arguments against are likely to come from your class discussions or your own ideas such as:
   - the argument ignores the evidence that the universe is not created by God, for example the Big Bang and evolution (see Topic 3.1.5)
   - only people who believe in God would think it matters, everyone else can quite happily accept that the world is just there. It does not matter because now the world is there we can live in it and treat it how we wish.

Exam focus

Evaluation questions
(part d on the examination)

- Decide what you think about the statement.
- Give at least three brief reasons, or two longer reasons, or a paragraph reason, supporting your point of view.
- Look at the opposite point of view and give at least three brief reasons, or two longer reasons, or a paragraph reason, for why people have this view.

The evaluation questions mean that you must always be aware not only of your own point of view about a topic, but also about the opposite point of view.

REMEMBER
One of your points of view should always be a Catholic one.

SUMMARY

Christians believe that God is the creator of the universe and all that is in it including human beings. This means that life is good and that life has a meaning and purpose given to it by God.

It is important to Christians that God is the creator of the world as it shows his power, his love and the relationship between God and humans. It is also important because if God created the world it means humans should regard it as holy and treat living things accordingly.

Topic 10.1.4 The meaning, and importance for Christians, of believing that Jesus is the Son of God

KEY WORDS

Atonement – reconciliation between God and humanity.

Compassion – a feeling of pity which makes one want to help the sufferer.

Incarnation – the belief that God took human form in Jesus.

Virgin Birth – the belief that Jesus was not conceived through sex.

Not everyone who says to me, 'Lord, Lord,' will enter the kingdom of heaven, but only he who does the will of my Father who is in heaven.

Matthew 7:21

Jesus said to them, 'I tell you the truth, it is not Moses who has given you the bread from heaven, but it is my Father who gives you the true bread from heaven.'

John 6:32

The meaning of believing that Jesus is the Son of God

- Jesus is God **incarnated**. This means Jesus is God on Earth living as a human and experiencing life as a human. This means that in the life of Jesus, humans can see the nature of God.
- As Son of God, Christians believe that Jesus was both fully human and fully divine. The Catechism says 'Jesus **Christ** possesses two natures, one divine and the other human, not confused, but united in the one person of God's Son' (481).
- As God's Son, Jesus had God's powers on Earth, which explains why he was able to work miracles, not only healing people, but also calming storms and walking on water, for example.
- Jesus was conceived by God. It was God's will that Jesus was incarnated, therefore Jesus was not conceived in the normal way. Christians believe that Jesus was conceived by the power of the Holy Spirit, therefore Mary remained a virgin and Jesus was born sinless. This is referred to as the **Virgin Birth**.
- As the Son of God, Jesus' death was not a normal death, but a **sacrifice** for the sins of the world, bringing God's salvation to humans.
- As Son of God, Jesus rose from the dead so bringing not only salvation from sin, but also eternal life.
- It means Christians can worship Jesus because he is God, the second person of the Trinity. The Bible teaches that only God should be worshipped and that **idolatry** is a sin. However, Jesus as the incarnate Son of God gives Christians a person to worship.
- Jesus is the Son of God. He was conceived by the action of the Holy Spirit and not by sex. This is an important part of Roman Catholic belief; they call it the Virgin Birth.

In this painting by Fra Angelico called *The Annunciation*, the Holy Spirit ▶ is visible in the left-hand corner and the image of God is in the centre above Mary and the Angel Gabriel. Do you think this is a good way to show Catholic beliefs about God the Son?

The importance for Christians of believing that Jesus is the Son of God

- Only the Son of God could bring salvation from sin. Sin prevented people from having a full relationship with God. The sacrifice of God the Son brought **forgiveness** of sins and **reconciliation** to God, which also gave people the chance to enter heaven.
- Believing in Jesus as the Son of God also gives Christians the chance to see what God is like. The love and **compassion** shown by God's Son inspires Christians today to share God's love.
- Believing that Jesus is the Son of God makes his life and teaching so much more important. If Christians follow the teachings of Jesus and try to live by his example, they know they are living as God wants them to.
- Believing that Jesus is the Son of God is a teaching of the **Creeds** and the Catechism of the Catholic Church, which all Catholics should believe.
- Believing that Jesus is the Son of God is important because only God's Son could institute the **Mass** – God comes into people's lives as Jesus becomes present in the bread and wine at Mass.

James J. Tissot, *The Baptism of Jesus* ▶ (1886–96). When Jesus was baptised a voice from heaven was heard to say, 'You are my Son, whom I love; with you I am well pleased.' Luke 3:22

> The title 'Son of God' signifies the unique and eternal relationship of Jesus Christ to God his Father: he is the only Son of the Father, he is God himself. To be a Christian, one must believe that Jesus Christ is the Son of God.
>
> **Catechism of the Catholic Church 454**

> Only God forgives sins. Since he is the Son of God, Jesus says of himself, 'The Son of man has authority on Earth to forgive sins' and exercises this divine power: 'Your sins are forgiven.' Further, by virtue of his divine authority, he gives this power to men to exercise in his name.
>
> **Catechism of the Catholic Church 1441**

Questions

b Do you think Jesus is God incarnated? Give two reasons for your point of view. **4**

c Explain why it is important for Christians to believe that Jesus is the Son of God. **8**

d 'Jesus is God.'
  i Do you agree? Give reasons for your opinion. **3**
  ii Give reasons why some people may disagree with you. **3**

Exam Tip

c 'Explain' means give reasons. To answer this question you should use four reasons from this topic, and make each of them into a short paragraph. For tips on Quality of Written Communication, look at page 107.

SUMMARY

Christian belief in Jesus as the Son of God means that Jesus was both man and God. He was conceived by the Holy Spirit and was God on Earth. His example and teaching show Christians how God wants them to live.

It is important that Jesus is the Son of God because:

- it explains that there is a special relationship between God and Jesus
- his life shows what God is like
- his life and death bring salvation and eternal life.

Topic 10.1.5 The meaning, and importance for Christians, of believing in the Holy Spirit

> *As soon as Jesus was baptised, he went up out of the water. At that moment heaven was opened, and he saw the Spirit of God descending like a dove and lighting on him.*
>
> **Matthew 3:16**

> *The Holy Spirit, who has led the chosen people by inspiring the authors of the Sacred Scriptures, opens the hearts of believers to understand their meaning. This same Spirit is actively present in the Eucharistic celebration.*
>
> **Pope Benedict XVI on World Youth Day, April 2006**

> *All of them were filled with the Holy Spirit and began to **speak in other tongues** as the Spirit enabled them.*
>
> **Acts 2:4**

> *The seven gifts of the Holy Spirit are wisdom, understanding, counsel, fortitude, knowledge, piety, and fear of the Lord. They belong in their fullness to Christ.*
>
> **Catechism of the Catholic Church 1831**

The meaning of believing in the Holy Spirit

- Christians believe that the Holy Spirit is the third person of the Trinity who, with the Father and the Son, is to be worshipped.
- Christians believe that the Holy Spirit is the means by which God communicates with humans revealing God's presence in the world. In the Old Testament, the Spirit is called ruah, meaning breath, air, **wind**, that is, a presence which can only be felt not seen.
- Christians believe that the Holy Spirit inspired the Bible by encouraging the writers of the Bible and guiding their writing to reveal the nature and will of God.
- Christians believe that the Holy Spirit is the means by which God assists the Church in its task of preserving the Apostolic Tradition and in helping the Magisterium to formulate teaching.
- Christians believe that the Holy Spirit is the means by which all the sacraments of the Church put believers into communion with Christ.
- Christians believe that through the presence of the Holy Spirit in their lives, God can strengthen and empower Christians today.

This icon of the descent of the Holy Spirit shows the gifts of the Holy Spirit being given to the apostles at **Pentecost**.

The importance for Christians of believing in the Holy Spirit

The Holy Spirit is important for Christians because:

- It is the third person of the Trinity and is God's presence in the world.
- Through the sacraments of baptism and reconciliation, it purifies people from sin, enabling them to have a relationship with God and enter eternal life.
- It inspires the teachings of the Church so the Church has a direct link to God and this means that the teachings of the Church should be obeyed as if they were the teachings of God.
- It gives guidance to the Church in the election of the Pope and the choice of the leaders of the Church, assuring Christians that the leaders are approved by God.
- Its gifts enable Christians to live lives full of **charity**, joy, peace, patience, kindness, goodness, generosity, gentleness, faithfulness, modesty, self-control and chastity. This power of the Holy Spirit is important as it helps Christians live the lives Jesus wants them to live.
- It gives power to people, enabling them to live their Christian vocations fully.

In this painting the Holy Spirit is shown as tongues of **fire** descending on the disciples at Pentecost.

Questions

b Do you think the Holy Spirit is important for Christians today? Give two reasons for your point of view.   **4**

c Explain what it means for Christians to believe in the Holy Spirit.   **8**

d 'The Holy Spirit is active in the world today.'
  i Do you agree? Give reasons for your opinion.   **3**
  ii Give reasons why some people may disagree with you.   **3**

Exam Tip

b You should already have thought about this, and you just have to give two reasons for your opinion. If you think the Holy Spirit is important for Christians today, you could use two reasons from why believing in the Holy Spirit is important from this topic.

SUMMARY

Believing in the Holy Spirit means believing in the third person of the Trinity. The Holy Spirit is the way God communicates with the world and who can be worshipped with the Father and the Son.

The Holy Spirit is important because Christians believe it:

- inspired the Bible
- guides the Church
- purifies from sin
- gives believers the presence and power of God.

Topic 10.1.6 The meaning and importance of Christian beliefs about salvation from sin

Sin is an offence against reason, truth, and right conscience; it is failure in genuine love for God and neighbour caused by a perverse attachment to certain goods. It wounds the nature of man and injures human solidarity. It has been defined as 'an utterance, a deed, or a desire contrary to the eternal law.'

Catechism of the Catholic Church 1849

Faith is necessary for salvation. The Lord himself affirms: 'Whoever believes and is baptised will be saved, but whoever does not believe will be condemned.' (Mark 16:16)

Catechism of the Catholic Church 183

The meaning of Christian beliefs about salvation from sin

Christians believe a sin is an action that breaks God's law. Sin is also the state of being that comes about by committing a sinful action. Sin makes it difficult to have a relationship with God because sin separates a person from God.

Sin can be original sin, which is inherited from the actions of Adam and Eve, or personal sin, which is the consequence of a person's own actions. All people are born with original sin – this is washed away at baptism.

People who die with unforgiven mortal sins (very serious sins such as murder) will go to **hell**. People who die with unforgiven venial sins (less serious sins such as selfishness) will go to **purgatory**.

Salvation means being saved from sin, which allows Christians to have eternal life with God. Christians believe that Jesus came to Earth in order for Christians to receive salvation. The death of Jesus was the sacrifice needed to bring salvation to the world, so Jesus is the saviour of the world.

Catholics believe that the salvation from sin brought by Jesus comes to the world today through the Church and is brought about by:

- receiving the sacraments of baptism and **confirmation**
- receiving the sacrament of reconciliation
- receiving the sacrament of the **Eucharist** (Holy Communion)
- leading a Christian life.

William Blake's picture of ▶ *Satan, Sin and Death* (1808). Is this how you imagine sin to be?

The importance of Christian beliefs about salvation from sin

- Salvation from sin is important because without salvation, a person's sins will prevent them from having a relationship with God in this life and send them to hell or purgatory after death.
- Salvation is important because it is the only way that Christians can have eternal life with God. This eternal life will be perfect and is beyond description.
- Salvation must be important because it was the reason why God became man. Salvation from sin was the purpose of the life, death and resurrection of Jesus. Jesus is the saviour of the world whose death on the cross brought forgiveness of sins and by his death opened the gates of heaven so that Christians can spend eternal life there.
- Salvation from sin is important for Catholics because it explains why the sacraments of baptism, reconciliation, confirmation, healing and the Mass are at the heart of Catholic life

> *Salvation comes from God alone; but because we receive the life of faith through the Church, she is our mother: 'We believe the Church as the mother of our new birth, and not in the Church as if she were the author of our salvation.' Because she is our mother, she is also our teacher in the faith.*
>
> **Catechism of the Catholic Church 169**

◄ The **Vatican**, where the governing body of the Catholic Church is based (the Holy See). Through following the teachings of the Church, Catholics hope to achieve salvation.

Questions

b Do you think we need salvation from sin? Give two reasons for your point of view. **4**

c Explain why salvation is important for Christians. **8**

d 'Salvation cannot be achieved just by going to Mass.'

  i Do you agree? Give reasons for your opinion. **3**

  ii Give reasons why some people may disagree with you. **3**

Exam Tip

c 'Explain' means give reasons. To answer this question you should use four reasons from the importance part of this topic, and make each of them into a short paragraph. For tips on Quality of Written Communication, look at page 107.

SUMMARY

Christians believe sin is what separates people from God and people who die with unforgiven sins will not go to heaven. They also believe that the sacrifice of Jesus brought salvation from sin, that is forgiveness and the promise of eternal life.

Catholics believe that salvation is important because it:

- saves people from hell and leads to eternal life with God
- was the purpose of the death of Jesus
- explains why we have the sacraments
- gives Christians a reason to live a holy life.

Topic 10.1.7 The meaning and importance of loving God and how love of God affects Christians' lives

The meaning of loving God

Jesus said that the two most important commandments are to love God and to love your neighbour as yourself. Many Christians would say that the most important thing that leads to salvation is to love God. This means that human values should take second place to God's values. Catholic Christians show their love of God by worshipping him through:

- going to weekly Mass and praying every day
- taking the other sacraments of the Church
- following the Christian life as outlined in the Bible, Apostolic Tradition and Magisterium.

> *Adoring God, praying to him, offering him the worship that belongs to him, fulfilling the promises and vows made to him, are acts of the virtue of religion which fall under obedience to the first commandment.*
>
> **Catechism of the Catholic Church 2135**

The photo on the left shows ▶ Catholics in the Philippines enacting the **crucifixion** at **Easter** which is one way in which their culture shows their love of God. Real nails are used for the crucifixions though the devotees generally stay on the cross for minutes, not days. The photo on the right shows a Sister of the Missionaries of Charity at work in Southwest Detroit. Which is the best way for Catholics to show their love of God?

The importance of loving God

- Jesus said that loving God is the Greatest Commandment. Christians should follow the instructions of Jesus because he is God's Son whose teachings tell Christians how to gain eternal life. If Jesus says that loving God is the greatest commandment, then it is tremendously important for Christians to love God.
- By loving God, Christians are living the life God wants, and doing what God wants will bring eternal life.
- It is important for Christians to love God as a response to how God has loved his people. God loved the world so much that he gave his Son as the sacrifice for sin in order that humans could have eternal life.

> *Everyone who believes that Jesus is the Christ is born of God, and everyone who loves the father loves his child as well. This is how we know that we love the children of God: by loving God and carrying out his commands. This is love for God: to obey his commands.*
>
> **1 John 5:1–3**

- The Church teaches that all believers should love God, and this is the basis of the Christian life according to the Catechism. It is important for Catholics to follow the teachings of the Church and the Catechism because they believe that this is the way to eternal life.
- Love for God is important as to love God one has to live a good Christian life by thinking of others before yourself, and so follow the second great commandment – love your neighbour.

How love of God affects Christians' lives

Loving God means that Christians should:

- use human abilities and talents as God intends so that others benefit from them and so that respect is shown to God in the way that we use them. This will affect a Christian's choice of career, marriage partner, use of money, etc.
- show respect towards God's creations. This will affect a Christian's life because they will have to be stewards of the world ensuring that the Earth and all the creatures on it are cared for. This also means treating other people fairly and standing up against oppression and injustice.
- follow the rules set by God, which means obeying the Ten Commandments and living by the rules set by Jesus in the **Sermon on the Mount**. This is bound to have a big effect on a Christian's life (see Topics 10.4.5 to 10.4.9).
- use their life to make the most of the vocations given to them, that is recognising God's call in life and responding to it. This will have a huge effect on a Christian's life if they are called to the priesthood, the religious life, or service to the poor.
- follow the teachings of the Church about how to love God. This is because Catholics believe that the teachings of the Church bring them closer to God. Following the Church's teachings will affect the whole of a person's life, because the Church teaches Christians how they should live.

> *God has loved us first. The love of the one God is recalled in the first of the ten words. The Ten Commandments then make explicit the response of love that man is called to give his God.*
>
> **Catechism of the Catholic Church 2083**

Questions

b Do you think loving God is easy? Give two reasons for your point of view. **4**

c Explain why love of God is important for Christians. **8**

d 'It is not hard to love God.'
  i Do you agree? Give reasons for your opinion. **3**
  ii Give reasons why some people may disagree with you. **3**

Exam Tip

d Use the answering evaluation questions advice from page 111. Arguments for could be the reasons why love of God is important in this topic. Arguments against could come from the way love of God affects Christians' lives in this topic

SUMMARY

Love of God is central to Christian belief. Jesus said love of God is the greatest commandment.

Love of God is important as it is commanded by Jesus, God's Son, and leads to living a good life, thinking of others before yourself, and salvation.

Love of God affects a Christian's life as they will have to show their love of God in their choice of career and their daily life.

Topic 10.1.8 The meaning and importance of Christian teachings on the love of others

Mark 12:29–31

Jesus says that the second commandment is to love your neighbour as you love yourself.

This Christian teaching means that the love that Christians need to have for their neighbours:
- needs to be as strong and as endless as it is for one's own self
- is very important to God, second only to love of God himself
- is what God wants from Christians, it is not just a nice idea, it is a commandment and so must be carried out.

This Christian teaching is important because:
- it is a commandment from Jesus, which means that it cannot be ignored
- by loving their neighbour Christians are doing God's will, which will lead to their reward in heaven
- it is not easy to do, as most people love themselves a lot. Jesus knew it would not be easy and yet still commanded it. This is important as it shows that Christian love for neighbour will be a struggle.

The Parable of the Good Samaritan
Luke 10:25–37

When asked who is our neighbour, Jesus told this parable:
A Jew was travelling from Jerusalem to Jericho when he was attacked by robbers and left half dead. Two Jewish people (a **priest** and a **Levite**) ignored him and hurried past. A Samaritan (who were a different race and religion and, according to the Gospels, hated Jews) stopped and helped the injured man.
This parable means that:
- Christians need to show love to everyone, not just those people who are their friends.
- Sometimes the person you need to show love for the most is your enemy, and this might not be easy.
- It is important that Christians love their neighbours because for the ill or less well off it could mean life or death.
- Love of neighbour is what God wants so that everyone is cared for and no one suffers.

'The most important one (commandment),' answered Jesus, 'is this: "Hear, O Israel, the Lord our God, the Lord is one. Love the Lord your God with all your heart and with all your soul and with all your mind and with all your strength." The second is this: "Love your neighbour as yourself." There is no commandment greater than these.'

Mark 12:29–31

A consistent theme of Catholic social teaching is the option or love of preference for the poor. Today, this preference has to be expressed in worldwide dimensions, embracing the immense numbers of the hungry, the needy, the homeless, those without medical care, and those without hope.

Solicitudo Rei Socialis
On Social Concern, Pope John Paul II, 1987

This parable is important because:

- It shows who is a person's neighbour: the answer given is everyone, including your enemy.
- It shows that loving your neighbour is important and that it is doing what God wants.
- It reassures Christians, because loving your neighbour as you love yourself is not easy to do in the parable (the good people have good reasons for not helping) and yet it tells Christians they have to try to do it.
- It explains that your neighbour is anyone, whatever their race or religion, who needs your compassion and help.

The Good Samaritan by Dr He Qi, a Chinese Christian artist

Anyone who needs me, and whom I can help, is my neighbour. The concept of 'neighbour' is now universalised, yet it remains concrete. Despite being extended to all mankind, it is not reduced to a generic, abstract and undemanding expression of love, but calls for my own practical commitment here and now.

Encyclical letter: *Deus Caritas Est*, Pope Benedict XVI, 25 December 2005

◀ The extract from the **encyclical** letter quoted in the margin was the first letter **Pope** Benedict XVI wrote to the Catholic community after he was inaugurated as Pope in 2005. Why do you think he chose this topic?

The Parable of the Sheep and the Goats
Matthew 25:31–46

Jesus told a story about the end of the world when everyone will be brought before the **Son of Man** to be judged. Jesus said that:

- He would separate the people like a shepherd separates sheep from goats.
- The sheep would be those who fed Jesus when he was hungry, gave him drink when he was thirsty, took him in when he was a stranger, clothed him when he needed clothes, looked after him when he was sick, visited him when he was in prison.
- The people will say they never did this, but Jesus will say that whatever they did for someone suffering like this, they did for him, so they can go to heaven.
- Jesus identifies himself with those who suffer in this parable, showing his humanity.
- However, the goats will be told that they did not do any of these things for other people and so they did not do them for Jesus. Because they did not love others, they will go to hell.

The Parable of the Sheep and the Goats separates the good from the bad. How does this show love?

This parable means that:

- Christians need to show love to everyone, especially those who are in need.
- By showing love for others you are showing love for God.
- People will be judged by God according to the way they act, the way they treat others and the way they choose to spend their time.
- Love of others is what God wants: it means that everyone is cared for and no one suffers.

- Because of Jesus' resurrection he is not bound in time or place, so in the needy it is Christ himself appealing to us through the person in front of us.

Young people working with CAFOD.

This parable is important because:
- It tells us that by showing love for others Christians are showing love for God and this is the most important commandment.
- It explains that loving others means caring for those people who are hungry, thirsty, strangers, short of clothes, sick or in prison.
- It shows that loving your neighbour is important and that it is doing what God wants.
- It shows Christians that there is a reward for showing love to those who are suffering: the reward is eternal life with God in heaven.
- It shows that those people who choose not to help those in need will be punished.

Questions

b Do you think Christians should show love for others? Give two reasons for your point of view. **4**

c Explain why the parable of the Good Samaritan is important for Christians. **8**

d 'Loving your neighbour is too hard.'
  i Do you agree? Give reasons for your opinion. **3**
  ii Give reasons why some people may disagree with you. **3**

Exam Tip

b You should already have thought about this, and you just have to give two reasons for your opinion. For example, if you agree, you could use two reasons from the importance of the two greatest commandments, or the Parable of the Good Samaritan, or the Parable of the Sheep and the Goats.

SUMMARY

All Christians think it is very important to love others because Jesus said that loving your neighbour is the second greatest commandment. Loving others means helping anyone in trouble, as seen in the Good Samaritan where the Samaritan helped an enemy in trouble, and in the Sheep and the Goats where Jesus said that those who do not help people in trouble will go to hell.

Topic 10.1.9 How love of God is expressed in the life of a religious community

Carmelite nuns are a mainly contemplative religious community who spend their lives in prayer and study. The Carmelites formed from a religious community living on Mount Carmel. In around 1215 they were given a rule for living by Albert, the **Patriarch** of Jerusalem, and moved away from Mount Carmel to smaller communities around the world. Carmelites as a whole are not just a **contemplative order**, some are active and some are lay people who live in or out of the **closed communities**.

Love for God is expressed by the Carmelite nuns in the following ways:

1. The nuns take the evangelical counsels (vows of poverty, chastity and obedience) – giving up their money, their sex life and their freedom to do as they want, to show their complete love of God.

2. The nuns follow the Carmelite Rule which says that the nuns must:
   - develop the contemplative dimension of their life, in an open dialogue with God
   - live in communities which means they should show care, love and be full of charity
   - meditate day and night on the Word of the Lord
   - pray together or alone several times a day
   - celebrate the **Eucharist** every day
   - do manual work, as Paul the Apostle did
   - purify themselves of every trace of sin
   - live in poverty, placing in common what little they may have
   - love the Church and all people
   - conform their will to that of God, seeking the will of God in faith, in dialogue and through discernment.

   Clearly, to follow this rule, they must show great love for God.

3. They spend almost twelve hours of every day in prayer, worship and contemplation of God showing their complete love for him (see a typical day in the margin on the left).

4. They show their love for God by living a life away from the world, concentrating on God alone, trying to come closer to God each day, by receiving the Eucharist during Mass, praying for the whole world and the needs of the world and as God requested in the teachings of Jesus.

Carmelite nuns give themselves to God and pray constantly for the needs of the world.

> *Prayer is Carmel's particular form of service to the Church. We spend an hour each morning and each evening in silent prayer. These times of special openness to God nourish an entire life of prayer that tends towards God in everything.*
>
> **From the Carmelite nuns of Notting Hill website, www.carmelitesnottinghill.org.uk**

Questions

b Do you think joining a religious community is the best way to show your love for God? Give two reasons for your point of view. **4**

c Explain how one religious community shows love for God. **8**

d 'Living in a religious community is the best way to show your love for God.'

   i Do you agree? Give reasons for your opinion. **3**

   ii Give reasons why some people may disagree with you. **3**

Exam Tip

d Use the answering evaluation questions advice from page 111. Arguments for the statement could come from how the Carmelites show love for God. Arguments against could come from class discussions and/or Topic 10.1.7.

SUMMARY

The Carmelites show love of God by separating themselves from the world, taking the evangelical counsels, spending most of their lives in prayer and worship including daily Mass, following the Carmelite Rule.

Topic 10.1.10 How love of others is expressed in the life of a religious community

> *We can make work a prayer. How can we do this? By doing our work with Jesus and for Jesus ... This is beautiful and it is what God wants. He wants our will and our desires to work for him, for our family, for our children, for our brethren and for the poor.*
>
> **Mother Teresa as quoted in** *A Life for God: The Mother Teresa Reader*

The Missionaries of Charity is one of the newest monastic orders. It was founded by Mother Teresa in 1950. It has over 4,500 nuns and monks working in 133 countries. The Missionaries of Charity express their love for others in many ways:

1. As well as taking the evangelical vows of poverty, chastity and obedience, the Missionaries take this extra vow: to give 'wholehearted and free service to the poorest of the poor'.

2. For between ten and twelve hours every day, the nuns and monks work in the various centres run by the order. They are able to show love to others because of their regular worship, daily Mass and contemplative prayer, which fill them with enough of God's love to share with others.

3. Some of the Missionaries run centres for the abandoned and dying of all castes and religions, bathing their wounds and helping those who are dying to die with dignity and surrounded by God's love.

Mother Teresa gave up her life to do God's work. She believed firmly that this was what God wanted her, and others, to do.

The Missionaries of Charity express God's love to others by running orphanages.

4. Some of the Missionaries run leprosy centres in **LEDCs**, giving not only love and care to people who are often driven out of their villages, but also providing them with the medical care that can now cure most forms of leprosy.

5. Some of the Missionaries run hostels in places such as London and Edinburgh, providing free accommodation for single homeless men who have been living rough. The Missionaries ensure that other charities (such as Alcoholics Anonymous) and state employment agencies are involved to try to get the men back into society.

6. Elsewhere the missionaries run orphanages, AIDS hospices, and care for refugees and victims of floods, epidemics and famine in order to share God's love with others.

◀ An Indian nun of the Missionaries of Charity distributing lunch to volunteers at the 'Sishu Bharan' children's home.

Questions

b Do you think Christians should join a religious community to show love for others? Give two reasons for your point of view. **4**

c Choose one religious community and explain how the members of that community show love for others. **8**

d 'It is easier to show love for others when you live in a religious community.'
  i Do you agree? Give reasons for your opinion. **3**
  ii Give reasons why some people may disagree with you. **3**

Exam Tip

c 'Explain how' means you should explain how four of the activities of the Missionaries of Charity each shows love for others. For tips on Quality of Written Communication, look at page 107.

SUMMARY

The Missionaries of Charity are a religious community founded by Mother Teresa. They express love of others in an extra vow to help the poorest of the poor and in their daily work of caring for the dying left on the streets of slums, caring for orphans, AIDS victims and lepers, for example.

Topic 10.1.11 How a Christian church shows love of God and love of others in a local area

Love of God in a local area (parish)

A Catholic church shows love of God:

- through being the focal point of worship. It is where people go to show their devotion to God in the celebration of Mass.
- by keeping the Blessed Sacrament in the tabernacle for **adoration**. By providing opportunities to adore the **Body of Christ** the church encourages the congregation to show love of God.
- through offering the sacraments to the people. This allows people to show their love of God through baptism, First **Confession** and Communion, regular confessions, confirmation and marriage.
- through the liturgy of the word. By giving regular Bible readings and homilies explaining those readings to the people, a church gives the people a chance to learn more about God and how they should behave to show their love for him.
- by enabling people to share in worship with the Catholics of the **parish**, the church not only shows love of God, but also enables the people to grow in love of God and show their love of God.

Love of others in a local area (parish)

A Catholic church shows love of others in a local area by:

- giving Catholics in the local area a sense of belonging. A church shows its love by making sure that a Catholic grows up surrounded by people who not only share the same beliefs but also love them as brothers and sisters in Christ.
- providing the sacraments that are essential if the people of the parish are to lead a good Catholic life and gain eternal life.
- supporting the local Catholic primary and secondary schools, providing children's liturgies, providing classes in First Confession and Communion and confirmation. This shows the Church's love of parents and children as it helps children to grow up in the love of God and helps parents to keep their baptismal promises.
- providing opportunities for Christians to learn more about their faith, for example discussion and prayer groups.
- providing social facilities such as youth clubs, uniformed organisations, Mother and Toddler groups, showing love for the entire parish by fulfilling people's need to socialise and make friends .

> The church, the house of God, is the proper place for the liturgical prayer of the parish community. It is also the privileged place for adoration of the **real presence** of Christ in the Blessed Sacrament. The choice of a favourable place is not a matter of indifference for true prayer.
>
> **Catechism of the Catholic Church 2691**

- providing help for the needy through such groups as the St Vincent de Paul Society (SVP), CAFOD groups (CAFOD is a Catholic charity that works to relieve poverty in developing countries), lunch clubs for the elderly, and so on. By these means the church shows love for those in need as requested by Jesus in the Parable of the Sheep and the Goats.

◀ Farishes provide sacramental preparation lessons, showing love and helping parents in raising the children in the Catholic faith.

You could find out about the ways your local church shows love for God and love for others by interviewing your parish priest and active members of the congregation.

A parish is a definite community of the Christian faithful established on a stable basis within a particular church; the **pastoral** *care of the parish is entrusted to a pastor as its own shepherd under the authority of the diocesan* **bishop***. It is the place where all the faithful can be gathered together for the Sunday celebration of the Eucharist.*

Catechism of the Catholic Church 2179

Questions

b Do you think Christians spend too much of their time showing love for God? Give two reasons for your point of view. **4**

c Explain how a Christian church can show love for others in the area. **8**

d 'The local church should do more to show love for others.'
  i Do you agree? Give reasons for your opinion. **3**
  ii Give reasons why some people may disagree with you. **3**

Exam Tip

d Use the answering evaluation questions advice from page 11. Arguments for saying a local church should do more to show love of others are likely to be based on class discussion or your own ideas such as:
  - there are always some people in need who are not helped
  - some age groups may feel their needs are not catered for
  - most church activities are aimed at Catholics who are active in the parish.

Arguments against saying the local church should do more to show love of others could be three of the love of others examples in this topic.

SUMMARY

The church shows love of God by being a place of worship of God and by providing the Mass and the sacraments.

The church shows love of others by helping parents raise their children as good Catholics, by helping the needy through SVP and CAFOD groups and by providing social facilities.

How to answer exam questions

Question A What is compassion? 2 marks

A feeling of pity which makes one want to help the sufferer.

Question B Do you think Jesus is the Son of God?
Give two reasons for your point of view. 4 marks

Yes I do think he is the Son of God, because in the Bible during the baptism of Jesus the voice of God says that 'this is my son', so Jesus must be the Son of God.

I also believe he is because this is what is said in the creed, so it is the teaching of the Church and should be believed.

Question C Explain why belief in the Trinity is important for Christians. 8 marks

Belief in the Trinity is important because it explains what Christians believe about what God is like. It explains that although God is known in three ways (Father, Son and Holy Spirit), Christians only believe in one God. God the Father is the Creator, God the Son is the Saviour and God the Holy Spirit is the presence of God in the world. This is important because it helps Christians to understand what God does for them.

Belief in the Trinity is taught in the Creeds and the Catechism, which are the authoritative teachings of the Church. All Christians believe in the Creeds and all Catholics should believe the teaching of the Catechism.

Question D 'Salvation is no longer the most important thing for Christians.'

  i Do you agree? Give reasons for your opinion. 3 marks

  ii Give reasons why some people may disagree with you. 3 marks

i I disagree. Being saved from sin is the ultimate aim of a Christian as you can then have eternal life with God in heaven. Also, salvation was the purpose of the life, death and resurrection of Jesus. The death of Jesus on the cross brought forgiveness of sins and as Christianity is based on believing in Jesus, then salvation is very important to Christians. Finally, salvation is important because without salvation, you will not have eternal life as you will die in sin.

ii Others might agree with this because they think that there are many other things that are more important to Christians like showing love to God and each other and that salvation might be the result of doing this but it is not important.

Also they may think that for most Christians salvation is unimportant as they don't think about it because salvation is too difficult an idea to understand and they concentrate on being a good Christian instead.

Finally, they might say that because Christians believe God loves them, that he would not want anything bad to happen to them after their death and so they will have eternal life with God after they die whether they have been saved from their sins or not.

QUESTION A
A high mark answer because it is a correct definition of the key word.

QUESTION B
A high mark answer because an opinion is backed up by two developed reasons.

QUESTION C
A high mark answer because two reasons for the importance of the Trinity are developed, the first very fully. A formal style of English is used and there is good use of specialist vocabulary such as three ways, Father, Son, Holy Spirit, Creator, Saviour, Creeds, Catechism, authoritative.

QUESTION D
A high mark answer because it states the candidate's own opinion and backs it up with three clear reasons for thinking that salvation is important. It then gives three reasons for people disagreeing and believing that salvation is unimportant.

Section 10.2 **Community and tradition**

Introduction

This section of the examination specification requires you to look at issues surrounding community and tradition in the Catholic Church.

The Church
You will need to understand the effects of, and give reasons for your own opinion about the meaning and importance for Catholics of:
- the Church as the means to faith and salvation
- the Church as the Body of Christ
- the Church as the communion of saints.

Authority
You will need to understand the effects of, and give reasons for your own opinion about:
- why the Bible has authority and importance for Catholics
- the meaning of the Apostolic Tradition and Apostolic Succession and their importance for Catholics
- the role and importance of the Magisterium for Catholics
- the meaning of Protestant beliefs about the authority of the Church and their importance for Protestant Christians.

Priesthood
You will need to understand the effects of, and give reasons for your own opinion about:
- the role and importance of the Pope and bishops in the Catholic Church
- the role and importance of the priest in the local parish
- why Christians have different attitudes to the celibacy of the clergy
- the role and importance of the Virgin Mary for Catholics.

Topic 10.2.1 The meaning, and importance for Catholics, of the Church as the means to faith and salvation

When Catholics refer to the Church, with a capital C, they mean everyone who is a member of the Church: the ordained and ordinary lay people.

What does 'the Church as the means to faith' mean?

Catholics believe that the Church is the means to faith as it is through the Church that people come to believe in Christianity. This is because:

- the Church has kept the true faith of Christianity through the **Apostolic Succession**; the apostles were taught by Jesus and so through the Church people can learn the true faith from Jesus through his apostles.
- Catholics believe that the Pope and the **bishops** can interpret the faith of the Bible and Apostolic Tradition for today's world through the **Magisterium** of the Church. So it is only through the Church that true faith can be found.
- In the preparation for baptism, First Confession and **First Communion**, and confirmation, Catholics are taught Christian beliefs and learn to have faith in God.
- In the Bible readings and **homily** in Sunday Mass, Catholics learn more about their faith and can deepen their faith. So the Church is the means to faith for them.
- The **sacraments** of the Church not only proclaim the faith of the Church, but also give spiritual strength to believe and to live out the faith in daily life. So the Church is the means to faith through its celebration of the sacraments.

KEY WORDS

Apostolic – the belief that the Church can only be understood in the light of the apostles.

Bishops – priests specially chosen by the Pope who are responsible for all the churches in a diocese.

Catholic – universal or worldwide.

Magisterium – the Pope and the bishops interpreting the Bible and tradition for Roman Catholics today.

The Church is catholic: she proclaims the fullness of the faith. She bears in herself and administers the totality of the means of salvation. She is sent out to all peoples. She speaks to all men. She encompasses all times. She is 'missionary of her very nature'.

Catechism of the Catholic Church 868

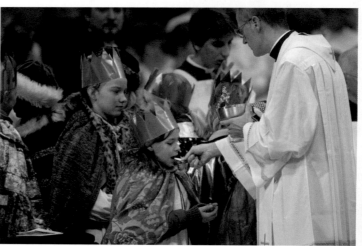

Catholics believe children should be brought up in the Church so that they gain faith and salvation.

Why the Church as the means to faith is important for Catholics

- It is important to Catholics that their faith is the true faith, and if the Church is the means to faith, then what the Church teaches is the 'one true faith', handed down from the apostles through the Church.
- It is important because the faith of the Church brings salvation as belief in Christ leads to eternal life in heaven.
- It is important that there is a place where people can learn about the Catholic faith and the Church, through local parish churches, provides the means to faith
- It is important that people are guided into faith and the Church, through its worship and teaching, provides that guidance.
- It is important that people are provided with support and strength as they seek to believe and the Church provides this through the sacraments and through the help of priests and ordinary members of the parish.

> *It is the Church that believes first, and so bears, nourishes and sustains my faith ... It is through the Church that we receive faith and new life in Christ by Baptism.*
>
> **Catechism of the Catholic Church 168**

These young people are participating in Mass as altar servers. Catholics learn more about their faith when they participate in some way.

What does 'the Church as the means to salvation' mean?

> *Faith is necessary for salvation. The Lord himself affirms: 'He who believes and is baptised will be saved; but he who does not believe will be condemned'. (Mark 16:16)*
>
> **Catechism of the Catholic Church 183**

As we have already seen (Topic 10.1.6) salvation means being saved from sin through the sacrifice of Christ. The Church is the means to salvation through:

- The sacrament of baptism which washes away original sin and makes a person a member of the Church, so opening up the possibility of salvation.
- The sacrament of reconciliation where, if a person truly repents of their sins and determines to live a new life, the priest can give **absolution** declaring forgiveness of sins (a person who has no sins will receive salvation). This forgiveness, however, comes through the Church not just the priest: 'The Father of mercies is the source of all forgiveness. He effects the reconciliation of sinners through the Passover of his Son and the gift of his Spirit, through the **prayer** and ministry of his Church.' Catechism 1449
- The **penitential rite** of the Mass which gives people a chance to confess their sins and receive absolution from God through the Church via the priest, again opening up the possibility of salvation.
- The sacrament of confirmation which allows a Catholic to affirm for themselves the **vows** taken on their behalf at baptism. It also makes them a full member of the Church and gives the gifts of the Holy Spirit to help them on their way to salvation.

Bishops have to ensure that Catholics receive the correct teaching of the Church.

- The sacrament of the anointing of the sick which can give a person an opportunity when sick or near the end of their life to receive God's forgiveness through the Church and to be prepared for the final journey to **heaven**. The final absolution and the food for the journey to heaven given in this sacrament is the means of salvation given by the Church.

Why the Church as the means to salvation is important for Catholics

- The Church as the means to salvation is important because without salvation, a person's sins will prevent them from having a close relationship with God in this life and send them to hell or purgatory after death.
- The Church as the means to salvation is important because it is the only way that Christians can have eternal life with God.
- The Church as the means to salvation is important because it gives Catholics a clear route to salvation. If Catholics take part in the sacraments of the Church and follow the teachings of the Church, they will be saved.
- The Church as the means to salvation is important because it gives Catholics second chances. It shows that salvation is a process rather than happening just once at baptism. Life is a journey to salvation and the Church gives Catholics opportunities to get back on the right path through the sacraments of reconciliation and anointing, and the Mass.

Questions

b Do you think the Church is the means to faith? Give two reasons for your point of view. **4**

c Explain why it is important for Christians to believe that the Church is the means to salvation. **8**

d 'The Church is the means to salvation for everyone in the world.'
  i Do you agree? Give reasons for your opinion. **3**
  ii Give reasons why some people may disagree with you. **3**

Exam Tip

c 'Explain' means give reasons. To answer this question you should use four reasons from the importance of believing the Church is the means to salvation and make each of them into a short paragraph. For tips on Quality of Written Communication look at page 107.

SUMMARY

The Church is the way to faith for Catholics because the Church has kept the faith of Apostles and teaches it through worship and the sacraments. It is important to know the true faith and to be guided into it by the teaching and support of the Church.

The Church is the way to salvation because the faith it teaches and the sacraments given by the Church bring forgiveness and so salvation from sin and death.

Topic 10.2.2 The meaning, and importance for Catholics, of the Church as the Body of Christ

> The body is a unit, though it is made up of many parts; and though all its parts are many, they form one body. So it is with Christ. For we were all baptised by one Spirit into one body—whether Jews or Greeks, slave or free—and we were all given the one Spirit to drink.
>
> **1 Corinthians 12:12–13**

What does 'the Church as the Body of Christ' mean?

The Church is described as the Body of Christ in both the New Testament and the Catechism. This means that:

- All Christians continue the work of Christ on Earth. They are his physical body as he is no longer physically present with us.
- The teaching that the Church is the Body of Christ means that the work of Christ on Earth did not finish with the **Ascension**; Jesus lives on through his followers, he still lives in the Church which is his body on Earth.
- Christians become part of the Church and so part of the Body of Christ through baptism which means they are united with each other and with Christ.
- All Catholics receive the Body of Christ weekly through the action of the Church in Mass (for Catholics the sacrament of the Eucharist is the Body of Christ). This joins Catholics with all the other Christians around the world receiving the sacrament.

> The Church is the Body of Christ. Through the Spirit and his action in the sacraments, above all the Eucharist, Christ, who once was dead and is now risen, establishes the community of believers as his own Body.
>
> **Catechism of the Catholic Church 805**

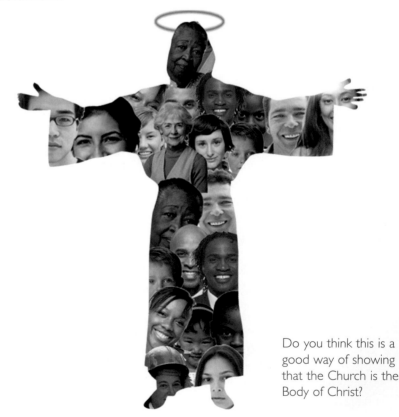

> Baptism makes us members of the Body of Christ: 'Therefore ... we are members one of another.' Baptism incorporates us into the Church.
>
> **Catechism of the Catholic Church 1267**

Do you think this is a good way of showing that the Church is the Body of Christ?

Why the Church as the Body of Christ is important for Catholics

- This is how the Church is described in the New Testament. It is a term used by **St Paul** in 1 Corinthians 6:15: 'You know that your bodies are parts of the body of Christ'.

- It explains why the Mass is so important for Catholics. By sharing the consecrated host at communion, Catholics share in the Body of Christ through **transubstantiation**, and are re-affirmed as part of Christ's body. They are strengthened each week by the grace of this sacrament.

- It shows how Christians can continue the physical helping and teaching work of Jesus today because they are the Body of Christ on Earth. This also shows that Christ is still active in the world he came to save.

- It shows how Christians can perform different tasks and yet be a unity. Each person within the Church has a different talent that they can use for the good of the Church in the same way that each part of a body has a different talent that is used for the good of the body. There can be diversity of talents and tasks (just as the body has different limbs and organs) and yet the Church remains a unity because all are working together as the body of Christ.

The bread and wine used during the Mass.

Questions

b Do you think the Church behaves like the Body of Christ? Give two reasons for your point of view. **4**

c Explain why belief in the Church as the Body of Christ is important for Christians. **8**

d 'The Church is no longer good enough to call itself the Body of Christ.'
  i Do you agree? Give reasons for your opinion. **3**
  ii Give reasons why some people may disagree with you. **3**

Exam Tip

b You should already have thought about this, and you just have to give two reasons for your opinion. For example, if you think the Church behaves like the Body of Christ you could use reasons from Topic 10.1.11 how the Catholic Church shows love of God and love of others.

SUMMARY

Catholics believe that the Church is the Body of Christ on Earth because the Church carries on the work of Jesus on Earth, and is one body even though it has lots of different parts.

This is important because:

- it is what the New Testament says
- it explains the importance of the Mass
- it shows how Christ is still active in the world.

Topic 10.2.3 The meaning, and importance for Catholics, of the Church as the communion of saints

> I believe in
> The Holy Spirit;
> The Holy Catholic Church;
> The Communion of Saints
>
> **The Apostles' Creed**

> We believe in the communion of all the faithful of Christ, those who are pilgrims on Earth, the dead who are being purified, and the blessed in heaven, all together forming one Church; and we believe that in this communion, the merciful love of God and his saints is always [attentive] to our prayers.
>
> **Catechism of the Catholic Church 962**

> Exactly as Christian communion among our fellow pilgrims brings us closer to Christ, so our communion with the saints joins us to Christ, from whom as from its fountain and head issues all grace, and the life of the People of God itself.
>
> **Catechism of the Catholic Church 957**

Saints are not just those people who have been officially made saints by the Church (**canonised**), but are all faithful Christians.

What does 'the communion of saints' mean?

The Church as the **communion of saints** means that all members of the Church are **holy** and that all members of the Church are joined together. This means that:

- There is no division between the Church on Earth and the Church in heaven. All members of the Church are joined together: those on Earth, those in purgatory and those in heaven.
- Christians on Earth can offer prayers through the official saints. The official saints are in heaven rather than purgatory and so are closer to Christ to intercede with him for their brothers and sisters in the Church on Earth.
- All faithful Christians are part of the Church and God communicates his riches to them through the sacraments. So if there is a communion of holy things, there must also be a communion (sharing and fellowship) among holy people.
- Catholics can pray for the dead as they are still part of the communion of saints. This means that Christians on Earth can pray for their dead relatives/friends in purgatory.
- Christians on Earth can have comfort and support from the prayers for them.

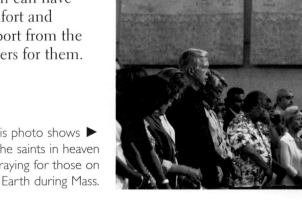

This photo shows ► the saints in heaven praying for those on Earth during Mass.

Why the Church as the communion of saints is important for Catholics

- It is the teaching of the **Creeds** and the **Catechism** which are the basis of Christian faith and which all Catholics should believe.
- It gives Catholics direct contact with the official saints allowing Catholics to have help, comfort and support from great Christians of the past.
- It allows prayers to be offered for the dead so that those in purgatory can ascend to heaven and those in heaven can pray for those on Earth.
- It is important because it means that all Christians are equally important, all are joined and can pray for one another. No one Christian is more important than another.
- There is a communion among holy people because everyone in the Church shares in the gifts of the Holy Spirit. This means the gifts can be used for everyone's benefit. Just as the saints helped on earth so they do in heaven.

▶ Catholics believe that when they pray they are joined together and the saints in heaven will also join in their prayers.

Questions

b Do you think Catholics on Earth can contact the saints in heaven? Give two reasons for your point of view. **4**

c Explain why belief in the Church as the communion of saints is important for Catholics. **8**

d 'Saints cannot pray for those on Earth.'
  i Do you agree? Give reasons for your opinion. **3**
  ii Give reasons why some people may disagree with you. **3**

Exam Tip

d Use the answering evaluation questions advice from page 111. Arguments for are likely to come from class discussions and your own ideas such as saints do not exist and so cannot pray for those on Earth; only people on Earth can pray. Arguments against should come from the importance of the communion of saints in this topic

SUMMARY

The communion of saints means that Christians on Earth and Christians in heaven are in contact with each other and share their gifts and prayers with each other.

This is important because it means that Catholics on Earth can ask the saints in heaven for help and Catholics in purgatory can be helped by the prayers of Catholics on Earth.

Topic 10.2.4 Why the Bible has authority and importance for Catholics

The Bible is the holy book of Christianity. The first part of the Bible is called the Old Testament and contains God's laws for the Jews, prophecies about the coming of Jesus, and the history of the Jewish people before Jesus. The second part of the Bible is called the New Testament and contains the four Gospels (Matthew, Mark, Luke, John) about the life and death of Jesus, the Acts of the Apostles about the founding of the Church, and letters of early Church leaders such as St Peter and St Paul and the Book of Revelation, which is the last book of the New Testament.

Why the Bible has authority for Catholics

Catholics believe the Bible has authority because it:

- is inspired by the Holy Spirit which means it comes from God and is therefore holy and considered authoritative (giving the truth and to be accepted and followed) by Catholics
- reveals God. God speaks through both the Old Testament and New Testament showing his character and commands, so it should be followed.

The scriptures are read during most Church services, as the Bible has authority to guide Christians how to live.

The Bible can be used in many ways. Do you think all ways lead to an increase in faith and love of God?

- contains God's laws on how to behave, such as the Ten Commandments. These rules are there to help people live as God intends so it has authority by showing them how God wants them to live.
- contains the teachings of Jesus on how to live the Christian life. They believe Jesus is the second person of the Holy Trinity so what he taught has authority, which means that the Bible that records his teaching also has authority.
- the Bible can bring people into a closer relationship with God by learning about what God wants and how God cares for them.

Why the Bible is important for Catholics

- The Bible records the teaching of Jesus during his **ministry** on Earth. These teachings (especially the **Sermon on the Mount**) are essential for Christians to know how to live and how to make decisions.
- The Bible records the life, death and **resurrection** of Jesus which is of supreme importance because Jesus' work of salvation is the basis of the Christian faith and the story of the early church.
- The Bible contains the Ten Commandments which are important for Catholics because they are God's basic guidelines on how to live.
- The Bible reveals what God is like and what he does for Christians. This is important because it is only by knowing what God is like and what he does that Christians can fulfil the first of the great commandments to love God.
- Through using the Bible in private devotion and reading about God's actions and reading Gods words, God is revealed to Christians. This is important as it leads to a closer relationship with God.
- Through using the Bible in public worship (including its interpretation by the priest in the homily), Christians learn how to live the type of life God wants them to in today's world.

> To compose the sacred books, God chose certain men who, all the while he employed them in this task, made full use of their own faculties and powers so that, though he acted in them and by them, it was as true authors that they consigned to writing whatever he wanted written, and no more.
>
> **Catechism of the Catholic Church 106**

> The Bible, which has had such an enormous impact on the life of so many people and nations, has enriched the English language with its momentous words and phrases, and continues to inspire literature, art, music and film. These Holy Scriptures, which have their place at the heart of our liturgy and prayer, remain an extraordinary gift of God for us today.
>
> *The Gift of Scripture* **Bishops of England and Scotland (Catholic Truth Society)**

Questions

b Do you think the Bible is important? Give two reasons for your point of view.   **4**

c Explain why the Bible is important for Catholics.   **8**

d 'Everyone should obey what the Bible says.'
  i Do you agree? Give reasons for your opinion.   **3**
  ii Give reasons why some people may disagree with you   **3**

Exam Tip

c 'Explain' means give reasons. To answer this question you should use four reasons from the importance of the Bible for Catholics and make each of them into a short paragraph. For tips on Quality of Written Communication, look at page 107.

SUMMARY

The Bible has authority because it is inspired by God and contains the teachings that come from God.

The Bible is important for Catholics because it reveals God, contains God's commands on how Christians should behave, and shows Christians what Jesus did on Earth.

Topic 10.2.5 The Apostolic Tradition and Apostolic Succession

> *And I tell you that you are Peter, and on this rock I will build my church, and the gates of Hades will not overcome it. I will give you the keys of the kingdom of heaven; whatever you bind on Earth will be bound in heaven, and whatever you loose on Earth will be loosed in heaven.*
>
> **Matthew 16:18–19**

> *The Lord made St Peter the visible foundation of his Church. He entrusted the keys of the Church to him. The Bishop of the Church of Rome, successor to St Peter, is head of the college of bishops, the Vicar of Christ and Pastor of the universal Church on Earth.*
>
> **Catechism of the Catholic Church 936**

The meaning of Apostolic Tradition

The Apostolic Tradition means that:
- The Church believes that Jesus gave the apostles his message and authority to begin the Church. The Church teaches that the Gospel was handed on not just in the writings of the New Testament, but also in the oral message of the apostles.
- The apostles preached the Gospel and established the first Churches as they were inspired to by Jesus.
- The teachings they used and handed down were given to the apostles directly from Jesus so the teaching Catholics have today should be followed if they wish to live as Jesus intended.
- The tradition handed down by the apostles to the Church today comes directly from Jesus.

The importance of Apostolic Tradition

The Apostolic Tradition of the Church is important to Catholics because:
- it gives the Church the authority of Jesus to teach the faith.
- it means that the teaching of the Church is the teaching that was given to the apostles by Jesus. This is important because it gives Catholics confidence in the true faith taught by the Church.
- it guarantees that the teaching Catholics follow is correct. It has not been changed since Jesus gave it. It is the true faith.
- not everything that Jesus did and said is recorded in the Gospels. The unwritten message of Jesus was preserved by the apostles and has been passed on to the present day through the Apostolic Tradition.

The meaning of Apostolic Succession

Catholics believe that the tradition from the apostles has been handed down in the Church through the Pope and the bishops. This is known as the Apostolic Succession.

How does this picture of the Last Supper by Jacopo Bassano in 1542 show the importance of the Apostles?

Jesus appointed St Peter to be the founder of the Church and gave him the keys of the kingdom of heaven with the authority to lead the Church and to forgive people's sins. St Peter was the first Bishop of Rome, and Catholics believe that all subsequent Bishops of Rome (all Popes are also the Bishop of Rome) have Peter's authority as head of the apostles to be head of the college of bishops. This succession is assured by the **cardinals** electing the Pope under the guidance of the Holy Spirit.

Apostolic Succession has been conferred by the sacrament of holy orders; when a bishop is ordained the grace of God is given to them to continue Apostolic Succession.

Apostolic Succession means that:
- The same teaching that the apostles gave their congregations is given to congregations today. The teaching is what God requires and is unchanged since the apostles.
- Only priests who have been ordained by a bishop ordained in the line of Apostolic Succession are true priests with Christ's authority to administer the sacraments.

The importance of the Apostolic Succession

- The authority of St Peter has been passed down by the Apostolic Succession to the current Pope. This is important because it means that the Pope has the same authority that Christ gave to St Peter.
- The Apostolic Succession is important because when the Pope and the College of Cardinals proclaim the Magisterium of the Church, they are speaking as the successors of the apostles and are proclaiming the message of Jesus.
- The Apostolic Succession preserves the faith of the apostles which is important because it makes sure that the faith of the Church today is the same faith as that of the apostles.
- The power to confer (give) the sacraments is passed down through the Apostolic Succession, meaning the power has come from Jesus and that the sacraments are authentic ways to pass on God's grace to Catholics today.
- The Apostolic Succession is one way by which Jesus fulfils his promise to stay with his Church.

> *Thus the risen Christ, by giving the Holy Spirit to the apostles, entrusted to them his power of sanctifying: they became sacramental signs of Christ. By the power of the same Holy Spirit they entrusted this power to their successors. This 'apostolic succession' structures the whole liturgical life of the Church and is itself sacramental, handed on by the sacrament of holy orders.*
>
> **Catechism of the Catholic Church 1087**

Questions

b Do you think it is important for Catholics to believe in the Apostolic Succession? Give two reasons for your point of view. **4**

c Explain what the Apostolic Tradition means for Catholics. **8**

d 'You can't be a Catholic if you don't believe in the Apostolic Succession.'
  i Do you agree? Give reasons for your opinion. **3**
  ii Give reasons why some people may disagree with you. **3**

Exam Tip

b You should already have thought about this, and you just have to give two reasons for your opinion. For example, if you think it is important for Catholics to believe in the Apostolic Succession you could use two reasons from this topic.

SUMMARY

Catholics believe that the authority of the Church comes from the Bible and the tradition of the Apostles. Catholics believe the Pope has special authority because he is the successor of St Peter, chosen by the Holy Spirit to lead the Church.

Topic 10.2.6 The role and importance of the Magisterium for Catholics

> *The Roman Pontiff and the bishops are authentic teachers, that is, teachers endowed with the authority of Christ, who preach the faith to the people entrusted to them, the faith to be believed and put into practice. The ordinary and universal Magisterium of the Pope and bishops in communion with him teaches the faithful the truth to believe, the charity to practise, the beatitude to hope for.*
>
> **Catechism of the Catholic Church 2034**

It is the duty of the Church to interpret the Bible and the Apostolic Tradition for the life of Christian people today. This task of interpreting is carried out by the Pope and the college of bishops under his leadership. When the Pope and bishops act as interpreters they are called the Magisterium (the living teaching office of the Church).

The role of the Magisterium

- The main role is to interpret the Bible and the Apostolic Tradition for the life of Christian people in the twenty-first century.
- When there are developments in medicine (for example, genetic engineering, IVF treatments) it is the role of the Magisterium to tell Catholics how they should treat such developments.

The Magisterium is made up of the Pope and the college of bishops.

> *Church teaching on moral matters is founded not only on reason and argument, but also on Scripture and the Christian tradition developed through reflection on Christian practice, and through the teachings of saints, popes and councils, under the guidance of the Holy Spirit.*
>
> **Article 34, *Cherishing Life***

- It is the role of the Magisterium to define the beliefs (**dogmas**) of the Catholic Church. This has been done through the writing, authorising and publishing of the Catechism of the Catholic Church (latest edition 1994).
- It is the role of the Magisterium to ensure that its teachings are communicated to all the bishops who can then pass them on to all the parish priests in their **diocese** so that the **laity** are fully informed about the beliefs and teachings of the Church.

The importance of the Magisterium for Catholics

- The Magisterium is the supreme authority for Catholics telling them what to believe. If the Magisterium states something to be true then it is true. There is no higher earthly authority than the Magisterium (unless the Pope makes an *ex cathedra* definitive statement on doctrine).
- The Magisterium can address issues that did not exist in the time of the apostles, for example same-sex partnerships. This is important as Catholics cannot look in the Bible to find answers to these issues.
- It is important because following the teachings of the Magisterium points the way to salvation. As the Magisterium is the Pope and college of bishops guided by the Holy Spirit, its teachings must be correct and holy.
- The Magisterium is important because it provides clear guidelines for Catholics on what to believe and how to behave as Catholics in today's world.
- The Magisterium ensures that the teaching of the Church is updated but does not change the Apostolic Tradition. This means it is always correct to follow the teachings of the Magisterium. If Catholics do this, they will not be led to believe or do things that are against the will of God.

Pope Benedict XVI waves as he leaves his residence in the Vatican.

> *It is this Magisterium's task to preserve God's people from deviations and defections and to guarantee them the objective possibility of professing the true faith without error. Thus, the pastoral duty of the Magisterium is aimed at seeing to it that the People of God abides in the truth that liberates.*
>
> **Catechism of the Catholic Church 890**

Questions

b Do you think the Magisterium is needed today? Give two reasons for your point of view. **4**

c Explain why the Magisterium is important for Catholics. **8**

d 'The Magisterium is out of touch with the lives of modern Catholics.'
   i Do you agree? Give reasons for your opinion. **3**
   ii Give reasons why some people may disagree with you. **3**

Exam Tip

c 'Explain why' means give four brief, or two developed, reasons why the Magisterium is important for Catholics from the bullet points given in this topic. For tips on Quality of Written Communication, look at page 107.

SUMMARY

The Magisterium is the living teaching office of the Church today.

Catholics believe that the authority of the Church comes from the Bible and the tradition of the Apostles. These sources of authority are interpreted for Catholics by the Pope and the bishops in the Magisterium of the Church.

Topic 10.2.7 The meaning and importance of Protestant beliefs about the authority of the Church

KEY WORDS

Anglican Churches – Churches that are in communion with the Church of England.

Nonconformist Churches – Protestant Christians separated from the Church of England.

Unless I am convinced by proofs from Scriptures or by plain and clear reasons and arguments, I can and will not retract, for it is neither safe nor wise to do anything against conscience. Here I stand. I can do no other. God help me. Amen.

The words of Martin Luther at the Diet of Worms after he was asked to deny that salvation came from faith rather than the Church

Martin Luther 1486–1546

Protestant beliefs about the authority of the Church

Protestant Churches (or **Nonconformist Churches**) are those that broke away from Rome in the sixteenth century (Lutheran, Calvinist, Baptist and **Anglican**) and those that have broken away from these Churches at later dates (**Methodists**, **Quakers**, **Pentecostals**, **Salvation Army**). Although there are some differences between different Protestant Churches, the main beliefs are:

- There is only one authority for Christians, the Bible (often called Scripture), which can be understood by anyone if they have faith. Therefore the Church does not have the authority to interpret the Bible for Christians.
- The Church is the community of believers who are all of equal value. Therefore, only decisions agreed to by all the members of the Church can have authority. For this reason Protestant Churches are ruled democratically and vote on issues. For example, the Methodist Church has an annual conference at which elected members take decisions.
- Each Protestant Church has an agreed statement of beliefs that members are expected to accept (for example, most Protestant Churches accept the **Apostles'** and **Nicene Creeds** and the **Chalcedonian Definition** of the nature of Jesus).

- Any guidance offered by the Church is guidance, not a command, and so can be interpreted by members in the light of their own interpretation of the Bible's teaching.
- The Church has the authority to decide on how the Church shall be organised, to choose ministers, and so on, but it does not bring salvation. Salvation comes through the Bible alone.

◄ The General Synod is the national assembly of the Church of England.

Why these beliefs are important

- They are important for Protestant Christians because they allow them to have an input into the decisions and beliefs of the Church.
- They explain why there are so many different Protestant Churches. If the Church does not have complete authority, and salvation is dependent on an individual reading of the Bible, then there will be disagreements and new Churches will be set up.
- They show why the Protestant Churches broke away from Rome and why they still cannot accept the authority of the Pope or the Magisterium.
- They explain why there are different attitudes to the sacraments among Protestant Christians (most Protestants believe baptism and communion are the only sacraments, though some Anglicans believe in the seven sacraments, and Quakers and the Salvation Army have no sacraments).
- They explain why there are so many differences between Protestant Churches (for example, some have ministers, some have pastors; some have weekly communion, some only have communion once a year) because there is no agreed Church authority.
- In England the beliefs about the authority of the Church help to explain the differences within the **Church of England** where some Anglicans believe in seven sacraments, priests and bishops, for example Anglo-Catholics, while others believe in two sacraments and ministers.

> *Baptists understand the Church as a community of believers who gather together for worship, witness and service ... In Baptist churches the final authority rests not with the ministers or deacons but with the members gathered together in church meetings. It is the church meeting which, for instance, appoints ministers, elders, deacons, and others who exercise various forms of leadership within a local congregation, agrees financial policy and determines mission strategy ... The minister functions as a church member with special responsibilities in caring for the members and leading in the church's mission.*
>
> **Taken from the website of Dartford Baptist Church**

Questions

b Do you think the Church is important for Protestants? Give two reasons for your point of view. **4**

c Explain why beliefs about the authority of the Church are important for understanding Protestant Christians. **8**

d 'The Bible is the only authority a Christian needs.'
  i Do you agree? Give reasons for your opinion. **3**
  ii Give reasons why some people may disagree with you. **3**

Exam Tip

d Use the answering evaluation questions advice from page 111. The arguments that might agree with this statement could come from this topic. Arguments against could come from topics 10.2.1, 10.2.5 and 10.2.6.

SUMMARY

Within the Protestant Churches the Church leads and guides and has authority on Church organisation; however the Bible is the only true source of authority and salvation.

These beliefs are important because they explain why there are different Protestant Churches with different beliefs, and why the Protestant Churches broke away from Rome.

Topic 10.2.8 The role and importance of the Pope and bishops in the Catholic Church

KEY WORDS

Laity – all the people of the Church who are not chosen to be bishops, priests or deacons.

Ordination – making someone a priest, bishop or deacon by the sacrament of holy orders.

Papacy – the office of the Pope.

The role of the Pope in the Catholic Church

The Pope:

- has to carry out his duties as the Bishop of Rome caring for his diocese and ensuring that all the parishes are correctly run
- organises the Magisterium and ensures that it considers all the issues that are needed to guide Catholics in their beliefs
- acts as the ultimate authority for Catholics. He has the ability to speak *ex cathedra*, which means that when he makes these announcements he is infallible – he cannot be wrong
- appoints and ordains new cardinals and bishops, ensuring that there are enough to care for the **laity** and that their teaching is correct
- must ensure that Catholics are kept up to date with issues that may arise for both the laity and the priesthood
- leads the worldwide Church, ensuring that its unity is maintained and that the community of the Church is cared for. He is helped in this by the **Curia**
- is responsible for Vatican City, an independent state with its own police force, diplomatic service, coinage, post office, etc.

The importance of the Pope in the Catholic Church

The Pope is important for Catholics because he:

- is responsible for the Magisterium and therefore the beliefs and teachings of the Catholic Church that affect all Catholics
- is the successor of St Peter and so passes on the authentic teachings of Christ to Catholics in the same way that St Peter did
- is the Head of the Church who appoints and ordains cardinals and bishops as leaders. They are extremely important to both priests and lay people
- gives guidance and inspiration to Catholics through his encyclicals, letters, addresses and pastoral visits around the world
- is chosen by the cardinals guided by the Holy Spirit so he has been chosen by God. This is important so that Catholics know they are being led correctly
- is infallible under certain circumstances (when he speaks *ex cathedra*) – this means that on these occasions he can make statements that Catholics must believe.

Pope Benedict XVI, Supreme Pontiff and Vicar of Christ, addresses people in St Peter's Square. Which role do you think he is carrying out here?

The role of bishops in the Catholic Church

A bishop:

- is responsible for ensuring the needs of all the priests and laity in their diocese are attended to
- is in charge of all the priests in their diocese. He must make sure that there are sufficient priests in every part of the diocese and that they are correctly carrying out their role
- is responsible for appointing, ordaining and disciplining the priests and deacons in their diocese. If any priest wants to change parish this has to be organised through the bishop
- is responsible for passing information concerning matters of faith from the national Bishops' Conference to his diocese. He must ensure that everyone is always aware of the Church's teachings and that any important issues of faith are correctly explained
- acts as the link between parishes and the Vatican, allowing the Pope to be in contact with the whole Church, as it would not be possible for all priests to be in direct contact with the Vatican.

The importance of bishops in the Catholic Church

- Bishops are responsible, with the Pope, for establishing the Magisterium, which means they participate in deciding upon the beliefs and teachings of the Church.
- Cardinals are chosen from bishops. This means that bishops are important in the hierarchy of the Church.
- Only bishops can administer the sacrament of **holy orders** (**ordination**) and they usually ordain the priests in their diocese.
- Bishops make sure their diocese is following the faith of the Church. It is the bishop's responsibility to ensure that the teachings given to the laity are correct and they have to correct and discipline any priest who teaches or acts incorrectly.

> *The Pope, Bishop of Rome and Peter's successor 'is the perpetual and visible source and foundation of the unity both of the bishops and of the whole company of the faithful. For the Roman Pontiff, by reason of his office as Vicar of Christ, and as pastor of the entire Church has full, supreme, and universal power over the whole Church, a power which he can always exercise unhindered.'*
>
> **Catechism of the Catholic Church 882**

SUMMARY

The **papacy** is the Head of the Catholic Church worldwide, appointing and ordaining cardinals and bishops and making sure that they teach the true faith. The Pope must organise the Magisterium, act as Bishop of Rome and give guidance to Catholics on the issues of the day.

The Pope is important because he is the Head of the Church, the successor of St Peter and the ultimate authority for Catholics.

Bishops are in charge of a diocese and must make sure the priests and people are well looked after and are taught the true faith. A bishop acts as a communicator between the Pope and the priests and people. Bishops are important because only they can ordain priests. They make sure a diocese has the true faith and they help with the Magisterium.

Questions

b Do you think the Pope is important? Give two reasons for your point of view. **4**

c Explain the role of bishops are important for the Catholic Church. **8**

d 'The Pope is the best person to decide what Christians should believe.'

    i Do you agree? Give reasons for your opinion. **3**

    ii Give reasons why some people may disagree with you. **3**

Exam Tip

b You should already have thought about this, and you just have to give two reasons for your opinion. For example, if you think the Pope is important you could use two reasons from this topic.

Topic 10.2.9 The role and importance of the priest in the local parish

> Priests therefore, as educators in the faith, must see to it either by themselves or through others that the faithful are led individually in the Holy Spirit to a development of their own vocation according to the Gospel, to a sincere and practical charity, and to that freedom with which Christ has made us free.
>
> **Presbyterorum Ordinis**
> **Pope Paul VI, 1965**

The role of the priest in the local parish

A priest is in charge of the local area around his church, called a parish. A parish priest has to:

- lead daily Mass and special occasion liturgies. The priest must celebrate Mass to consecrate the bread and wine, the laity cannot do this
- teach the people of the parish about the faith, through his sermons and through other education groups
- administer the sacraments of baptism, **marriage**, reconciliation and healing, ensuring that people fully understand them
- conduct funerals and care for the bereaved through visiting them so that they receive spiritual counselling
- ensure that people are prepared fully for the sacraments. This may involve running special classes
- pray for the congregation and the whole Church through his daily office
- pray with the members of the congregation privately and publicly, through regular worship and one-off events
- make sure that the church building is looked after and maintained
- look after the people within the parish, providing advice and counselling
- build links with other local faiths and churches.

This priest is consecrating the wine. ▶
Priests are able to consecrate the bread and wine to make it become the body and blood of Jesus.

The importance of the priest in the local parish

Priests are important because a priest:

- fulfils the role of Jesus in the Mass and transubstantiates the bread and wine – feeding the people with the body and blood of Christ
- brings the people together through the rite of communion

- is the 'shepherd of his flock'. He ensures they are cared for, and the church runs smoothly. Without the priest the parish might not be run for the benefit of the entire congregation equally
- gives the gift of grace to his parishioners through the sacraments and especially through Mass. The parish needs this grace in order to achieve salvation and go to heaven
- can give advice on matters of faith and personal problems in order to help people. This advice is essential in the spiritual life of people as they face the challenges that life brings
- can help organise material care for people through money and charity (for example, SVP). This kind of care is essential to the needy as without it they would suffer greatly
- is a link between the bishop and the parish so that new teachings and messages are given to the people
- helps people with the important stages of their life – baptism, confirmation, marriage, funerals. This is important as faith is a journey and people's understanding of their faith is constantly changing so they need a priest to guide them on the correct path.

Because it is joined with the episcopal order the office of priests shares in the authority by which Christ himself builds up and sanctifies and rules his Body. Hence the priesthood of priests, while presupposing the sacraments of initiation, is nevertheless conferred by its own particular sacrament. Through that sacrament priests by the anointing of the Holy Spirit are signed with a special character and so are configured to Christ the priest in such a way that they are able to act in the person of Christ the head.

Catechism of the Catholic Church 1563

◄ A priest has a number of roles and all are needed when running a parish.

Questions

b Do you think that every parish needs a priest? Give two reasons for your point of view. **4**

c Explain the role of a parish priest. **8**

d 'Priests are essential to a parish.'
  i Do you agree? Give reasons for your opinion. **3**
  ii Give reasons why some people may disagree with you. **3**

Exam Tip

d Use the answering evaluation questions advice from page 111. Reasons for this statement should come from this topic. Reasons against the statement are likely to come from class discussion and/or your own ideas such as: all the roles of a priest could be performed by the laity; some parishes do not have a parish priest; priests are not the best people to do things like teaching – teachers are.

SUMMARY

The main functions of the priest are to administer the sacraments, represent Christ at the Mass and help the Catholics in the parish.

The priest is important practically, socially and spiritually. He is essential to a local church because he can offer the Mass and perform the sacraments.

Topic 10.2.10 Why Christians have different attitudes to the celibacy of the clergy

In the Catholic Church priests and bishops have to be celibate. Married men may be ordained deacons, but may not be ordained priests or bishops, nor may priests marry after ordination. The exception to this is when non-Catholic clergy who are married become Catholic priests.

Most non-Catholic Churches allow their priests to marry.

Why Catholics teach that the clergy must be celibate

- It is tradition handed down from St Paul who taught that 'an unmarried man is concerned about the Lord's affairs' (1 Corinthians 7:32).
- Jesus remained single and it is important that priests should follow his example.
- It allows the priests to be completely devoted to God and their vocation. They are then not distracted by worldly problems and have more time for their parishoners.
- Unmarried priests are free to deal with the needs of their parish rather being than tied to family matters. If they were married the needs of their family would necessarily be important.
- It means priests sacrifice their lives to God in the same way that Jesus did. Jesus gave up everything including his home, stability, the chance of a married life and having children when he was following his mission and therefore so do priests.

For spiritual as well as practical reasons, the Catholic Church in the West also requires priests and bishops to live lives of permanent celibacy, unless they have been given special dispensation. The priests and bishops of the Church, in following the example of Jesus, the good shepherd, seek to give themselves wholeheartedly to the service of the Gospel. Freedom from special family responsibilities allows them to make a greater commitment of time and energy to the demands of their pastoral role.

Article 116, *Cherishing Life*

Why other Christians allow priests to marry

Catholic priests take a vow where they promise not to marry. Do you think this is needed?

- St Peter was married; towards the beginning of his ministry Jesus healed Peter's mother-in-law.
- Priests can be devoted to God and their families. There are many married priests and they manage to do both things, in the same way that other people are able to fulfil more than one role.

Most non-Catholics allow their clergy to marry. What are the advantages of a married priesthood?

- Married priests have first hand experience of recognising and dealing with married people's problems. If a priest is married, arguably someone who is having marriage problems will feel more comfortable talking to them.
- Early Christian priests were married, although there is some discussion about when this was. It seems from documentation that married priests were allowed in the early Church until **celibacy** became the norm.
- There would be a shortage of priests if they had to be celibate. Non-Catholic churches do not have a shortage of priests, but the Catholic Church in Europe does, perhaps because many men are put off joining the celibate priesthood.

> *In the Eastern Churches a different discipline has been in force for many centuries: while bishops are chosen solely from among celibates, married men can be ordained as deacons and priests. This practice has long been considered legitimate; these priests exercise a fruitful ministry within their communities. Moreover, priestly celibacy is held in great honour in the Eastern Churches and many priests have freely chosen it for the sake of the Kingdom of God. In the East as in the West a man who has already received the sacrament of holy orders can no longer marry.*
>
> **Catechism of the Catholic Church 1580**

Questions

b Do you think priests should be celibate? Give two reasons for your point of view. **4**

c Explain why some Christians expect priests to be celibate, and some do not. **8**

d 'Celibate priests make better priests.'

   i Do you agree? Give reasons for your opinion. **3**

   ii Give reasons why some people may disagree with you. **3**

Exam Tip

c For this 'explain' question you should give at least two reasons why some Christians expect priests to be celibate and two reasons why some Christians do not. Use the reasons given in this topic. For tips on Quality of Written Communication, look at page 107.

SUMMARY

Catholic priests have to be celibate in order to copy what Jesus did, maintain tradition and be able to give their whole life to the Church. Other Christians allow their priests and ministers to marry as they feel there are many advantages to allowing priests to marry should they want to.

Topic 10.2.11 The role and importance of the Virgin Mary for Catholics

Many people show devotion to Mary ▶ at the grotto in Lourdes. Why do you think Lourdes is so important for Catholics (see page 5)?

> The Virgin Mary, who at the message of the angel received the Word of God in her heart and in her body and gave Life to the world, is acknowledged and honoured as being truly the Mother of God and Mother of the Redeemer. Redeemed by reason of the merits of her Son and united to Him by a close and indissoluble tie, she is endowed with the high office and dignity of being the Mother of the Son of God, by which account she is also the beloved daughter of the Father and the temple of the Holy Spirit.
>
> **Lumen Gentium**
> **Pope Paul VI, 1964**

> Finally the Immaculate Virgin, preserved free from all stain of original sin, when the course of her earthly life was finished, was taken up body and soul into heavenly glory, and exalted by the Lord as Queen over all things.
>
> **Catechism of the Catholic Church 966**

Catholics pay special devotion to the Virgin Mary. All Catholic churches have a statue of Mary, sometimes in a special Lady chapel. There are special feasts of the Church dedicated to the Virgin Mary (for example, the **Immaculate Conception**, the **Annunciation** and the **Assumption**), and Catholics are encouraged to use the Virgin Mary as a role model for their own lives because of her openness to God's will for her.

The role of the Virgin Mary for Catholics

- For many Catholics, Mary's main role is to act as an intercessor. Prayers are said to Mary, for example, Hail Mary and the Angelus. These are not said to worship her but rather to ask for her prayers (**intercession**) because of her special relationship with God. Prayers can be offered to Mary because she said in the **Magnificat**, 'All generations will call me blessed' (Luke 1:48).
- Mary is a role model for Christians. She shows them how to live a good Christian life because she obeyed God's plan for her: she did not question what was to happen to her, rather she accepted that it was God's will.
- Mary is also a role model for how to live a pure life. She was conceived without sin (Immaculate Conception) and remained a pure virgin throughout her life. By following her example, Catholics can also try to live pure lives.
- Mary is also a role model of love for Jesus. She loved her son and was with him right to the end, even sharing in his sufferings on the cross. This is how Christians should love Christ.
- Mary was present at Pentecost and helped the apostles begin the early Church.

Why the Virgin Mary is important for Catholics

◀ Michelangelo's *Pieta* shows the love Mary had for her son.

- Mary was special from before her birth as she had an immaculate conception. This meant that she was sinless and predestined to be the mother of God. This is important because it means that Jesus was totally sinless because his mother was born without original sin and his father was God.

- Mary was specially chosen by God to be the mother of his Son. Without her acceptance of God's will Jesus would have not been incarnated. This is very important because without the incarnation there would be no Christianity and no salvation.

- Because of the virgin birth, Mary gave birth to God and so she is 'the Mother of God'. Although Jesus was conceived by the power of the Holy Spirit, Mary gave birth to Jesus naturally so she is his real birth mother. As the mother of God, Mary must be the most important human being ever to have lived.

- At the end of her life, she was taken up to heaven instead of dying (the Assumption of the Blessed Virgin Mary). This means she did not suffer death like everyone else. This shows how important Mary is in the eyes of God because no one else has been assumed into heaven.

- In heaven, she is able to pray for the souls of Christians on Earth and to intercede to God on behalf of Christians on Earth. This makes Mary tremendously important to Christians on Earth because she can make their prayers more effective and give them more chance of God's help.

> 'All generations will call me blessed': The Church's devotion to the Blessed Virgin is intrinsic to Christian worship. The Church rightly honours the Blessed Virgin with special devotion. From the most ancient times the Blessed Virgin has been honoured with the title of 'Mother of God,' to whose protection the faithful fly in all their dangers and needs … This very special devotion … differs essentially from the adoration which is given to the incarnate Word and equally to the Father and the Holy Spirit.
>
> **Catechism of the Catholic Church 971**

Questions

b Do you think Catholics should pray to the Virgin Mary? Give two reasons for your point of view. **4**

c Explain why the Virgin Mary is important for Catholics. **8**

d 'The Virgin Mary is the most important role model for Catholics.'
  i Do you agree? Give reasons for your opinion. **3**
  ii Give reasons why some people may disagree with you. **3**

Exam Tip

d Use the answering evaluation questions advice from page 11. Arguments for this statement could come from this topic. For arguments against you could use reasons for Jesus being the most important role model from Topic 10.1.4.

SUMMARY

Catholics believe that the role of the Virgin Mary is to help their prayers to be accepted by God. She also acts as a role model to show Catholics how to live good lives, how to love Christ and how to be obedient to God.

The Virgin Mary is important because she was totally obedient to God; she was the Mother of God, making sure Christianity began. She was taken up to heaven instead of dying and she can pray for the souls of Christians on Earth.

How to answer exam questions

Question A What does catholic mean?   **2 marks**

Universal or worldwide.

Question B Do you think Catholics should pray to the Virgin Mary?
Give two reasons for your point of view.   **4 marks**

Yes I do think Catholics should pray to the Virgin Mary as she can take their prayers to God and ask that they are answered. This is called interceding, and Catholics think it is a very powerful way of praying.

I also believe Catholics should pray to Mary as she is the mother of God's son and so is the most important human.

Question C Explain why the Magisterium is important for Catholics.   **8 marks**

The Magisterium is important for Catholics because it is the supreme authority for Catholic teaching. If the Magisterium states something to be true, then it is true. There is no higher earthly authority than the Magisterium.

The Magisterium is important because it can make decisions about issues that did not exist in the time of the Apostles, for example same-sex partnerships, or fertility treatments. This is important as Catholics cannot look in the Bible to find answers.

It is important because following the teachings of the Magisterium points the way to salvation. As the Magisterium is the Pope and college of bishops guided by the Holy Spirit, its teachings must be correct and holy.

The Magisterium is important because it provides clear guidelines for Catholics on what to believe and how to behave as Catholics in today's world.

Question D 'The Pope is the best person to decide what Christians should believe.'

i Do you agree? Give reasons for your opinion.   **3 marks**

ii Give reasons why some people may disagree with you.   **3 marks**

i *I am a Catholic and so I agree with this statement. The Pope is the successor of St Peter and so passes on the authentic teachings of Christ to Catholics in the same way that St Peter did. He is chosen by the cardinals guided by the Holy Spirit so he has been chosen by God. Also, when the Pope speaks ex cathedra, he is infallible, which means he cannot be wrong. This means he must be the best person to decide what Catholics should believe.*

ii *Some people, such as Protestants, might disagree with me because they do not accept the authority of the Pope. They believe there is only one authority for Christians, the Bible, which can be understood by anyone if they have faith. Therefore the Pope does not have the authority to make decisions for Christians. They also believe that the Church is the community of believers who are all of equal value. Therefore, only decisions agreed to by all the members of the Church, not just the Pope, can have authority.*

QUESTION A
A high mark answer because it is a correct definition of the key word.

QUESTION B
A high mark answer because an opinion is backed up by two developed reasons.

QUESTION C
A high mark answer because four reasons why the Magisterium is important for Catholics have been developed. A formal style of English is used and there is good use of specialist vocabulary such as supreme authority, earthly authority, Bible, Pope, salvation, college of bishops, Holy Spirit.

QUESTION D
A high mark answer because it states the candidate's own opinion and backs it up with three clear reasons for thinking that the Pope is the best person. It then gives three reasons for people disagreeing and believing that the Pope is not the best person.

Section 10.3 **Worship and celebration**

Introduction

This section of the examination specification requires you to look at the meaning and importance of worship and celebration.

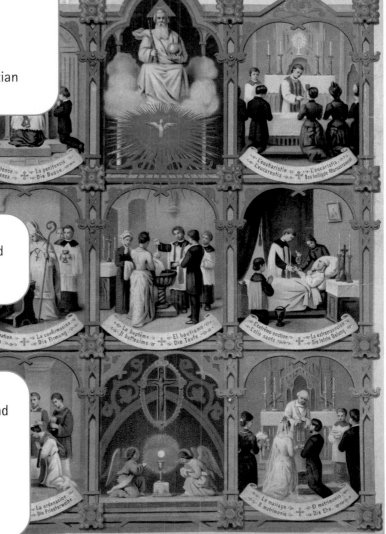

Sacraments
You will need to understand the effects of, and give reasons for your own opinion about:
- the meaning and importance for Catholics of the sacraments of:
  - baptism
  - confirmation
  - reconciliation
  - anointing of the sick
  - Mass
- the meaning of the Eucharist in other Christian traditions.

Church features
You will need to understand the effects of, and give reasons for your own opinion about why Catholic churches have certain features.

The liturgical year
You will need to understand the effects of, and give reasons for your own opinion about the meaning and importance of:
- Christmas
- Lent
- Holy Week
- Easter.

Topic 10.3.1 The meaning and importance of the sacrament of baptism

KEY WORDS

Chrism – the oil used in baptism, confirmation and ordination.

Sacrament – an outward sign through which invisible grace is given to a person by Jesus.

Baptism is birth into the new life in Christ. In accordance with the Lord's will, it is necessary for salvation, as is the Church herself, which we enter by Baptism.

Catechism of the Catholic Church 1277

In explicit terms He Himself affirmed the necessity of faith and baptism and thereby affirmed also the necessity of the Church, for through baptism as through a door, men enter the Church.

Lumen Gentium **Vatican II, 1964**

Baptism, which is necessary for salvation, is the sign and the means of God's prevenient love, which frees us from original sin and communicates to us a share in divine life.

Instruction on Infant Baptism, Sacred Congregation for the Doctrine of the Faith, 1980

Sacraments are celebrations. They mark stages in life and are outward signs and symbols which show that an inward gift from God has been given. There are seven sacraments in the Catholic Church. These are baptism, reconciliation (**penance**), Holy Communion (**Eucharist**), confirmation, the anointing of the sick, holy orders and marriage.

The meaning of the sacrament of baptism

- The word baptism comes from the Greek 'baptisen' which means to dip, bathe or wash. It refers to the washing away of the old life and entering a new one, free of sin. Catholics are usually baptised as babies and their parents make promises on their behalf during the ceremony.
- When a person receives the sacrament of baptism it means that the person becomes part of the Christian Church. The sacrament is done in public so it is recognised by the whole Church community. The Magisterium through the Catechism says that baptism 'constitutes the *sacramental bond of unity*' so through baptism a person can be called a Christian and is joined in faith with other Christians.
- Baptism is the first of the sacraments of initiation (the other two are Eucharist and confirmation) and is a recognition of the fact that the person, who is usually a child, needs to grow in faith, and will continuously need grace from God to increase their faith. Baptism is the first step in sacramental life and is essential in a Catholic's life.
- As part of baptism parents and **godparents** say vows which show that they believe in the Catholic faith and are willing to bring the child up according to the Church's teachings. This means baptism is a solemn contract; the Church through the sacrament gives grace to help them fulfil this promise.
- During baptism all sins are washed away and the person is left pure. This means that the original sin with which the child is born is washed away, leaving the baptised person free of sin. This means the sacrament is a sign of God's forgiveness and love. The baptism of young people and adults also frees them from the sins they have already committed.
- Baptism is a powerful sign that the child is chosen by Christ to be a believer. This is symbolised in the anointing with oil, especially **chrism**, and the candle that is lit and given to the parents/godparents. The Church describes baptism as putting an indelible sign on a person's soul which shows that the person has been claimed by Christ.

The importance of baptism

Baptism is important for Catholics because:

- The Catechism teaches that it is the basis of the Christian life and, without it, a person cannot receive the other sacraments. Baptism is the way a person enters the Church and is often described as a door. It is therefore important as it allows the person entry to the other sacraments. It is through receiving the sacraments that a person can receive grace to live a holy and Christian life.

- Through this sacrament the person becomes a full member of the Church, which means he or she enters into a **covenant** (promise) with the Church to grow in faith and belief. The Church then helps the person grow in faith and the person is taught to follow the teachings of the Church. Baptism is said to give the person new life in the Holy Spirit.

- Baptism washes away original sin and, in young people and adults, any other sins the person may have committed, thereby making the person pure. As a result of this forgiving action the person becomes closer to God and more likely to achieve salvation.

- Baptism is seen as necessary for a person to receive salvation. Salvation means being saved from sin and it is required so that the person can enter heaven. The Magisterium through the Catechism of the Catholic Church says that baptism is necessary for salvation.

> *He said to them, 'Go into all the world and preach the good news to all creation. Whoever believes and is baptised will be saved, but whoever does not believe will be condemned.'*
>
> **Mark 16:15–16**

> *The Lord himself affirms that Baptism is necessary for salvation. He also commands his disciples to proclaim the Gospel to all nations and to baptise them. Baptism is necessary for salvation for those to whom the Gospel has been proclaimed and who have had the possibility of asking for this sacrament.*
>
> **Catechism of the Catholic Church 1257**

◀ This photo shows the priest pouring **water** over the child's head, symbolising the washing away of sin. Although priests and deacons normally baptise, any Christian can baptise as long as they say, 'I baptise you in the name of the Father, and of the Son, and of the Holy Spirit', whilst pouring water over the person's head, and have the right intention.

Questions

b Do you think babies should be baptised? Give two reasons for your point of view. **4**

c Explain why baptism is important for Catholics. **8**

d 'Baptism is the most important sacrament.'
  i Do you agree? Give reasons for your opinion. **3**
  ii Give reasons why some people may disagree with you **3**

Exam Tip

c 'Explain' means give reasons. To answer this question you should use four reasons for baptism being important, and make each of them into a short paragraph. For tips on Quality of Written Communication, look at page 107.

SUMMARY

Catholics believe that people have to be baptised to become members of the Church. Catholic parents and godparents make promises on behalf of the child. Baptism is important because it removes original sin and makes a child part of the Church.

Topic 10.3.2 The meaning and importance of the sacrament of confirmation

The meaning of the sacrament of confirmation

- The sacrament of confirmation is the final sacrament of initiation and means that the person has fully joined with the Catholic Church and has received the grace given (conferred) as part of the initiation sacraments. His or her faith will continue to grow as part of the journey as fully initiated adults.
- The sacrament gives grace which is needed in order to live a Christian life and so eventually receive salvation.
- Confirmation joins people more closely to the Church so that they learn to live in the way the Church teaches. Living in this way leads to salvation.
- Confirmation is a sacrament which marks the growth of a Christian into a mature member of the Church. By retaking the baptismal vows for themselves, Catholics bear witness to their faith. It is a public declaration of belief to the community.

The importance of confirmation

Confirmation is important for Catholics because:
- according to Canon (Church) law, it makes the person a full member of the Church.
- Only those who are full members of the Catholic Church can take on **lay ministries**.
- As with baptism, confirmation leaves a spirited mark on the person that cannot be removed. Confirmation is therefore important as it spiritually identifies a believer in Christ.

Most Catholics decide they want to be confirmed when they are between eleven and eighteen years old. A bishop must visit parishes to ensure that young people are taught the faith correctly and to administer the sacrament of confirmation.

- Part of confirmation is the gift of the Holy Spirit. This is important as it inspires the recipient to have faith and be a witness to their faith.
- It is a public declaration of the person's faith as the baptismal vows are renewed and a declaration is made that they believe and will practise the Catholic faith. In baptism this declaration was made by the person's parents and godparents, while in confirmation it is the individual's own choice to declare his or her belief.

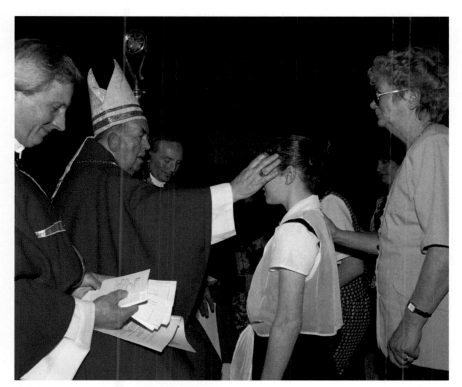

The community witnesses the person's choice to become a full member of the Church.

From this fact, confirmation brings an increase and deepening of baptismal grace:
- *it roots us more deeply in the divine filiation which makes us cry, 'Abba! Father!';*
- *it unites us more firmly to Christ;*
- *it increases the gifts of the Holy Spirit in us;*
- *it renders our bond with the Church more perfect;*
- *it gives us a special strength of the Holy Spirit to spread and defend the faith by word and action as true witnesses of Christ, to confess the name of Christ boldly, and never to be ashamed of the Cross.*

Catechism of the Catholic Church 1303

Questions

b Do you think Catholic Christians need to be confirmed?
Give two reasons for your point of view. **4**

c Explain why the sacrament of confirmation is important for Catholics. **8**

d 'Confirmation is the most important sacrament.'
  i Do you agree? Give reasons for your opinion. **3**
  ii Give reasons why some people may disagree with you. **3**

Exam Tip

b You should already have thought about this, and you just have to give two reasons for your opinion. For example, if you agree that Catholic Christians need the sacrament of confirmation you should use two reasons for the importance of confirmation from this topic.

SUMMARY

When a person is old enough to make their own decisions they are expected to renew their baptismal vows in the sacrament of confirmation.

Confirmation is important because it gives the gifts of grace and the Holy Spirit which completes the sacraments of initiation and makes the person a full member of the Church.

Topic 10.3.3 The meaning and importance of the sacrament of reconciliation

The spiritual effects of the sacrament of penance are:
- *reconciliation with God by which the penitent recovers grace;*
- *reconciliation with the Church;*
- *remission of the eternal punishment incurred by mortal sins;*
- *remission, at least in part, of temporal punishments resulting from sin;*
- *peace and serenity of conscience, and spiritual consolation;*
- *an increase of spiritual strength for the Christian battle.*

Catechism of the Catholic Church 1496

Anyone conscious of a grave sin must receive the sacrament of reconciliation before coming to communion.

Catechism of the Catholic Church 1385

The sacrament of reconciliation is also known as the sacrament of confession or the sacrament of **penance**.

The meaning of the sacrament of reconciliation

- The sacrament of reconciliation allows someone to recognise that they have, by their own actions, separated themselves from a close relationship with God (**contrition**) and that they need God's forgiveness for their wrongdoings (sins) and God's help in the form of grace to learn not to commit sins again.
- The sacrament gives grace, which is needed in order to live a Christian life and so avoid sins that lead away from salvation.
- As part of the sacrament, the penitent (person receiving reconciliation) is given advice about how to overcome temptation, and follow the path to salvation.
- The Catechism of the Catholic Church explains that reconciliation leads to 'peace and serenity of conscience'. This means that the person feels better and has an increase in self-worth.
- Receiving the sacrament of reconciliation at least once a year is one of the **Precepts of the Church**, which means it is one of the rules that Catholics are expected to follow, but receiving it more frequently is actively encouraged. It is therefore essential

These pictures show the sacrament of reconciliation in a confessional (left) and as an open confession (right). Reconciliation provides an opportunity for the penitent to receive advice on how to live a Christian life. Why might some people prefer to do this in private and others in public?

that Catholics receive reconciliation in order to maintain their relationship with the Church. Catholics believe that belonging to the Church and following its teaching will lead to salvation.

The importance of reconciliation

Reconciliation is important for Catholics because:

- it gives the opportunity for the penitent to strengthen their relationship with God. By attending the sacrament and receiving God's forgiveness they become closer to God.
- The gift of grace is given during the sacrament and, according to the Catechism, this gives 'an increase of spiritual strength for the Christian battle' against evil and temptation making it easier for the penitent to live a Christian life.
- Attending the sacrament allows reconciliation with the community. When Jesus appeared after his resurrection he encouraged the disciples to continue forgiving each other, and said 'If you forgive anyone his sins, they are forgiven; if you do not forgive them, they are not forgiven.' (John 20:23)
- The sacrament of reconciliation brings forgiveness of sins. Since early Christian times, this has been the main purpose of the sacrament, to forgive those sins which are committed by a person after their sins were forgiven during the sacrament of baptism. Once serious sins are forgiven Catholics can receive the Eucharist and they are also closer to receiving salvation and thus entering heaven.

> *The whole power of the sacrament of penance consists in restoring us to God's grace and joining us with him in an intimate friendship. Reconciliation with God is thus the purpose and effect of this sacrament. For those who receive the sacrament of penance with contrite heart and religious disposition, reconciliation is usually followed by peace and serenity of conscience with strong spiritual consolation.*
>
> **Catechism of the Catholic Church 1468**

> *By the will of Christ, forgiveness is offered to each individual by means of sacramental absolution given by the ministers of penance.*
>
> **Apostolic Exhortation *Reconciliation And Penance* John Paul II, 1984**

Questions

b Do you think Catholics need to attend the sacrament of reconciliation? Give two reasons for your point of view. **4**

c Explain why the sacrament of reconciliation is important for Catholic Christians. **8**

d 'The sacrament of reconciliation is not needed today.'
  i Do you agree? Give reasons for your opinion. **3**
  ii Give reasons why some people may disagree with you. **3**

Exam Tip

d Use the answering evaluation questions advice from page 111. The arguments for this should come from your class discussions and your own ideas. They might include such thoughts as:
  - God loves us and so will forgive sins when we say sorry.
  - All sins are forgiven at baptism, this means future sins as well as ones already committed.

Arguments against should come from reasons for its importance in this topic.

SUMMARY

Catholics believe that the sacrament of reconciliation forgives a person's sins and brings them into a closer relationship with God. The sacrament is also important because it is a Precept of the Church that it is essential to receive the sacrament.

Topic 10.3.4 The meaning and importance of the sacrament of anointing of the sick

The Anointing of the Sick 'is not a sacrament for those only who are at the point of death. Hence, as soon as anyone of the faithful begins to be in danger of death from sickness or old age, the fitting time for him to receive this sacrament has certainly already arrived.'

Catechism of the Catholic Church 1514

The meaning of the sacrament of anointing of the sick

- The sacrament of anointing of the sick is a strengthening sacrament, and is given to those in danger of death from sickness or old age.
- The sacrament is a gift of grace that helps the person deal with their illness; if a person's condition gets worse the sacrament can be repeated.
- The sacrament is used to mark the end of a person's life on Earth and it is used to prepare them for death.
- The sacrament is a way of joining the sick person with the community. The community prays for the sick person and in turn asks the person receiving the sacrament to pray for them.
- The sacrament copies the actions of Jesus when he healed by using both touch and word. In following the actions of Jesus, the sacrament reminds the sick person and the community that the Church today can still heal like Jesus and the disciples in the early Church.

The sick who receive this sacrament, 'by freely uniting themselves to the passion and death of Christ, contribute to the good of the People of God.' By celebrating this sacrament the Church, in the communion of saints, intercedes for the benefit of the sick person, and he, for his part, through the grace of this sacrament, contributes to the sanctification of the Church and to the good of all men for whom the Church suffers and offers herself through Christ to God the Father.

Catechism of the Catholic Church 1522

This photo shows Pope John Paul II towards the end of his life. He was given the sacrament of anointing of the sick several times before he died. Do you think he needed it?

The importance of anointing of the sick

Anointing of the sick is important to Catholics because:

- By using words and touch, the sacrament bestows grace and gives spiritual strength and healing to the person, including restoration to health, and so this is frequently a very supportive sacrament.
- The Catechism of the Catholic Church (1522) points out that the sacrament joins the person with the 'people of Christ'. The sacrament therefore makes all Christians holy, not only the person receiving the sacrament.
- The sacrament is a reassuring one by showing the love of the parish for the sick person. The Catechism (1532) says that through the grace given in the sacrament the person receives 'strengthening peace and courage'.
- The sacrament allows the person's sins to be forgiven, which means that the gift of the Holy Spirit in the sacrament will heal the soul and forgive all sins.
- Catholics believe that in suffering and dying they are joining with Christ in his passion. The final anointing in the sacrament reflects both the anointing they received in baptism and the anointing of Christ before he died. It is a reminder of their life with Jesus.

> *Is any one of you sick? He should call the elders of the church to pray over him and anoint him with oil in the name of the Lord. And the prayer offered in faith will make the sick person well; the Lord will raise him up. If he has sinned, he will be forgiven. Therefore confess your sins to each other and pray for each other so that you may be healed. The prayer of a righteous man is powerful and effective.*
>
> James 5:14–16

◄ *The Healing of the Blind Man* by Duccio di Buoninsegna 1255–1319 The sacrament of anointing of the sick follows the healing actions of Jesus by touching the sick person and praying with them.

Questions

b Do you think the sacrament of anointing of the sick should be given more than once? Give two reasons for your point of view. **4**

c Explain why the sacrament of the anointing of the sick is important for Catholic Christians. **8**

d 'All sick people should be anointed.'
  i Do you agree? Give reasons for your opinion. **3**
  ii Give reasons why some people may disagree with you. **3**

Exam Tip

c 'Explain' means give reasons. To answer this question you should use four of the reasons for why Catholics believe the sacrament of the anointing of the sick is important and make each of them into a short paragraph. For tips on Quality of Written Communication, look at page 107.

SUMMARY

The sacrament of the anointing of the sick gives seriously ill people the strength to face serious illness and death. It is important because it gives spiritual help as the person receives the Holy Spirit and grace from God which forgives their sins and strengthens their faith. The sacrament also joins the recipient with the Christian community and with the suffering of Christ.

Topic 10.3.5 The nature and importance of the Mass

KEY WORDS

Liturgy of the Eucharist – the re-enactment of the Last Supper during which the bread and wine are transubstantiated.

Liturgy of the word – the Bible readings in the second part of the Mass.

Penitential rite – the confession and absolution at the beginning of Mass.

Rite of communion – receiving the body and blood of Jesus.

Transubstantiation – the belief that the bread and wine become the body and blood of Jesus.

The Eucharist is the source and summit of the Christian life. The other sacraments, and indeed all ecclesiastical ministries and works of the apostolate, are bound up with the Eucharist and are oriented toward it.

Catechism of the Catholic Church 1324

The nature of the Mass

- The Mass is a re-enactment of the Last Supper and a celebration of the resurrection of Jesus. It is celebrated every day of the week except Good Friday and Holy Saturday morning.
- The first part of the Mass, the **penitential rite**, makes Catholics aware that they are sinners and need the forgiveness of God on a regular basis. If they have committed a serious sin they are expected to go to confession before receiving Holy Communion.
- The second part of the Mass contains Bible readings and is called the **liturgy of the word**. The readings usually have a common theme, frequently linked to the time of year, such as Advent, Lent, Christmas and **Easter**. The priest or deacon often gives a homily explaining the readings and relating them to Catholic life today. The congregation will then recite the creed and join in prayers of intercession.
- The third part of the Mass, the **liturgy of the Eucharist**, is when the bread and wine are brought to the altar and the priest says the Eucharistic Prayer which re-enacts the Last Supper and changes the bread and wine by **transubstantiation** into the body and blood of Christ. This is then distributed to the people in the **rite of communion**.
- In the fourth and final part of the Mass, Catholics give thanks for what they have received and they are given a blessing to help them in the week ahead.
- Catholics are expected to attend Mass every Sunday and on holy days. It is an obligation and is the first Precept of the Church.

The importance of Mass

The Mass is important to Catholics because:

- During Mass bread and wine are turned into the body and blood of Christ. This process is called transubstantiation. Catholics believe Jesus is really present with them during Mass.

When a person receives the Eucharist for the first time it is a very special occasion.

- The Eucharist is a sacrament. It is a daily or weekly gift of grace that Catholics wish to receive, and by receiving this grace they are strengthened in their faith so that they can grow closer to God.

- The Mass is a celebration of the resurrection. It shows all Catholics that there is eternal life, so Catholics attend Mass to remember this and pray that one day they too will be able to receive eternal life.

- Catholics attend Mass to be in the real presence of Christ and receive the body and blood of Christ. This is important as it joins them with Jesus, and so brings them closer to salvation.

- According to the Gospels Jesus rose from the dead on a Sunday. This became known as the Lord's Day by the early Christians and was celebrated as a day of rest in the same way that the **Sabbath** was by the Jews.

- It is the duty of all Catholics to attend Mass on Sundays and Holy Days. It is at the centre of Catholic life as it is when they meet as a community to worship and learn the teachings of the Church.

- The Mass is a communal activity. During Mass the congregation join together to show their love of God. This is important as by doing this together they strengthen their faith and copy the community of apostles around Jesus at the Last Supper.

- It is important that Catholics attend Mass since it was commanded by Jesus when he said at the Last Supper 'Do this in memory of me'. The Catechism says it is a sin to knowingly miss Sunday Mass and Mass on holy days of obligation.

We must therefore consider the Eucharist as:
- *thanksgiving and praise to the* **Father***;*
- *the sacrificial memorial of* **Christ** *and his Body;*
- *the presence of Christ by the power of his word and of his* **Spirit.**

Catechism of the Catholic Church 1358

Participation at Sunday Mass must be seen by a Catholic not as an imposition or a weight, but as a need and joy. To meet with brothers, to listen to the Word of God and to be nourished of Christ.

Pope Benedict XVI, 2005

◀ Catholics participating in Mass. There are many reasons why Catholics attend Mass, what do you think is the most important reason?

Questions

b Do you think Mass is important? Give two reasons for your point of view. **4**

c Explain why Mass is important for Catholic Christians. **8**

d 'Sunday Mass is the most important celebration a Catholic takes part in.'

   i Do you agree? Give reasons for your opinion. **3**

   ii Give reasons why some people may disagree with you. **3**

Exam Tip

c You should already have thought about this, and you just have to give two reasons for your opinion. For example, if you agree that Mass is important you should use two reasons from this topic.

SUMMARY

The Mass is a re-enactment of the Last Supper and a celebration of the resurrection of Jesus. It is important for Catholics because it is a chance for them to meet as a community in the presence of God, to give thanks to God, to remember the sacrifice of Jesus, to receive the Eucharist and to receive the grace of God to help them grow in faith.

Topic 10.3.6 The meaning of the Eucharist in other Christian traditions

KEY WORD

Commemoration – the belief that the Eucharist is simply a remembrance of the Last Supper.

The word Eucharist means thanksgiving and although there are different meanings of what the Eucharist is, it is celebrated by the majority of Christians. Some regard it as a sacrament and some do not, some say that it is the real presence of Christ while others disagree, and some people say that it should be celebrated regularly while others do not.

The Eucharist in the Eastern Orthodox Church

For the Eastern Orthodox Church the meaning of the Eucharist is that:

- The bread and wine become the body and blood of Jesus. This change is not explained by the Church or called a sacrament but is termed a holy mystery.
- The Eucharist is part of the Divine Liturgy during which heaven comes to Earth in the body and blood of Jesus. This is symbolised by the priest consecrating the elements behind a screen (iconostasis) representing heaven and bringing them out to the people on Earth.
- The Eucharist gives spiritual nourishment to the congregation, filling them with the presence of Christ and with every grace and blessing from God.
- The Eucharist is celebrated following the actions and words of Jesus during the Last Supper and remembering the sacrifice of Christ on the cross.

The Eucharist in most Nonconformist Protestant Churches

Most **Nonconformist** Protestants call the Eucharist, Holy Communion. They only believe in two sacraments – baptism and Holy Communion. Nonconformists believe that:

- Holy Communion is a **commemoration** of the Last Supper, and of God's mercy. The bread and wine do not change, they are symbols of the presence of Christ.

This sacrament is an act of worship in which we share ordinary material things (bread and wine – the latter is always non-alcoholic in a Methodist Church). Through God's grace, the bread, the wine and the gathered people come to embody the transcendent love of God in Christ.

John Wesley encouraged Methodists to share in Holy Communion regularly. It is a feast in which we encounter Christ present with us now. It is one of the most important ways in which we learn, over time, what it means to be a Christian disciple. And we learn through being nourished and fed.

Source: Official website of the Methodist Church of Great Britain www.methodist.org.uk

Methodists receive grape ▶ juice rather than wine. Do you think it is good that different Christian denominations have different beliefs about the Eucharist?

- Holy Communion gives spiritual nourishment, filling Christians with the presence of Christ and with every grace and blessing from God.
- Holy Communion brings unity as the worshippers share the one Body of Christ.
- Holy Communion is a reminder of the Last Supper and the **crucifixion** of Christ.

The Eucharist in the Church of England

There are different attitudes to the Eucharist in the Church of England.

- Those Anglicans (members of the Church of England) who believe in priests and seven sacraments have very similar beliefs to Catholics.
- Those Anglicans who believe in ministers and two sacraments (baptism and Holy Communion) have Nonconformist Protestant beliefs about the Eucharist.

The Eucharist in the Salvation Army and Quakers

The Salvation Army and Quakers have no Eucharist and no sacraments because:

- They believe Jesus is the only priest so there is no need for rituals, especially as these have caused divisions between Christian groups.
- They believe worship should be direct contact with God without symbols like bread and wine.
- They believe they can lead spiritually holy lives without the use of sacraments.

A major difference between The Salvation Army and other religious **denominations** *is that it does not include the use of sacraments (mainly Holy Communion, sometimes called the Lord's Supper, and baptism) in its form of worship.*

The Salvation Army has never said it is wrong to use sacraments, nor does it deny that other Christians receive grace from God through using them. Rather, the Army believes that it is possible to live a holy life and receive the grace of God without the use of physical sacraments and that they should not be regarded as an essential part of becoming a Christian.

Salvationists see the sacraments as an outward sign of an inward experience, and it is the inward experience that is the most important thing.

Source: Official website of the Salvation Army in the UK and Ireland www1.salvationarmy. org.uk/uki/www_uki.nsf

Questions

b Do you think Christians should all believe the same things about the Eucharist? Give two reasons for your point of view. **4**

c Explain the main differences between Catholic and Protestant understandings of the Eucharist. **8**

d 'The Eucharist is not important to Christians.'
  i Do you agree? Give reasons for your opinion. **3**
  ii Give reasons why some people may disagree with you. **3**

Exam Tip

c 'Explain' means give four brief, or two developed, differences in understanding. For example, re-enactment of the Last Supper or as a reminder of it; transubstantiation or symbols. For tips on Quality of Written Communication, look at page 107.

SUMMARY

Christians understand the Eucharist in different ways and refer to it using different names. Eastern Orthodox Christians believe the bread and wine changes to the body and blood of Jesus by a holy mystery; most Protestants believe the bread and wine do not change, but do believe that during the celebration of Holy Communion Jesus becomes spiritually present.

Topic 10.3.7 Why Catholic churches have certain features

A Catholic church is the place of worship where Catholics gather as a community to celebrate their faith. The Catechism (2691) says that it 'is the proper place for the liturgical prayer of the parish community'. Churches are designed to have certain features to assist in spiritual development and worship. These are:

The church faces east

This reminds Catholics of their belief that Jesus rose from the dead bringing new life just as the sun rises from the east. The Mass contains prayers that remind Catholics that by living good holy lives they will share in the resurrection of Christ.

The altar

This is a focus of attention in a Catholic church. It is prominent because the priest offers Mass on the altar as a symbol of Christ offering himself as a sacrifice to God on the cross. The priest takes the place of Jesus who, on the night before his death, shared bread and wine with his followers. The altar is positioned so that the priest can face the congregation as he celebrates the Mass. On or near the altar are candles that shine and give light representing the Christian belief that Jesus is the light of the world.

> *The altar, around which the Church is gathered in the celebration of the Eucharist, represents the two aspects of the same mystery: the altar of the sacrifice and the table of the Lord. This is all the more so since the Christian altar is the symbol of Christ himself, present in the midst of the assembly of his faithful, both as the victim offered for our reconciliation and as food from heaven who is giving himself to us.*
>
> **Catechism of the Catholic Church 1383**

The altar is found at the front of the church and the congregation will sit facing it. The crucifix can clearly be seen hanging behind the altar, reminding the congregation of the suffering Jesus went through.

The crucifix

In Catholic churches, there is always a crucifix, a cross with an image of the crucified Christ on it. This may be on or near the altar. It is a visual reminder of the suffering and death of Jesus. Catholics believe that the death of Jesus was the price he had to pay for their salvation. Catholics, like other Christians, believe that Jesus died for them to forgive their sins and give them eternal life.

The tabernacle

This is where the consecrated hosts are conserved. These hosts have undergone transubstantiation and Catholics believe they are now the body and blood of Christ. In Catholic churches the **tabernacle** has a place of honour usually adjacent to the altar. Catholics believe that Jesus is really present in the blessed sacrament reserved in the tabernacle for distribution to the sick. Catholics show their reverence for Jesus by genuflecting (bending on one knee to kneel or bowing, usually making the sign of the cross at the same time) towards the tabernacle whenever they walk past it. The tabernacle is also a reminder of the Tent of Meeting (tabernacle) in which Moses kept the Ark of the Covenant which contained the tablets of the Ten Commandments. This reminds Catholics that Jesus has become the New Covenant.

◄ This tabernacle is from the high altar at Saint Jean Baptiste Church in France. On it are designs showing the Passion, John the Evangelist and Saint Peter.

The baptismal font

The baptismal font is usually at the entrance (the back) of the church to remind Catholics that baptism is what makes a person a member of the Church. The font contains holy water and it is where Catholics are baptised with the water. This is a reminder of baptism, the first sacrament which forgives sins, to those who have already been baptised.

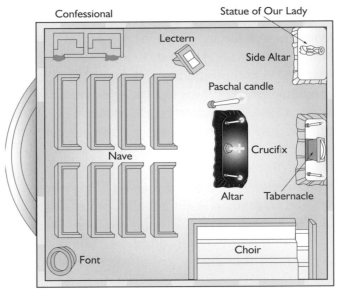

The layout of a traditional Catholic church. How does each of the features of this traditional church help spiritual development or worship?

The confessional

This is a small room in which the sacrament of reconciliation (confession) may take place. The fact there is a room set aside for this shows the importance of the sacrament of reconciliation: by penance and absolution, Catholics are reconciled to God and to each other.

The lectern

This is a book stand where the priest, deacons and ministers of the word (readers) stand to read to the congregation. It is often decorated and shows the Catholic belief that faith and truth come from the Bible (the readings) and the teaching of the Church (the homily).

The stations of the cross

These fourteen pictures from the **Passion of Christ** are a reminder of the importance of the death and suffering of Jesus

The Stations of the Cross ▶ in San Antonio San Fernando Cathedral in Texas, USA.

for the salvation of all people. They are especially used during **Lent** when Catholics focus their worship on the passion of Christ. Some people pray to the stations of the cross each Friday to remember Jesus' death on Good Friday.

Statues

Different churches will have a variety of different statues. They are visual aids to assist worship, and remind the congregation of the various beliefs about Mary and the saints. They are to help the congregation in their prayer. Catholics do not pray to the statues.

Water stoop

When Catholics enter the church they bless themselves with the water from the holy water stoop and make the sign of the cross. This reminds them of the Trinity and the death of Jesus, and of their baptism into the Church. It also puts them into a reverent frame of mind as they enter the church.

Statues are frequently found in Catholic churches. They are to help when praying to God and are not to be worshipped themselves. Why do you think some people think Catholics worship statues?

Questions

b Do you think statues are needed in a Catholic church? Give two reasons for your point of view. **4**

c Explain why the features of a Catholic church are important for Catholic Christians. **8**

d 'The features of a Catholic church are essential for Catholic worship.'
  i Do you agree? Give reasons for your opinion. **3**
  ii Give reasons why some people may disagree with you. **3**

Exam Tip

d Use the answering evaluation questions advice from page 111. The arguments for this are the reasons for three features given in this topic, for example, altar, font, tabernacle. Arguments against are likely to come from class discussion or your own ideas, and could include:
  • Catholics can worship anywhere and in any building so the features found in churches are not required.
  • The features are distracting so a plain building could make worship easier.

SUMMARY

A Catholic church has many different features which show important Catholic beliefs such as transubstantiation, the new life brought by baptism, the importance of the Bible and the teachings of the Church.

Topic 10.3.8 The meaning and importance of Christmas

> *To become children of God, we must be 'born from above' or 'born of God'. Only when Christ is fully formed in us will the mystery of Christmas be fulfilled in us. Christmas is the mystery of this marvellous exchange.*
>
> **Catechism of the Catholic Church 526**

> *All that Jesus did and taught, from the beginning until the day when he was taken up to heaven, is to be seen in the light of the mysteries of Christmas and Easter.*
>
> **Catechism of the Catholic Church 512**

> *At Christmas, the Almighty becomes a child and asks for our help and protection. His way of showing that he is God challenges our way of being human. By knocking at our door, he challenges us and our freedom; he calls us to examine how we understand and live our lives.*
>
> *Urbi et Orbi*
> **Pope Benedict XVI**
> **Christmas 2005**

The meaning of Christmas

Christians celebrate the birth of Jesus Christ on 25 December each year.

- **Christmas** is the celebration of the incarnation when Christians believe God became a human being in Jesus.
- Catholics believe that before the incarnation, it was only possible to have a partial relationship with God because of the effects of sin. However, through the incarnation (which led to the life, death and resurrection of Jesus) the power of sin was cancelled so that it became possible for humans to have a full relationship with God and go to heaven after death.
- Christmas tells Christians that God cared so much about the world that he sent his Son to show humans what God is like and to teach them how to live.
- Christmas is a time each year to start afresh, to remember the salvation offered in the birth of Jesus. It is a time when Catholics are asked to look at their lives and examine whether they are living in a holy way.
- Christmas is a time when the community gather in worship and thanks. Each of the special Masses focuses on the birth of Christ. It is a time of hope and peace, when Catholics pray for the coming of the **Kingdom of God**.

Why do you think many people have a nativity scene in their homes during Christmas?

The importance of Christmas

Christmas is important for Catholics because:

- Without the birth of Jesus Christ, there would be no Christianity. Christmas celebrates the beginnings of the Christian faith.
- Christmas is an opportunity to remember and thank God for the incarnation of Jesus, when God became human.
- Through the incarnation, God began the process of salvation from sin, so making it possible for humans to have a full relationship with him and go to heaven after death.
- Through celebrating the birth of Christ, Catholics recognise that he was born not only to teach and work miracles, but also to suffer and die to save humans from sin.
- It allows Catholics to feel united and celebrate as a worldwide community. The celebrations such as Christmas Mass and the papal blessing *Urbi et Orbi* remind Catholics that they all share a common faith.
- It is a time to celebrate families, reflecting that Jesus was born into a human family. At Christmas, Catholics remember the humility and strength of Mary and Joseph, and in their worship remember to try to be spiritually like them.

*In the **liturgical year** the various aspects of the one Paschal mystery unfold. This is also the case with the cycle of feasts surrounding the mystery of the incarnation (Annunciation, Christmas, Epiphany). They commemorate the beginning of our salvation and communicate to us the first fruits of the Paschal mystery.*
Catechism of the Catholic Church 1171

◀ The candles are lit each Sunday during **Advent** to show that the 'light of the world' (Jesus) is coming.

Questions

b Do you think Christmas is an important celebration? Give two reasons for your point of view. **4**

c Explain why Christmas is important for Catholic Christians. **8**

d 'Christmas is the most important celebration a Catholic takes part in.'
  i Do you agree? Give reasons for your opinion. **3**
  ii Give reasons why some people may disagree with you. **3**

Exam Tip

b You should already have thought about this, and you just have to give two reasons for your opinion. For example, if you agree that Christmas is important you should use two of the reasons given in this topic.

SUMMARY

Christmas is important for Christians because without the birth of Jesus there would be no Christianity and no salvation from sin. Christmas is an opportunity to remember God's gift to humanity and to worship God accordingly.

Topic 10.3.9 The meaning and importance of Lent

The meaning of Lent

Lent is the time that Christians spend in preparation for the celebration of Easter. Lent lasts forty days (without Sundays). It begins on Ash Wednesday and ends on Holy Thursday.

- It is the time of year when all Catholics remember the time that Jesus spent in the desert preparing for his active ministry.
- On Ash Wednesday, Catholics go to church for a special Penitential Mass. As a sign of their penitence they have a cross of ashes smeared on their forehead by the priest. These ashes are from palms used in the previous year's Palm Sunday celebration. The cross of ashes reminds them of the Lenten practices of prayer, fasting and **almsgiving**. Catholics fast and give money to charity to remind them not to be so dependent on material possessions.
- The importance of penitence in Lent is shown by the fact that if Catholics do not take part in the sacrament of reconciliation at any other time of the year, they will do so during Lent.
- There is often a CAFOD (Catholic Fund for Overseas Development) Family Fast Day. On Family Fast Day Catholics try not to eat so much and the money they save by not eating is donated to CAFOD.
- Catholics try to give up something to make them into better people and show devotion to God. They will often give the money they save to charity.
- Catholics try to pray more and strengthen their faith by acts of mercy such as visiting the sick and housebound.

Lent is a special time for giving up things. Is it right to do this?

- Special Lenten services may be held such as Lenten prayer groups, where groups of Christians (often from different denominations) meet to pray together and/or study Bible passages. The stations of the cross are also used to help people reflect on the different episodes of the passion of Christ.
- There are often special meetings or study groups (often with other Christian Churches) to think about Easter and what it means to be a Christian today.

The importance of Lent

Lent is important for Catholics because:

- It is a time when Catholics concentrate on improving their Christian lives.
- It is a time when Catholics receive the sacrament of reconciliation and hope that by becoming better Christians they will receive salvation.
- It is a time when Catholics reflect upon the teachings of Jesus and what they mean for Christians living today.
- The readings during Mass are based upon the later part of Jesus' life. They also look at the temptations and difficulties that listeners may face. These help Catholics work out what they need to do in their lives in order to achieve salvation.
- It is a time for thinking more about what it means to be a Christian today. Catholics celebrate in their community and try to increase in faith through attending the liturgies, prayer groups and celebrating additional charitable actions.

> *The seasons and days of penance in the course of the liturgical year (Lent, and each Friday in memory of the death of the Lord) are intense moments of the Church's penitential practice. These times are particularly appropriate for spiritual exercises, penitential liturgies, pilgrimages as signs of penance, voluntary self-denial such as fasting and almsgiving, and fraternal sharing (charitable and missionary works).*
>
> **Catechism of the Catholic Church 1438**

Questions

b Do you think Lent is the most important time of year for Catholics? Give two reasons for your point of view. **4**

c Explain why Lent is important for Catholic Christians. **8**

d 'Lent is not important for Catholics.'

   i Do you agree? Give reasons for your opinion. **3**

   ii Give reasons why some people may disagree with you. **3**

Exam Tip

d Use the answering evaluation questions advice from page 111. The arguments for this should come from your class discussion and may include such ideas as:

- Attending Mass is important but Lent does not really make much difference to a Catholic's life.
- Lent reminds Catholics of the Passion of Christ which Catholics can be reminded of in many different ways, such as saying the rosary.

Arguments against should come from the reasons for the importance of Lent in this topic.

SUMMARY

Lent is forty days of preparation for Easter beginning with Ash Wednesday. It reflects the time Jesus spent in the desert preparing spiritually for his ministry. Lent is important because during Lent, Catholics try to change their lives so that they can enter the kingdom of heaven. They give up things, pray more often and meet with other Christians to think about what Jesus did and what it means to be a Christian today.

Topic 10.3.10 The meaning and importance of Holy Week

KEY WORD

Holy Week – the week before Easter Sunday.

Jesus' entry into Jerusalem manifested the coming of the kingdom that the King-Messiah was going to accomplish by the Passover of his Death and Resurrection. It is with the celebration of that entry on Palm Sunday that the Church's liturgy solemnly opens Holy Week.

Catechism of the Catholic Church 560

The Easter Triduum, the three days that begin on Holy Thursday with the Mass of the Lord's Supper, celebrates the Paschal event and the newness of life which flows from the crucified, buried and risen Christ.

The Sunday Missal

The meaning of Holy Week

- **Holy Week** is the week in the Catholic liturgical calendar before Easter Sunday. It begins on Palm Sunday, includes Maundy Thursday and Good Friday and ends on Holy Saturday.

- During Holy Week Catholics remember the last week of the life of Jesus. It gives them an opportunity to recall what Jesus did and taught from his entrance into Jerusalem on Palm Sunday to his death on Good Friday, such as The Last Supper when Jesus washed his apostles' feet.

- During Holy Week there are special liturgies which, unlike Sunday and Holy Days, are not an obligation for Catholics but are frequently attended. Special liturgies such as the Stations of the Cross are intended to build up to the great event of the Resurrection on Easter Sunday. During the **Easter Triduum** the congregation will re-enact the Last Supper (on Maundy Thursday) and the arrest, trial and crucifixion of Jesus (Good Friday).

- Holy Week is a time of reflection and prayer. Catholics remember that Jesus suffered and was tortured until he died. Catholics worship him especially during Holy Week because they are taught that he did these things so that they could be saved from sin and enter the kingdom of heaven.

Foot washing on Maundy Thursday. Why do Catholics re-enact this? What does it remind them they have to do?

The importance of Holy Week

Holy Week is important for Catholics because:

- Catholics renew and deepen their faith in Jesus through remembering the events of Holy Week. They are reminded that they need to serve one another and put themselves last as well as be public witnesses to their faith.
- They remember how Jesus faced adulation (on Palm Sunday), then rejection and crucifixion. This should inspire Catholics to think about their role in the world, especially when they are asked to stand up for others in the cause of **justice** and peace.
- Holy Week reminds Catholics of the suffering Jesus experienced which will give them strength with the suffering they may face.
- It reminds them of the salvation brought by Jesus. The death of Christ on the cross forgave the sins of the world and enabled people to have a full relationship with God. It was the death of Jesus that overcame sin, and during Holy Week Catholics try to do things to make up for their sinfulness (reparation).

> *At the sixth hour darkness came over the whole land until the ninth hour. And at the ninth hour Jesus cried out in a loud voice, 'Eloi, Eloi, lama sabachthani?', which means, 'My God, my God, why have you forsaken me?'*
>
> **Mark 15:33–34**

The crucifixion is described as ▶ happening on Good Friday. What is good about 'Good Friday'?

Questions

b Do you think it is important for Catholics to take part in Holy Week celebrations? Give two reasons for your point of view. **4**

c Explain why Holy Week is important for Catholic Christians. **8**

d 'Holy Week is not important.'
  i Do you agree? Give reasons for your opinion. **3**
  ii Give reasons why some people may disagree with you. **3**

Exam Tip

c 'Explain' means give four brief, or two developed, reasons for the importance of Holy Week given in this topic and perhaps use some of the evidence supplied in the margin. For tips on Quality of Written Communication, look at page 107.

SUMMARY

Holy Week is last week of Lent. It is a week when Catholics re-enact and remember the last week of Jesus' life. It is important because Catholics use this week to try to make up for their sins and try to make themselves spiritually pure.

Topic 10.3.11 The meaning and importance of Easter

> *He is not here; he has risen! Remember how he told you, while he was still with you in Galilee: 'The Son of Man must be delivered into the hands of sinful men, be crucified and on the third day be raised again'.*
>
> **Luke 24:6–8**

> *For all the baptised, children or adults, faith must grow after baptism. For this reason the Church celebrates each year at the Easter Vigil the renewal of baptismal promises.*
>
> **Catechism of the Catholic Church 1254**

> *Jesus answered them, 'Destroy this temple, and I will raise it again in three days.' The Jews replied, 'It has taken forty-six years to build this temple, and you are going to raise it in three days?' But the temple he had spoken of was his body. After he was raised from the dead, his disciples recalled what he had said. Then they believed the Scripture and the words that Jesus had spoken.*
>
> **John 2:19–22**

The meaning of Easter

- Easter is the most important celebration in the Christian calendar. It celebrates the resurrection of Christ which Christians believe proves the identity of Jesus. If Jesus rose from the dead, he must have been both human and divine, thus showing the two natures of Jesus as taught in the creeds and the Catechism.
- The resurrection is the final part of the **Paschal mystery**. Through his life, miracles, teachings and death, Jesus was trying to bring people back to God. The resurrection is the final part of this because through the resurrection, forgiveness of sins is assured and people can be restored to God.
- The resurrection proves that death has been overcome and assures Christians that this life is not all there is. Easter celebrates the fact of eternal life for those who follow Jesus.
- The resurrection also gives Catholics the assurance that Jesus is not dead, he is alive to help and guide his Church and to be with individual Christians.
- The basis of all Christian faith is that Jesus was able to overcome death and rise to life. Easter is an opportunity for Catholics to reflect upon the mysteries of their faith and deepen their personal belief.

The importance of Easter

Easter is important for Catholics because:

- It celebrates the resurrection of Jesus which is the ultimate proof that Jesus is really God, since no one but God could rise from the dead.
- It proves that there is eternal life. Since Jesus rose from the dead, his faithful followers are assured that they too will have life after death with God in his kingdom.

The service of light outside a church, marking the beginning of Easter and the end of Lent.

◄ The Paschal candle is used throughout the year during baptisms and it is a reminder that Christ, the light of the world, is risen.

- It celebrates Jesus' victory over death and evil, which is why new Catholics are often baptised on Easter Sunday and why baptismal vows are renewed.
- The **renewal of baptismal vows** at Easter is important because it makes Catholics re-commit themselves to the Christian life.
- Easter proves that the predictions Jesus made about his death and resurrection (for example, John 2:19–22) were true, and therefore Christians can believe the other things he said.
- It proves that Jesus is still alive and working in his Church. This means that Catholics can call upon God in prayer and know that Jesus and the Holy Spirit will be with them.

Questions

b Do you think Easter is the most important celebration in the Christian year? Give two reasons for your point of view. **4**

c Explain why Easter is important for Catholic Christians. **8**

d 'Easter should only be celebrated by Christians.'
  i Do you agree? Give reasons for your opinion. **3**
  ii Give reasons why some people may disagree with you. **3**

Exam Tip

b You should already have thought about this, and you just have to give two reasons for your opinion. For example, if you agree that Easter is the most important celebration in the Christian year you could use two reasons for its importance given in this topic.

SUMMARY

Easter Day celebrates the resurrection of Jesus; Jesus rising from the dead on the Sunday after Good Friday. Catholics celebrate with the Easter Vigil when they renew their baptismal vows. It is important because it proves Jesus is the Son of God and gives Christians the hope of eternal life.

How to answer exam questions

Question A **What is a creed?**   2 marks

An official statement of religious belief.

Question B **Do you think Christmas is important for Catholic Christians?**
Give two reasons for your point of view.   4 marks

Yes I do think Christmas is important as it is a time when Catholics remember that Jesus was incarnated, meaning God became man.

I also believe Christmas is important for Catholics because it is a celebration that unites all Christians around the world and in the belief that Jesus was born to save them from sin.

Question C **Explain why the sacrament of baptism is important for Catholic Christians.**   8 marks

Baptism is important for Catholics as it is the way a person enters the Church. After baptism the person is allowed entry to the other sacraments and through receiving the sacraments a person can receive grace to live a holy and Christian life.

Baptism gives a person the gift of grace which helps the person grow in faith. Baptism is said to give the person new life in the Holy Spirit.

Baptism is important because it washes away original sin and any other sins a person may have committed, and makes the person pure.

Baptism is seen as essential for the person to receive salvation and enter the kingdom of heaven. The Catechism of the Catholic Church says that baptism is necessary for salvation.

Question D **'Confirmation is not important to Christians.'**

 i Do you agree? Give reasons for your opinion.   3 marks
 ii Give reasons why some people may disagree with you.   3 marks

i *I disagree. Confirmation is important as according to Canon (Church) law it makes the person a full member of the Church. Confirmation is also important as it marks the person as someone chosen by God and gives the gift of the Holy Spirit. Finally, by retaking the baptismal vows for themselves Catholics become witnesses to their faith.*
ii *Others might disagree with me and think that confirmation is not important because they think that baptism is the only sacrament that is important because this makes you a member of the Church. The sacrament of baptism puts a spiritual mark on your soul that identifies you as one of God's children. Finally they might say that Christians might think that you increase your faith and become a full member of the Church by how you live your life, not by taking a sacrament.*

QUESTION A
A high mark answer because it is a correct definition of the key word.

QUESTION B
A high mark answer because an opinion is backed up by two developed reasons.

QUESTION C
A high mark answer because four reasons why the sacrament of baptism is important are developed. A formal style of English is used and there is good use of specialist vocabulary such as sacraments, grace, Holy Spirit, original sin, salvation.

QUESTION D
A high mark answer because it states the candidate's own opinion and backs it up with three clear reasons for thinking that confirmation is important. It then gives three reasons for people disagreeing and believing that confirmation is unimportant.

Section 10.4 Living the Christian life

Introduction

This section of the specification requires you to look the meaning and importance of living a Christian life.

Vocation
You will need to understand the effects of, and give reasons for your own opinion about:
- the meaning of vocation and why it is important for Christians
- how and why Christians show vocation in daily life and work
- how and why some Christians show vocation by taking holy orders
- how and why some Christians are involved in working for social and community cohesion.

Teachings on living a Christian life
You will need to understand the effects of, and give reasons for your own opinion about how and why Christians use:
- the Ten Commandments (respect for God and respect for others) as a guide for living
- the teachings of the Sermon on the Mount on the re-interpretation of the Law of Moses (Matthew 5:21–42) as a guide for living
- the teachings of the Sermon on the Mount on displaying religion (Matthew 6:1–18) as a guide for living
- the teachings of the Sermon on the Mount on Christians and money (Matthew 6:19–34) as a guide for living
- the teachings of the Sermon on the Mount on Judgement and the Golden Rule (Matthew 7:1–12) as a guide for living.

One Catholic organisation
You will need to understand the effects of, and give reasons for your own opinion about:
- how one Catholic organisation helps to relieve poverty and/or suffering in the United Kingdom
- the reasons why the organisation does this work.

Topic 10.4.1 The meaning of vocation and why it is important for Christians

The meaning of vocation

The word **vocation** means calling. It can be described as an inner feeling of what you have to do or a way that you have to live. Christians believe they have a calling from God to be followers of Jesus, to be his disciples, to be members of the Church and to live their lives on Earth in the Christian way so that when they die, they enter heaven.

Vocation used to mean whether a person was called to live a religious life by entering the priesthood or a **religious community**. This is still one type of vocation, and some Catholics would say it is the most important one as it is a full dedication to giving one's life to God.

However, since Vatican II (the second Ecumenical Council of the Vatican) vocation has been extended to include the way that a person can show their faith through the way they live, and so Christian vocation can be shown in marriage, single and family life, or in daily life and work. In daily life Christians can show their vocation by being loving, fair and honest.

Christians often refer to their vocation as a call to discipleship. This means that all Christians are called for a special purpose in the same way that the apostles were. All Christians still have to learn about Jesus in the same way that the first disciples learnt from Jesus.

When the Counsellor comes, whom I will send to you from the Father, the Spirit of truth who goes out from the Father, he will testify about me. And you also must testify, for you have been with me from the beginning.

John 15:26–27

Jesus sends his disciples out ▶ to spread his teachings to the world. Christians today still believe they must continue to tell others about their faith.

Vocation also means that all Christians must do what God calls them to do in the same way that Jesus did his Father's will. Therefore all Christians must show their vocation by showing their faith through their lives. When Christians describe their vocation as a call to witness they mean that it is to show others the love of God, their faith in Jesus and the power of the Holy Spirit in their lives.

Why vocation is important for Christians

- It means that Christians are called to live a life of discipleship, and that all Christians are called and chosen for a special purpose or role just as the Apostles were.
- It means that all Christians must do what God calls them to do in the same way that Jesus did his Father's will so that they can achieve salvation. Christians believe that vocation is given by God and by doing it you are doing God's will.
- Vocation means that all Christians must be a witness to Christ in their lives; they show their faith to others through the lives they lead. In John's Gospel, Jesus says 'you must testify'. By following a vocation Christians are not only doing what God wants them to do, they are bringing more people to God by their example.
- Vocation is important because it links present-day Christians with the Early Church. The vocations to discipleship and witness were the same in the time of Jesus as they are today. The struggles faced by the apostles and the teachings Jesus gave to them can be used to assist Christians today when they struggle with their vocation.
- Christians believe that a person's vocation is a chance to serve God and to listen to what God wants for them as Samuel did in the Old Testament (1 Samuel 3). By serving God through following a vocation a Christian will lead a holy life and work towards salvation.

> *He called his twelve disciples to him and gave them authority to drive out evil spirits and to heal every disease and sickness.*
> **Matthew 10:1**

> *Pope John Paul II in his teaching Christifideles Laici (1988) explained that everyone's vocation is important:*
> *'All are called to work for the coming of the Kingdom of God according to the diversity of callings and situations, charisms and ministries. This variety is not only linked to age, but also to the difference of sex and to the diversity of natural gifts, as well as to careers and conditions affecting a person's life. It is a variety that makes the riches of the Church more vital and concrete.'*

Questions

b Do you think that all Christians should teach others about Christ? Give two reasons for your point of view. **4**

c Explain why Christians believe vocation is important. **8**

d 'The call to holy orders is the only real vocation.'
  i Do you agree? Give reasons for your opinion. **3**
  ii Give reasons why some people may disagree with you. **3**

Exam Tip

c 'Explain' means give reasons. To answer this question you should use four reasons why Christians think vocation is important found in this topic and make each of them into a short paragraph. For tips on Quality of Written Communication, look at page 107.

SUMMARY

A Christian's vocation is a call to discipleship and to be a witness to his or her faith. Vocation is important because Christians believe that it leads them into a life where they serve God, serve others and live in the way that God wants. This will eventually lead to a life in God's Kingdom.

Topic 10.4.2 How and why Christians show vocation in daily life and work

> *The vocation to marriage is written in the very nature of man and woman as they came from the hand of the Creator. Marriage is not a purely human institution despite the many variations it may have undergone through the centuries in different cultures, social structures, and spiritual attitudes.*
>
> **Catechism of the Catholic Church 1603**

How Christians show vocation in daily life and work

By the way that Christians treat each other on a daily basis they are acting as witnesses to the teaching of Jesus, especially through their marriage and family life and work. This can be shown in the following ways:

- By their choice of career, Christians can show their vocation. They may act as a witness to the faith by choosing a caring profession such as a doctor, nurse, carer, teacher, counsellor, or a person working for equal opportunities.
- Christians can also show discipleship in their career choice by choosing a career that involves sharing the message of Jesus, for example teacher, **catechist**, charity worker or missionary worker.
- Marriage is a vocation because the couple choose to have God's blessing on their relationship and are acting as witnesses to God by doing his will. They also bring up children in a Christian family which means parents are acting as disciples through teaching the faith.
- The family is a unit which is a witness to the faith because within the family each person shows love and care for the others in the way that the Church asks them to do.
- Simply by the way that Christians treat each other they are acting as witnesses to the teaching of Jesus. For example, in daily life Christians can become involved in discussion about topics relevant to society, and by putting across the Christian view they are acting as disciples.

> *Parents have the mission of teaching their children to pray and to discover their vocation as children of God.*
>
> **Catechism of the Catholic Church 2226**

There are many different ways to fulfil a vocation. Is any one vocation more important than the others?

- In their work Christians can show discipleship by being honest, giving a fair day's work to their employer, being fair to employees, and standing up for justice if they think a fellow employee is being unfairly treated.

Why Christians show vocation in daily life and work

Christians need to show their vocation in their daily life because:
- They believe that vocation is about the whole of life and that they therefore need to show that they are serving God in all that they do.
- They believe that when Jesus asked the disciples to go and 'baptise all nations', he meant that they should show their Christian faith in all their actions and in what they say to others.
- Christian vocation is the call to love God and love one's neighbour in the whole of life as Jesus commanded his disciples in the greatest commandment. So Christians must show their vocation in daily life and work.
- Christian vocation cannot be restricted to church or Sundays. The call to be a Christian must involve everything a Christian does. Jesus did not say you should only love God on the Sabbath Day

At the root of every vocational journey there is the Emmanuel, the God-with-us. He shows us that we are not alone in fashioning our lives, because God walks with us, in the midst of our ups-and-downs, and, if we want him to, he weaves with each of us a marvellous tale of love, unique and irreproducible, and, at the same time, in harmony with all humanity and the entire cosmos.

Message of the Holy Father for the 28th World Day of Prayer for Vocations Pope John Paul II, 2001

Christian revelation recognises two specific ways of realising the vocation of the human person, in its entirety, to love: marriage and virginity or celibacy. Either one is in its proper form an actuation of the most profound truth of man, of his being 'created in the image of God.'

Familiaris Consortio **Pope John Paul II, 1981**

Questions

b Do you think Catholic Christians need to show their vocation in their daily life? Give two reasons for your point of view. **4**

c Explain how Christians show vocation in their daily life. **8**

d 'Most Catholics forget about their vocation when they are not at church.'
  i Do you agree? Give reasons for your opinion. **3**
  ii Give reasons why some people may disagree with you. **3**

Exam Tip

b You should already have thought about this, and you just have to give two reasons for your opinion. For example, if you agree that Catholic Christians need to follow a vocation in their daily life, you should use two reasons from this topic.

SUMMARY

Christians show vocation in their daily life and work in many different ways. It can be by the job they choose such as a doctor, or carer. Or it can be the way they treat people and live their life.

It is important for Christians to show their vocation in their daily life because vocation means serving God in everything you do.

Topic 10.4.3 How and why some Christians show vocation by taking holy orders

Two other sacraments, holy orders and Matrimony, are directed towards the salvation of others; if they contribute as well to personal salvation, it is through service to others that they do so. They confer a particular mission in the Church and serve to build up the People of God.

Catechism of the Catholic Church 1534

But 'the members do not all have the same function.' Certain members are called by God, in and through the Church, to a special service of the community. These servants are chosen and consecrated by the sacrament of holy orders, by which the Holy Spirit enables them to act in the person of Christ the head, for the service of all the members of the Church. The ordained minister is, as it were, an 'icon' of Christ the priest.

Catechism of the Catholic Church 1142

How some Christians show vocation by taking holy orders

Some Christian men follow their vocation by taking **holy orders**. In doing this they are copying the work of the apostles when they gave up everything to follow Jesus. When they take holy orders they show discipleship, and they promise to serve. They do this to copy the way that Jesus served people. By taking holy orders men show witness to other people that is visible to the entire world:

- by the roles that they undertake and showing God's love and compassion to those who suffer
- because they try to build the Kingdom of God on Earth by evangelising and running parish communities.

Why some Christians show vocation by taking holy orders

Men take holy orders because:

- It is their vocation. They have a special calling from God to devote the whole of their life to his service through the **ordained ministry**.
- It is a calling that most priests could not ignore. When priests talk about why they have taken holy orders, they often say that they tried to ignore God's call, but it was so persistent that in the end they had to accept it.
- As the Catechism of the Catholic Church states, it is the way

Most priests take the **evangelical counsels**. Why do they do this?

in which they can 'share in the mission that Christ entrusted the apostles' (1565).

- They want to serve the Church by carrying out the vital work of celebrating the sacraments that give spiritual food and strength to the people.
- Some men also feel called to serve the needs of the people in their own parish.

> ... those of the faithful 'who have received holy orders, are appointed to nourish the Church with the word and grace of God in the name of Christ.'
> **Catechism of the Catholic Church 1119**

> The priesthood is not conferred for the honour or advantage of the recipient, but for the service of God and the Church; it is the object of a specific and totally gratuitous vocation: 'You did not choose me, no, I chose you; and I commissioned you ... ' (John 15:16)
> Inter Insigniores
> **Sacred Congregation for the Doctrine of the Faith 1976**

This man is being ordained. When a man takes holy orders he continues the work of the apostles.

Questions

b Do you think some Catholics need to take holy orders? Give two reasons for your point of view. **4**

c Explain why some men show their vocation by taking holy orders. **8**

d 'Holy orders are the most important vocation.'
  i Do you agree? Give reasons for your opinion. **3**
  ii Give reasons why some people may disagree with you. **3**

Exam Tip

d Use the answering evaluation questions advice from page 111. The arguments for could be from the reasons in this topic and the important role of priests in Topic 10.2.9. Arguments against could be from the general nature of vocation in Topic 10.4.1 and vocation in daily life in Topic 10.4.2.

SUMMARY

Some men receive a special vocation from God to take the sacrament of holy orders and devote their life to God as a deacon, priest or bishop.

Holy orders means that a man has a vocation of discipleship and witness and he does this by serving the Church as an ordained minister.

Topic 10.4.4 How and why some Christians are involved in working for social and community cohesion

> School communities aim to foster appropriate attitudes: for example, respect for the truth, respect for the views of others; awareness of the spiritual, of moral responsibility, of the demands of religious commitment in everyday life and especially of the challenge of living in a multicultural, multifaith society. In order to build and sustain a cohesive society it is vital that children and young people listen to and learn from others, both within the Catholic and wider community.
>
> *Catholic Schools and Community Cohesion: CES Guidance,* **14th February 2008**

> The Catholic Church now sees itself as working alongside and often in alliance with other bodies, secular and religious, state and voluntary, on behalf of the common good.
>
> **The Common Good and the Catholic Church's Social Teaching,** Catholic Bishops' Conference of England and Wales, 1996.

> For the more closely the world comes together, the more widely do people's obligations transcend particular groups and extend to the whole world.
>
> **The Church in the Modern World, (30).**

How some Christians are involved in working for social and community cohesion

1. Many Christians work as individuals to ensure that communities work together towards a common vision and shared sense of belonging for all groups in society. To achieve this they:
   - have friendships with people of different faiths and ethnic groups
   - work with groups dedicated to community cohesion
   - support any community cohesion policies in their workplace, school, or local area
   - oppose any racist or religiously discriminatory people they meet or hear.

2. The Catholic Education Service (CES) has encouraged Catholic schools to be at the forefront of working towards social and community cohesion by:
   - ensuring that Catholic schools teach their students about non-Christian faiths practised in the UK so that Catholics are more tolerant and understanding
   - signing up to the National Framework in RE which has a large community cohesion aim and content
   - ensuring that Catholic schools are open to all ethnic groups
   - ensuring that racism is not tolerated in Catholic schools.

3. Churches Together in Britain and Ireland represents all the Christian Churches from Catholic to Black Pentecostal and promotes community cohesion by:
   - working with member Churches to share resources and learn from each other's experiences

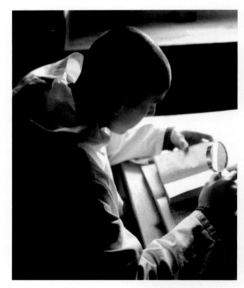

Birinus, St. Joseph's Community Project. Supporting Families in Nechells, Birmingham, www.birinus.org.uk

- working with member Churches to make joint responses to social and community issues both locally and nationally
- bringing different ethnic groups together to promote mutual understanding and friendship
- working for racial justice through the Churches' Racial Justice Network.

4. Some Christians form their own groups to promote social and community cohesion. For example, Birinus is a Roman Catholic organisation that works on a local level in the Archdiocese of Birmingham. It helps to promote community cohesion by encouraging parishes to:

- engage with local activities, regeneration, business, other faiths and minority groups and public services to improve the quality of life in communities.
- assist parishes' work with others to meet local priorities such as health and social care, housing, education and training, youth and community and social cohesion
- develop projects through training and capacity building where premises, volunteers and workers can serve the common good in partnership with others.

Why some Christians are involved in working for social and community cohesion

There are many reasons why Christians and particularly Roman Catholics work towards social cohesion:

- In the Parable of the Good Samaritan (Luke 10:25-37), Jesus taught that Christians should love their neighbours and that neighbour means people of all races.
- St Peter was given a vision by God (Acts 10) in which Peter believed that God was showing him that God treats all races the same and accepts the worship of anyone who does right whatever their race.
- St Paul taught that as God created all nations from one man, Adam, all ethnic groups are therefore equal to each other.
- There are Christians of every race and colour of skin, and the Church is dedicated to fighting racism in all its forms.
- All the Christian Churches have issued statements encouraging Christians to work for social and community cohesion (for example 'The Common Good') and Christians should follow the advice of their Church.
- The Catechism teaches that it is the duty of Catholics to promote unity within society and give all people equal rights and respect.
- In order for there to be harmony, and a world that is peaceful, that they must work for social and community cohesion.

SUMMARY

Individual Christians work for cohesion by making friends with people of different ethnic groups and religions. The Catholic Education Service does it by encouraging study of non-Christian religions and banning racism in schools. Churches Together encourages different ethnic groups to work together and organises joint Christian responses to social and community issues. Some Christian groups like Birinus support local projects.

Christians do this work to follow the teachings of the Bible and Jesus and because it is the teaching of the Church.

Topic 10.4.5 How and why Christians use the Ten Commandments as a guide for living

The Jewish Torah (Genesis, Exodus, Leviticus, Numbers and Deuteronomy) contains many commandments that Jews believe were given to **Moses** by God. Christians believe that only the Ten Commandments (Exodus 20:1–17, Deuteronomy 5:6–21) need to be followed by Christians. Catholics follow the numbering of Deuteronomy 5, whereas Protestants follow the slightly different numbering of Exodus 20.

How Christians use the Ten Commandments as a guide for living

- Christians worship one God only in the way set down by the Church. By their prayers and worship Christians show that they are following the first three commandments.
- Many Christians use the commandment not to take God's name in vain to avoid swearing, and in particular not to swear using God's name.
- Catholics use the commandment to honour the Sabbath day as a reason for attending Mass every Sunday. Since the beginning of the Church, Christians have taken this commandment to refer to Sunday (the Lord's Day when Jesus rose).
- The commandment to honour parents is used to help Christians in their family life and in the upbringing of children as good Christians.
- Christians use the last six commandments to help them make moral decisions as they give Christians very clear moral guidance: do not steal, do not kill, do not commit **adultery**, do not lie and do not desire other people's things.

> *The Ten Commandments state what is required in the love of God and love of neighbour. The first three concern love of God and the other seven love of neighbour.*
>
> **Catechism of the Catholic Church 2067**

> *The Council of Trent teaches that the Ten Commandments are obligatory for Christians and that the justified man is still bound to keep them; the Second Vatican Council confirms: ... that all men may attain salvation through faith, Baptism and the observance of the Commandments.*
>
> **Catechism of the Catholic Church 2068**

> *The Sabbath is at the heart of Israel's law. To keep the commandments is to correspond to the wisdom and the will of God as expressed in his work of creation.*
>
> **Catechism of the Catholic Church 348**

I am the LORD your God: you shall not have strange Gods before me

You shall not take the name of the LORD your God in vain

Remember to keep holy the Lord's Day

Honour your father and your mother

You shall not kill

You shall not commit adultery

You shall not steal

You shall not bear false witness against your neighbour

You shall not covet your neighbour's wife

You shall not covet your neighbour's goods

Which of the Ten Commandments do you think are important to follow?

Why Christians use the Ten Commandments as a guide for living

Christians use the Ten Commandments as a guide for living because:

- They are used by Christians because they are a precise list of rules that have come from God for good Christian behaviour.
- If Catholics (or any Christians) follow the first three commandments, they will be worshipping and respecting the one God of the Apostles' Creed.
- Following the Ten Commandments means Christians will also be giving God special worship and respect one day a week. According to the Catholic Catechism Catholics must attend Mass on Sundays.
- If Christians follow the next seven commandments, they will have a good relationship with their neighbours. By not killing and not stealing, they will be rejecting violence.
- Following the Ten Commandments means Christians will respect their parents, and will not commit adultery or desire other people's partners. Through this they will promote marriage and family life.
- Following the Ten Commandments means Christians will not lie or cheat people. By doing this they will be promoting the truth.
- Following the Ten Commandments means Christians should not covet or desire other people's possessions, and they should act against all forms of greed and materialism.
- Historically, the commandments are the basis for many of the United Kingdom's laws such as those about ownership and murder, although clearly some laws have changed due to the pressures of society, for example, laws on **abortion**.

> *The Ten Commandments are not an arbitrary imposition of a tyrannical Lord. They were written in stone; but before that, they were written on the human heart as the universal moral law, valid in every time and place. Today as always, the Ten Words of the Law provide the only true basis for the lives of individuals, societies and nations.*
>
> **Celebration of the Word at Mount Sinai**
> **Pope John Paul II, 2000**

Catholics must attend Mass on Sunday but there are many other things young people would rather do. Which do you think is more important, attending Mass or enjoying leisure time?

Questions

b Do you think the Ten Commandments are important? Give two reasons for your point of view. **4**

c Explain why Christians use the Ten Commandments as a guide for living. **8**

d 'The Ten Commandments are not needed by today's Christians.'
  i Do you agree? Give reasons for your opinion. **3**
  ii Give reasons why some people may disagree with you. **3**

Exam Tip

b You should already have thought about this, and you just have to give two reasons for your opinion. For example, if you agree that the Ten Commandments are important you should use two reasons, such as those given in this topic.

SUMMARY

Christians use the Ten Commandments to help them worship one God, avoid swearing, honour parents and live a good Christian life.

They use the commandments as a guide for living because they are precise rules about how to respect God, how to behave and how to regard possessions.

Topic 10.4.6 How and why Christians use the teachings of the Sermon on the Mount on the re-interpretation of the Law of Moses as a guide for living

Rejoice and be glad, because great is your reward in heaven, for in the same way they persecuted the prophets who were before you.

Matthew 5:12

Jesus did not abolish the Law but fulfilled it by giving its ultimate interpretation in a divine way: You have heard that it was said to the men of old … But I say to you … With this same divine authority, he disavowed certain human traditions of the Pharisees that were 'making void the word of God'.

Catechism of the Catholic Church 581

The main teachings of Jesus on how to live the Christian life are contained in **the Sermon on the Mount** in Matthew's Gospel. Jesus teaches his followers about the **Law of Moses** (Jewish teaching) and the commandments and how they should interpret them. Jesus taught that the Law of Moses was from God, but the teachers of the Law had interpreted it wrongly. Jesus' reinterpretation is a fulfilment of the Law of Moses which shows how Christians should live.

How Christians use the teachings as a guide for living

- If Christians find themselves thinking violent thoughts about others, they may refer to Jesus' teaching that to be angry with someone is the same response that can lead to murder, therefore, you must seek forgiveness and reconciliation.
- Married Christians may be guided by Jesus' teaching that lustful thoughts are as bad as committing adultery and must be avoided.
- Jesus' teaching that, although the Law of Moses allows divorce, if you re-marry after divorce you are committing adultery, is the basis of the Church's teaching on divorce and re-marriage.
- Some Christians take Jesus' teaching that the name of the Lord must not be used to make oaths (promises) to mean that Christians must not take the oath in court. But most Christians take it to mean that Christians should not use any form of swearing.
- Many Christians use Jesus' teachings about revenge to mean they should be pacifists. Jesus said Christians should react in a non-violent way and even pray for your attacker.

Why Christians use the teachings as a guide for living

Christians use the teachings as a guide for living because:
- This is the teaching of Jesus which is from God and must therefore be followed. It is given in a lot more detail than the Ten Commandments, making it easier to understand exactly what Jesus requires.
- The Sermon on the Mount shows that the old Jewish ways have been fulfilled by the new law of Jesus which means that Christians should use the Sermon on the Mount as guidance rather than just the Old Testament teachings.
- The Sermon on the Mount explains that the thoughts and feelings that people have are as important as their actions and this is not as clear in the Law of Moses.

- Christians should use the teaching Jesus gave in the Sermon on the Mount about the Law of Moses because Jesus realised his disciples needed this teaching and, if it was needed then, it must also be needed now.

The Sermon on the Mount by Fra Giovanni Angelico, 1387–1455. The teachings in The Sermon on the Mount were given to followers in the time of Jesus. Do you think they are still relevant to the followers of Jesus today?

> *The Law of the Gospel fulfils the commandments of the Law. The Lord's Sermon on the Mount, far from abolishing or devaluing the moral prescriptions of the Old Law, releases their hidden potential and has new demands arise from them: it reveals their entire divine and human truth. It does not add new external precepts, but proceeds to reform the heart, the root of human acts, where man chooses between the pure and the impure, where faith, hope, and charity are formed and with them the other virtues. The Gospel thus brings the Law to its fullness*
>
> **Catechism of the Catholic Church 1968**

Questions

b Do you think looking lustfully at someone is as bad as committing adultery with them? Give two reasons for your point of view. **4**

c Explain why Christians use Jesus' re-interpretation of the Law of Moses as a guide for living. **8**

d 'Christians should never fight back.'

  i Do you agree? Give reasons for your opinion. **3**

  ii Give reasons why some people may disagree with you. **3**

Exam Tip

c 'Explain why' means give four brief, or two developed, reasons on why Christians use the teachings of the Sermon on the Mount on the re-interpretation of the Law of Moses as a guide for living. For tips on Quality of Written Communication, look at page 107.

SUMMARY

Christians use the teachings of Jesus on the Law of Moses to decide how to react to such things as anger, lustful thoughts, divorce then re-marriage, making promises in the name of God, revenge and retaliation.

They use the teachings as a guide for living because they come from Jesus and are a development of the less detailed laws of Moses.

Topic 10.4.7 How and why Christians use the teachings of the Sermon on the Mount on displaying religion as a guide for living

KEY WORDS

Charity – voluntary giving to those in need.

Displaying religion – making a show of your religion, for example, by praying in the street.

Hypocrite – a person who acts in a way that contradicts what they say.

In the Sermon on the Mount Jesus also talked about religious practices, particularly about almsgiving, prayer and fasting. He said that if these are done in public deliberately to attract notice the person will not receive reward from God because public recognition has been the person's reward.

How Christians use the teachings as a guide for living

- Christians use the teachings as a guide for how to worship. The Sermon teaches Christians that worshipping God is a private action that is to be performed so that only God knows about it. This means Christians should not worship in order for other people to think they are holy but rather to improve their relationship with God.

- Christians use the teachings as a guide for how to behave when they are fasting or giving to **charity**. They should not make a display of what they are doing, so only God will know and they will receive their reward from God, not from the praise of people.

- Christians use the teachings as a guide for their prayer life. The Sermon on the Mount tells Christians that the way to pray to God is to use short prayers like the Our Father and, rather than praying on street corners for others to see, they should say prayers privately.

- Christians use the teachings to avoid making a display of their religion and being a **hypocrite** by showing off how much they go to church, but not actually treating people in a Christian way.

> *Be careful not to do your 'acts of righteousness' before men, to be seen by them. If you do, you will have no reward from your Father in heaven.*
>
> **Matthew 6:1**

> *And when you pray, do not be like the hypocrites, for they love to pray standing in the synagogues and on the street corners to be seen by men.*
>
> **Matthew 6:5**

This Catholic has received the sign of the cross in ashes on Ash Wednesday. Should Christians show their faith to others in this way?

Why Christians use the teachings as a guide for living

Christians use the teachings as a guide for living because:

- It is the teaching of Jesus which is from God and must therefore be followed. Jesus, as God's Son, is the best person to show Christians how to worship his father.
- The Sermon explains how Christians should show love of God when they worship, rather than love of public praise and recognition.
- The Sermon is a good guide for how to pray. The 'Our Father' in particular is a prayer that unites all Christian denominations.
- The teaching of the Sermon on the Mount about **displaying religion** can be used to tell Christians what they must not do and that they must show their love of God in a private way.

> *When you fast, do not look sombre as the hypocrites do, for they disfigure their faces to show men they are fasting. I tell you the truth, they have received their reward in full.*
>
> **Matthew 6:16**

◄ These people are praying in public and in a group. Do you think this is wrong?

Questions

b Do you think Catholics should not let anyone know when they are fasting? Give two reasons for your point of view. **4**

c Explain why Christians use Jesus' teachings on displaying religion as a guide for living. **8**

d 'Christians should only pray in private.'
　i Do you agree? Give reasons for your opinion. **3**
　ii Give reasons why some people may disagree with you. **3**

Exam Tip

d Use the answering evaluation questions advice from page 111. The arguments for this statement should come from this topic. Arguments against should come from class discussion and perhaps from Section 10.3 Worship and celebration. They might include such ideas as Christians gain support from other Christians and from Church leaders, so it is important that Christians pray together as a community.

SUMMARY

Christians use the teachings on displaying religion to decide how they should pray, fast, give to charity and worship God.

They use them because they are the teachings of God's Son Jesus, on how to live.

Topic 10.4.8 How and why Christians use the teachings of the Sermon on the Mount on Christians and money as a guide for living

> *Do not store up for yourselves treasures on Earth, where moth and rust destroy, and where thieves break in and steal.*
>
> **Matthew 6:19**

> *No-one can serve two masters. Either he will hate the one and love the other, or he will be devoted to the one and despise the other. You cannot serve both God and Money.*
>
> **Matthew 6:24**

> *Idolatry not only refers to false pagan worship. It remains a constant temptation to faith. Idolatry consists in divinising what is not God. Man commits idolatry whenever he honours and reveres a creature in place of God, whether this be gods or demons (for example, Satanism), power, pleasure, race, ancestors, the state, money, etc. Jesus says, 'You cannot serve God and mammon.'*
>
> **Catechism of the Catholic Church 2113**

The Sermon on the Mount teaches Christians about the use of money. When Jesus gave this part of the Sermon it was aimed at those people who thought that if someone had a lot of money it meant God had rewarded them for being a good person, and so they were better people than poor people.

How Christians use the teachings as a guide for living

- Christians use these teachings to guide them about the relationship between their attitude to money and their relationship with God. They learn that it is more important to gain spiritually than financially. A strong relationship with God will gain more rewards eternally, whereas possessions you have on Earth will be of no use after you die.
- They also use the teachings to see what they should do with their money. Christians learn from the Sermon not to hoard money (save it rather than using it), but to use it to help others.
- Christians use the teachings to see what their attitude to money should be. They learn not to make money their God (loving money rather than God).
- Christians also use the teachings to think about using money for the future. A few Christians do not save or have insurance policies because the Sermon teaches that Christians should not worry about what will happen in the future, but trust that God will care for them, as he does for the birds and the flowers.

The Bank of England. Do people ▶ think too much about money?

◀ Material goods become more important than God to some people.

Why Christians use the teachings as a guide for living

Christians use the teachings as a guide for living because:

- It is the teaching of Jesus that is from God and must therefore be followed. Jesus, as God's Son, is the best person to show Christians the relationship between money and God. If Jesus says you cannot worship God and money, then Christians should believe him.
- The teachings show Christians that possessions, money and treasure do not last forever. God, however, is eternal and by concentrating on him rather than money, Christians can gain eternal life.
- The teachings remind Christians how easily they can be distracted by wealth and forget about God. Therefore it is a useful guidance for their attitude to money in daily life.
- The teachings on hoarding wealth which does not last after death are a very useful guide for Christians, showing them that using money to love God and their neighbour is the way to eternal life.

Questions

b Do you think Christians can love God and be rich? Give two reasons for your point of view.   **4**

c Explain why Christians use the teachings of the Sermon on the Mount on Christians and money as a guide for living.   **8**

d 'The teachings of the Sermon on the Mount about money are too difficult to follow.'
   i   Do you agree? Give reasons for your opinion.   **3**
   ii Give reasons why some people may disagree with you.   **3**

Exam Tip

b You should already have thought about this, and you just have to give two reasons for your opinion. For example, if you agree that Christians cannot be rich and love God, you should use two reasons from this topic.

SUMMARY

Christians use the teachings on money to help them develop the right attitude to money and God. They use them because they are the guidance of God's Son, Jesus. They show Christians that serving God is more important than serving money because money dies but God is eternal and serving him brings eternal life.

Topic 10.4.9 How and why Christians use the teachings of the Sermon on the Mount on judgement and the Golden Rule as a guide for living

> *Do not judge, or you too will be judged. For in the same way you judge others, you will be judged and with the measure you use, it will be measured to you.*
>
> **Matthew 7:1–2**

> *Why do you look at the speck of sawdust in your brother's eye and pay no attention to the plank in your own eye? How can you say to your brother, 'Let me take the speck out of your eye,' when all the time there is a plank in your own eye? You hypocrite, first take the plank out of your own eye, and then you will see clearly to remove the speck from your brother's eye.*
>
> **Matthew 7:3–5**

> *The Golden Rule helps one discern, in concrete situations, whether or not it would be appropriate to reveal the truth to someone who asks for it.*
>
> **Catechism of the Catholic Church 2510**

The **Golden Rule** is what Christians today call the teaching of Jesus in Matthew 7:12:

'So in everything, do to others what you would have them do to you, for this sums up the Law and the Prophets.'

This teaching, which is also found in Luke's Gospel, is usually put into modern English as 'Treat others as you would like them to treat you'. It is used as a summary of all of Jesus' teachings in the Sermon on the Mount.

How Christians use the teachings as a guide for living

- Christians use Jesus' teaching on **judgement** to help them in their personal relationships. Jesus taught that if people judge someone, they must expect to be judged in the same way. So, before Christians criticise other people, they should think about the sort of things they do and whether they could also be criticised.
- Christians also use Jesus' teaching to think about the final judgement that they will face in front of God. In his teaching, Jesus said that Christians should not judge others if they do not want to be judged themselves. From this teaching, a few Christians refuse to have anything to do with courts as they involve judging others.
- Christians use the teaching on judgement to get their priorities right. By following Jesus' teaching, they concentrate on trying to improve themselves rather than picking on the small things that other people do wrong.
- Christians use the Golden Rule as a simple guideline for how they should behave. Lots of rules are difficult to follow, but many Christians find it easy to treat other people as they would like to be treated.
- Christians also use the Golden Rule to decide on major issues

Judging others is something we do ▶ naturally every day. Is it really wrong?

such as who to vote for. They look at the policies of the candidates and try to work out whether their policies will affect other people in the way the Christian would want to be affected if they were in that situation.

Why Christians use the teachings as a guide for living

Christians use the teachings as a guide for living because:

- It is the teaching of Jesus that is from God and must therefore be followed. Jesus, as God's Son is the best person to show Christians when to judge.
- If Jesus gives a rule to use in deciding what to do in every situation (the Golden Rule), it must be a rule worth using as a guide for living.
- Christians believe that they will be judged by God on how they have lived. Therefore any teachings of Jesus on judgement must be worth using as a guide for living.
- Everyone needs a guide for living and the Golden Rule provides a simple guide; following this will lead to eternal life.
- The Catechism says that the Golden Rule helps Christians to work out how to behave in difficult situations. As the Catechism is the teaching of the Magisterium, Catholics should follow it.

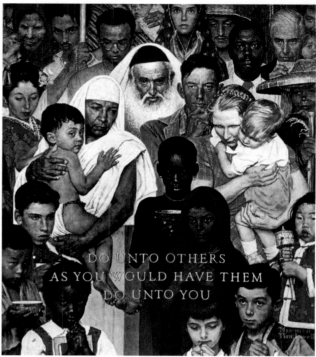

This poster by Norman Rockwell shows how the Golden Rule can be applied to everyday life. Can you think of some more ways?

Questions

b Do you think the Golden Rule is easy to follow? Give two
  reasons for your point of view.   **4**
c Explain why the Golden Rule is important for
  Catholic Christians.
d 'Christians should never judge other people.'
  i Do you agree? Give reasons for your opinion.   **3**
  ii Give reasons why some people may disagree with you.   **3**

Exam Tip

d Use the answering evaluation questions advice from page 11.
  The arguments for this should come from this topic on both how
  and why Christians use the teaching on judgement. Arguments
  against are likely to come from class discussion and your own
  ideas such as:
  - judgement is a natural thing and it can prevent a person from
    getting into trouble
  - everyone has to make judgements in life, for example deciding
    who gets a job or who will be your friend.

SUMMARY

Christians use the teachings on judgement to help them in their personal relationships and to work out how they can be judged well by God. They use the Golden Rule as a simple guide to decide what is the right thing to do.

They follow these teachings because they come from God's Son, Jesus, and they provide clear advice on how to live and gain eternal life.

Topic 10.4.10 How one Catholic organisation helps to relieve poverty and suffering in the UK

One of the main Catholic organisations that helps to relieve poverty and suffering in the United Kingdom is the St Vincent de Paul Society (SVP). Small groups of the SVP, known as conferences, are found in many parishes, schools, universities and hospitals. Each conference meets regularly and decides what needs to be done in their parish, such as:

- Regular visiting and personal care by the same people to help families who are finding it difficult to organise the home and/or family, to help the lonely and/or bereaved, to help the depressed, to help the housebound. All of these help to relieve some of the suffering in the UK.

- Organising diocesan children's camps for children from poor or broken homes, and holiday schemes to provide a break for family carers, to give poor families a holiday, to give people with disabilities a break, etc. This helps to relieve poverty and suffering by giving these children a holiday and increased self-esteem and confidence.

- Organising furniture stores for unwanted furniture, which can be used when housing the homeless, etc., so relieving their poverty.

- Organising Housing Associations to provide affordable housing for the homeless, overcrowded poor families, etc. This relieves the poverty of such groups and also helps to remove the sufferings of the homeless.

- Providing Drop-in Centres for lonely people to meet people and have an opportunity to socialise, so relieving their suffering.

This charity shop raises money for the work of the SVP and also provides cheap clothing and other household items for poor people.

◀ The Catholic Children's Society are another Catholic group working to relieve suffering in the UK. You can find out more about them on their website www.cathchild.org.uk.

◀ SVP members organise transport to pilgrimages for people who otherwise would not be able to go.

The aim of the St Vincent de Paul Society is the same today as it was at its conception in the nineteenth century: to tackle poverty in all its forms through the provision of practical assistance to those in need. The concept of need is broader than financial hardship, so visiting the sick, the lonely, the addicted, the imprisoned and those suffering from disabilities form a large proportion of the Society's work.

Source: www.svp.org.uk

Questions

b Do you think Catholic organisations do enough to relieve poverty and/or suffering in the United Kingdom? Give two reasons for your point of view. **4**

c Explain how one Catholic organisation helps to relieve poverty and/or suffering in the United Kingdom. **8**

d 'The government is better than religion at relieving poverty and suffering in the UK.'

   i Do you agree? Give reasons for your opinion. **3**

   ii Give reasons why some people may disagree with you. **3**

Exam Tip

Any organisation that is Catholic can be used for this topic. Be careful to check that it is a Catholic organisation and that it works for the relief of poverty or suffering in the United Kingdom rather than in the world. If you use any other non-Catholic organisation or an organisation that works outside the United Kingdom in your examination answers, you will not be awarded any marks.

c 'Explain how' means look at four types of work that the organisation of your choice does and explain how each type of work helps to relieve poverty or suffering in the United Kingdom. For the SVP look at the work listed in the bullet points above. For tips on Quality of Written Communication, look at page 107.

SUMMARY

The SVP or St Vincent de Paul Society is a Catholic organisation that works nationally in small groups mainly based in parishes. The members try to relieve poverty and suffering in many ways but mostly by visiting people and providing them with practical help and advice.

Topic 10.4.11 Why Catholic organisations help to relieve poverty and suffering in the UK

> *God blesses those who come to the aid of the poor and rebukes those who turn away from them ... Love for the poor is incompatible with immoderate use of riches, or their selfish use.*
>
> **Catechism of the Catholic Church 2443, 2445**

> *Only if I serve my neighbour can my eyes be opened to what God does for me and how much he loves me. The saints – consider the example of Blessed Teresa of Calcutta – constantly renewed their capacity for love of neighbour from their encounter with the Eucharistic Lord.*
>
> **Deus Caritas Est Encyclical of Pope Benedict XVI, 2006**

Catholic organisations help to relieve poverty and suffering in the UK because:

- According to the New Testament, riches must be used for the help of others, especially the poor.
- Christians believe that all humans are equal in the eyes of God, and that all the good things of the Earth have been given to humans by God to use to help each other.
- In the Parable of the Sheep and the Goats (see page 122) the good are sent to heaven because they fed the hungry, gave drink to the thirsty, clothed the naked and visited those in prison. The bad people were told they were going to hell because they had never fed the hungry, given drink to the thirsty, clothed the naked or visited those who were sick or in prison.
- In the Sermon on the Mount Jesus taught that Christians should share their time and possessions to help those in need.
- Throughout his life, Jesus did all he could to help the suffering and Christians should follow the example of Jesus.
- Helping to relieve poverty and suffering is a way of obeying the great commandment to love your neighbour.
- The Church teaches in the Catechism, and in many papal letters and encyclicals, that Christians have a duty to relieve poverty and suffering, and Catholics should follow the teachings and advice of the Church.

SUMMARY

Catholic organisations help to relieve poverty and suffering in the UK to try to follow the example of Jesus who healed the suffering. They are also trying to follow the teachings of Jesus in the Sermon on the Mount and parables like the Sheep and the Goats, that Christians should help the poor and suffering. They are also following the teaching of the Catechism and the advice of the Popes.

Questions

b Do you think Catholic organisations should work to relieve poverty and/or suffering in the United Kingdom? Give two reasons for your point of view. **4**

c Explain why Catholic organisations work to relieve poverty and/or suffering in the United Kingdom. **8**

d 'It is more important to worship and love God than to help relieve poverty and suffering.'
  i Do you agree? Give reasons for your opinion. **3**
  ii Give reasons why some people may disagree with you. **3**

Exam Tip

b You should already have thought about this, and you just have to give two reasons for your opinion. For example, if you agree that Catholic organisations should work to relieve poverty and suffering, you should use two reasons from this topic.

How to answer exam questions

Question A What is a hypocrite? 2 marks

A person who acts in a way that contradicts what they say.

Question B Do you think some Catholics need to take holy orders?
Give two reasons for your point of view. 4 marks

Yes I do because they feel called by God to serve the Church by becoming a priest.

I also believe that some Catholics need to take holy orders because the Church needs priests to administer the sacraments. Without a priest to celebrate Mass, Catholics cannot worship God properly.

Question C Explain why Christians use the Ten Commandments as a guide for living. 8 marks

Christians use the Ten Commandments as a guide for living because they are a precise list of rules that have come from God for good Christian behaviour.

The Commandments give guidance on how to worship and respect the one God of the Apostles' Creed. So Christians use these as a guide for loving God – the first great Christian duty.

The Commandments also give guidance on how to love your neighbour – the second great Christian duty.

Christians use them as a guide because if they follow them, they will respect their parents, will not commit adultery or desire other people's partners; through this they will promote marriage and family life. They will not lie or cheat people. By doing this they will be promoting the truth. They will not covet or desire other people's possessions, and so they will avoid greed and materialism.

Question D 'The teaching of the Sermon on the Mount about money is not important to Christians.'

i Do you agree? Give reasons for your opinion. 3 marks

ii Give reasons why some people may disagree with you. 3 marks

i I disagree. The teaching of the Sermon about money is important because it shows that Christians must be careful not to let money become more important than God. It also makes it clear that God will provide for people on Earth so Christians should not worry about gaining and hoarding material possessions. Finally it shows that concentrating on money can lead people away from God so that they cannot achieve salvation.

ii Others might disagree with me and think the teaching of the Sermon on the Mount about money is not important because they think that it is not practical in today's materialistic society to rely on God to provide for you. They may also think that it is possible to make lots of money and love God. Many people who say that they are Christians say they can, for example, Natasha Bedingfield and Bono. They may also believe that it shouldn't matter whether you have lots of money or how you get it as long as you go to church and have a close relationship with God.

QUESTION A
A high mark answer because it is a correct definition of the key word.

QUESTION B
A high mark answer because an opinion is backed up by two developed reasons.

QUESTION C
A high mark answer because four reasons why the Ten Commandments are used as a guide for living are developed. A formal style of English is used and there is good use of specialist vocabulary such as Christian duty, one God, Apostles' Creed, promote the truth, covet, greed, materialism.

QUESTION D
A high mark answer because it states the candidate's own opinion and backs it up with three clear reasons for thinking that the teaching of the Sermon on the Mount about money is important. It then gives three reasons for people disagreeing and believing that the teaching of the Sermon on the Mount about money is unimportant.

Glossary

Abortion The removal of a foetus from the womb before it can survive.

Abraham Regarded by Judaism as the founder of their faith and father of the Jewish people; regarded by Christians as the first great monotheist; regarded by Islam as a prophet and father of the Arab peoples.

Absolution Through the action of the priest, God grants pardon and peace.

Active life The life lived by religious orders who work in society as well as praying.

Adoration Worship of the consecrated Host.

Adultery A sexual act between a married person and someone other than their marriage partner.

Advent Four weeks set apart to remember the first coming of Jesus and the promise that he will come again.

Agnosticism Not being sure whether or not God exists.

Almsgiving Charitable giving of money or goods to the poor.

Anglican Churches Churches that are in communion with the Church of England.

Annulment A declaration by the Church that a marriage was never a true marriage and so the partners are free to marry.

Annunciation The announcement to the Virgin Mary by the angel Gabriel of the incarnation of Christ.

Apostle One who was sent out by Christ to preach his gospel.

Apostles' Creed A brief statement of the Christian faith traditionally composed by the apostles of Jesus.

Apostolic The belief that the Church can only be understood in light of the apostles.

Apostolic succession The belief that the bishops and the Pope continue the mission Jesus gave Peter and the apostles.

Apostolic tradition The oral Gospel passed on by the apostles to the bishops.

Ascension The celebration of the Ascension of Christ into heaven; Masses are held on the fortieth day after Easter.

Assisted suicide Providing a seriously ill person with the means to commit suicide.

Assumption The celebration in the Catholic Church of the Virgin Mary being taken up into heaven when her earthly life ended.

Atheism Believing that God does not exist.

Atonement Reconciliation between God and humanity.

'Back-street' abortionist Someone who carries out illegal abortions.

Baptism The Christian rite of initiation involving purification by water. It is one of the sacraments of the Church.

Baptists Members of evangelical Protestant Churches who believe in the baptism of believers.

Bible The word of God in the writings given by God to the Jewish people and to Christians.

Bigamy Marrying a person while still married to someone else.

Bishops Priests specially chosen by the Pope who are responsible for all the churches in a diocese.

Body of Christ Followers of Jesus live his life and in their various gifts Christ serves others through them. Also a description of the Church.

Born again An Evangelical Protestant phrase for personal conversion to Christianity.

Brain-dead When the brain is so damaged that doctors feel the patient's life has ended even though they are on a life-support machine.

Canon of scripture The list of books recognised by the Church as inspired by the Holy Spirit (the Bible).

Canonise To declare a dead person to be a saint.

Cardinal A specially chosen bishop who advises the Pope and elects new popes.

Cash crops Crops that LEDC countries can sell to gain foreign currency, for example coffee and cotton.

Catechism Official teaching of the Roman Catholic Church.

Catechist A person who instructs Catholics about their faith especially in preparation for the sacraments.

Catholic Universal or worldwide (the Church reaches out to all people).

Causation The idea that everything has been caused (started off) by something else.

Celibacy Living without engaging in any sexual activity.

Chalcedonian Definition That two natures, divine and human, are united in Christ.

Charity Voluntary giving to those in need.

Children's liturgy A celebration and explanation of the readings in Mass especially for children.

Chrism The oil used in baptism, confirmation and ordination.

Christ The Messiah or Anointed One.

Christmas Festival celebrating the birth of Christ.

Church of England The official state Church of England based on bishops with the monarch of England as its head.

Civil partnership A legal ceremony giving a homosexual couple the same legal rights as a husband and wife.

Closed community A religious community who have no or little physical contact with the outside world.

Cohabitation Living together without being married.

Commemoration The belief that the Eucharist is simply a remembrance of the Last Supper.

Communion Taking part in the Eucharist, or a group of Christians who all have the same beliefs.

Communion of Saints All Catholics, both alive and dead, are joined together (and can pray for one another).

Community cohesion A common vision and shared sense of belonging for all groups in society.

Compassion A feeling of pity which makes one want to help the

sufferer.

Concern To show compassion by being involved in other people's distress.

Confession Admitting to, and repenting of, one's sins. It is a major part of the Sacrament of Reconciliation, sometimes used to describe the sacrament itself.

Confirmation The sacrament admitting a baptised person to full participation in the Church.

Contemplative life The life of prayer and meditation lived by some religious orders.

Contemplative order A religious order whose vocation is to spend their lives in prayer and meditation.

Contraception Intentionally preventing conception from occurring. There are various forms of artificial contraception.

Contrition Sorrow for the sin committed and deciding not to sin again.

Convent A community of people in a religious order (especially nuns) living together.

Conversion When your life/religion is changed.

Covenant An agreement between God and his people.

Creed Statement of Christian beliefs.

Crucifixion A Roman death penalty suffered by Jesus when he was nailed to the cross.

Curia Governing body of the Roman Catholic Church.

Deacon Those called to assist bishops, especially in the caring for the needy.

Denomination A group of religious believers who have their own organisation and faith.

Design When things are connected and seem to have a purpose: for example, the eye is designed for seeing.

Diocese A Church area under the direction of a bishop.

Discrimination Treating people less favourably because of their ethnicity/gender/colour/sexuality/age/class.

Displaying religion Making a show of your religion, for example by praying in the street.

Dogmas The beliefs of the Catholic Church.

Dove A bird symbolising peace. When used as a symbol of the Holy Spirit, it implies an overshadowing by God.

Easter Festival celebrating the resurrection of Jesus.

EDC Economically developing countries (for example, Mexico).

Equality The state in which everyone has equal rights regardless of gender/race/class.

Ethnic minority A member of an ethnic group (race) which is much smaller than the majority group.

Eucharist A service celebrating the sacrificial death and resurrection of Jesus Christ using elements of bread and wine

Euthanasia The painless killing of someone dying from a painful disease.

Evangelical counsels The vows of poverty, chastity and obedience.

Evangelical Protestants Protestants who emphasise the sole authority of the Bible and the need to be born-again.

Exclusivism Those who believe Christianity is the only true religion.

Ex-nihilo That God created the universe out of nothing.

Extended family Children, parents and grandparents/ aunts/uncles living as a unit or very near to each other.

Extraordinary ministers A non-ordained man or woman who assists in the sacred ministry of priests, for example helping with the distribution of Holy Communion (ordinary ministers are priests).

Faith Firm belief without logical proof.

Faithfulness Staying with your marriage partner and having sex only with them.

Fire When used as a symbol of the Holy Spirit, it implies purifying power.

First Communion The first time a person receives the sacrament of the Eucharist.

Forgiveness To stop blaming someone and/or pardon them for what they have done wrong. (The willingness to seek no revenge and to take the first step in healing the relationship.)

Free will The idea that human beings are free to make their own choices.

Godparents A person who sponsors someone (the godchild) at baptism.

Golden Rule The teaching of Jesus that you should treat others as you would like them to treat you.

Gospel The Good News about Jesus. Usually refers to the four Gospels (Matthew, Mark, Luke and John) in the New Testament.

Heaven A place of paradise where God rules.

Hell A place of horrors where Satan rules.

Holy Of, or relating to God, sacred. When used to refer to the Church it means the Holy Spirit makes the followers of Jesus more and more like Jesus.

Holy orders The status of a priest, bishop or deacon.

Holy Week The week before Easter Sunday.

Homily A talk by the celebrant or other minister on how to apply the scripture readings in the daily life.

Homophobia A hatred or fear of homosexuals.

Homosexuality Sexual attraction to a same sex partner.

Hypocrite A person who acts in a way that contradicts what they say.

Idolatry The worship of idols.

Immaculate Conception The Catholic belief that God preserved the Virgin Mary from original sin from the moment she was conceived.

Immortality of the soul The idea that the soul lives on after the death of the body.

Incarnation The belief that God took human form in Jesus.

Inclusivism Believing that while only Christianity has the whole truth, non-Christian religions are searching for God and have some truth.

Intercession A prayer to God on behalf of another person.

Interfaith marriage Marriage where the husband and wife are from different religions.

Involuntary euthanasia See 'non-voluntary euthanasia'.

Judgement The act of judging people and their actions.

Just war A war that is fought for the right reasons in the right way (as set out by St Augustine and St Thomas Aquinas).

Justice The allocation of reward and punishment; maintaining what is right.

Kingdom of God The place where God rules, it is the aim of Christians to make the Earth God's Kingdom.

Laity All the people of the Church who are not chosen to be bishops, priests or deacons.

Law of Moses, The The laws God gave to Moses in the Old Testament.

Lay ministries Special ways of serving the Church open to the non-ordained.

Lector People who have a special calling to minister the word in Mass.

Lent Forty days set aside for prayer, fasting and generous giving.

LEDCs Less economically developed countries, which are very poor (for example, Bangladesh, Mali, etc.).

Levite Members of a Jewish tribe who acted as ministers of the Temple in Jerusalem.

Liberal Protestant Members of the Protestant Churches who interpret the Bible and Christian beliefs in the light of reason and the modern world.

Liturgical year The Church's year of worship, which contains different feasts and celebrations on an annual basis.

Liturgy of the Eucharist The re-enactment of the Last Supper during which the bread and wine are transubstantiated.

Liturgy of the Word Bible readings in the second part of the Mass.

Lord's Prayer (Our Father) A prayer asking for both daily food (which means the Eucharist) and the forgiveness of sins.

Magisterium The Pope and bishops being guided by the Holy Spirit to interpret the Bible and tradition for Roman Catholics today.

Magnificat The song of praise which the Blessed Virgin Mary sang when her cousin greeted her as the mother of God.

Marriage A man and woman legally joined so that they are allowed to live together and, usually, have children.

Mass The name given to the Eucharistic liturgy of the Catholic Church.

MEDC More economically developed countries (for example, USA).

Methodist A Christian who belongs to the Methodist Church founded by John Wesley in the eighteenth century.

Ministry A special way of serving the Church.

Miracle An event which seems to break a law of science and for which the only explanation seems to be God.

Mixed faith marriages See 'interfaith marriage'.

Monastery The residence of a religious community.

Monastic life, the Living as a monk or nun in a religious community.

Monotheism Belief in one God.

Moral evil Actions done by humans which cause suffering.

Moses The Old Testament prophet who led the Jews out of Egypt and received the Ten Commandments from God.

Multi-ethnic society Many different races and cultures living together in one society.

Multi-faith society Many different religions living together in one society.

Natural evil Things that cause suffering, but have nothing to do with humans, for example, earthquakes.

Near-death experience When someone about to die has an out-of-body or religious experience.

New Testament The second half of the Bible including the Gospels, and letters (epistles).

Nicene Creed A longer creed summarising Christian beliefs; first adopted in 325.

Nonconformist A Protestant in England who is not a member of the Church of England.

Nonconformist Churches Protestant Christians separated from the Church of England.

Non-voluntary euthanasia Ending someone's life painlessly when they are unable to ask, but when there is good reason for thinking they would want death, for example, switching off a life-support machine.

Nuclear family Mother, father and children living as a unit.

Numinous The feeling of the presence of something greater than you.

Old Testament The first half of the Bible including holy writings of the Jewish people and their history as the chosen people.

Omni-benevolent The belief that God is all-good.

Omnipotent The belief that God is all-powerful.

Omniscient The belief that God knows all that has happened and all that will happen.

Oppressed Those who are denied their rights and made to suffer by others (especially by governments and by rich and powerful leaders).

Ordained ministry Service to the Church, which can only be carried out by those who have received the sacrament of holy orders.

Ordination Making someone a priest, bishop or deacon by the sacrament of the holy orders.

Orthodox Churches National Churches which are in union with the Patriarch of Constantinople (for example, the Russian Orthodox Church).

Papacy The office of the Pope.

Papal encyclicals A papal letter sent to bishops of the Church to teach or explain a matter of belief.

Paranormal Unexplained things which are thought to have spiritual causes, for example, ghosts, mediums.

Parish A local church community.

Paschal mystery The suffering, death and resurrection of Jesus.

Passion of Christ The sufferings of Christ from the Last Supper to his death on the Cross.

Pastoral The work of caring for the souls of a parish usually carried out by a priest or bishop.

Patriarch The title given to the head of an Orthodox Church, for example, the Patriarch of Moscow is the head of the Russian Orthodox Church.

Penance An action showing contrition.

Penitential rite The confession and absolution at the beginning of Mass.

Pentecost The celebration of the Holy Spirit descending onto the Apostles.

Pentecostal A Christian belonging to those Churches which emphasise the gifts given to the Apostles at Pentecost.

Pluralism The belief that all religions are equal and are just different ways of finding God.

Pope The head of the Roman Catholic Church.

Prayer An attempt to contact God, usually through words.

Precepts of the Church Seven rules that Catholics are expected to follow.

Prejudice Believing some people are inferior or superior without even knowing them.

Pre-marital sex Sex before marriage.

Priests Specially called chosen people who are ordained to be ministers of the word and the sacraments.

Procreation Making a new life.

Promiscuity Having sex with a number of partners without commitment.

Purgatory A place where Catholics believe souls go after death to be purified.

Quaker A member of the Religious Society of Friends, a Christian group whose beliefs include meditation and pacifism.

Quality of life The idea that life must have some benefits for it to be worth living.

Racial harmony Different races/colours living together happily.

Racism The belief that some races are superior to others.

Real presence The bread and wine become the Body and Blood of Jesus.

Reconciliation Bringing together those who were bitterly divided.

Re-constituted family Where two sets of children (step-brothers and step-sisters) become one family when their divorced parents marry each other.

Reformation A sixteenth-century reform movement that led to the formation of the Protestant Churches.

Reincarnation The belief that, after death, souls are reborn in a new body.

Religious community A religious order who live together as a group, for example Benedictines, the Carmelites.

Religious experience An event where a person comes into contact with God in some way.

Religious freedom The right to practise your religion and change your religion.

Religious pluralism Accepting all religions as having an equal right to co-exist.

Re-marriage Marrying again after being divorced from a previous marriage.

Renewal of baptismal vows Confirming and deepening the solemn promises made at baptism.

Repentance The act of being sorry for wrongdoing and deciding not to do it again.

Resurrection The belief that, after death, the body stays in the grave until the end of the world, when it is raised.

Rite of communion Receiving the body and blood of Jesus.

Sabbath A day of rest and worship: Sunday for most Christians.

Sacrament An outward sign through which invisible grace is given to a person by Jesus.

Sacrament of penance One of the seven Catholic sacraments also called the Sacrament of Forgiveness, Reconciliation and Confession.

Sacrifice A surrender of something valuable for the sake of others; Jesus giving his life on the cross remembered in the Eucharist.

Saint A person who has died and has been declared a saint by canonisation.

Salvation The act of delivering from sin or saving from evil.

Salvation Army A charitable and religious organisation.

Sanctity of life The belief that life is holy and belongs to God.

Sermon on the Mount, The Jesus' description of the Christian way of living found in Matthew's Gospel.

Service to others Showing Christian values by helping other people.

Sexism Discriminating against people because of their gender (being male or female).

Sin An act that is against God's will.

Son of Man The title Jesus used of himself.

St Paul The first Christian missionary and the last Apostle appointed. St Paul wrote many of the New Testament letters.

Tabernacle A safe place in which is kept the Blessed Sacrament.

Ten Commandments The ten rules for living given by God to Moses.

Theological colleges Colleges that teach religion and prepare people for ordination.

Transubstantiation The belief that during Mass the bread and wine become the body and blood of Jesus by the power of the Holy Spirit.

Tridium The three days from the evening of Maundy Thursday to the evening of Easter Day.

Trinity The belief that God is three in one.

Unity God's way of being one.

URC United Reformed Church formed by the union of English Congregational and Presbyterian Christians.

Vatican The governing body of the Catholic Church and the Vatican or the residence of the Pope in the Vatican City.

Virgin birth The belief that Jesus was not conceived through sex.

Vocation A call from God to lead the Christian life.

Voluntary euthanasia Ending life painlessly when someone in great pain asks for death.

Vows Solemn promises made to God.

Water Used in baptism as a sign of purification and as a reminder of Christ's own baptism.

Wind When used as a symbol of the Holy Spirit, it implies power.

Photo credits and acknowledgements

Photo credits:

p.1 Peter Barritt/Alamy; **p.2** © ArkReligion.com/Alamy; **p.3** © Ilene MacDonald /Alamy; **p.5** *t* akg-images, *b* © images-of-france/Alamy; **p.7** *t* Jerome Delay/AP Photo/PA Photos, *b* ©Mike Baldwin/Cornered/ www.CartoonStock.com; **p.8** © Reuters/Corbis; **p.11** *t* © Corbis, *b* © Jill Watton; **p.12** Royal Observatory, Edinburgh/ AATB/Science Photo Library; **p.13** © Kevin Schafer/Corbis; **p.14** © Digital Vision/Getty Images; **p.16** Deep Light Productions/Science Photo, Library; **p.17** © Wesley Hitt/Alamy; **p.18** Romeo Gacad/AFP/Getty Images; **p.19** Anank Tono/AFP/Getty Images; **p.20** Bertram Henry/Getty Images; **p.21** *t* © Peter Turnley/Corbis, *b* Punit Paranjpe/Reuters/Corbis; **p.22** David E. Scherman/Time & Life Pictures/Getty Images; **p.23** © Gilberto Aviles/Reuters/Corbis; **p.24** Caritas Makeni/Cafod; **p.26** Tigeraspect productions; **p.27** Martin Jenkinson/Alamy; **p.29** *l* Stockfolio/Alamy, *r* Jill Watton; **p.31** Digital Art/Corbis; **p.32** Custom Medical Stock Photo/Science Photo Library; **p.33** *l & r* Action Press/Rex Features; **p.34** UPI; **p.35** Henry Westheim Photography/Alamy; **p.36** © Janine Wiedel/Photofusion; **p.37** Steve Bell/Rex Features; **p.39** Courtesy of LIFE; **p.40** AAP Image/Dave Hunt; **p.41** marc latzel/lookatonline; **p.42** © Images.com/Corbis; **p.43** John Cole/Science Photo Library; **p.45** © Shahaf Twizer/epa/Corbis; **p.47** Starmax/EMPICS Entertainment/PA Photos; **p.48** Rex Features; **p.49** © Attar Maher/Corbis Sygma; **p.50** Haydn West/Rex Features; **p.55** Victor Watton; **p.57** *t* © Photofrenetic/Alamy, *b* © Corbis; **p.58** Odd Andersen/AFP/Getty Images; **p.60** Bernadette Delaney/Alamy; **p.62** © Norbert Schaefer/Corbis; **p.63** © Images.com/Corbis; **p.65** © Steve Skjold/Alamy; **p.66** © Design Pics Inc/Photolibrary group; **p.67** Bruno Vincent/Getty Images; **p.68** © Jim Bourg/Reuters/Corbis; **p.69** © C. Lyttle/zefa/Corbis; **p.70** Garo/Phanie/Rex Features; **p.71** © Dr Cecilia Pyper & Jane Knight, Fertility UK 2009; **p.74** Azure Films/Isle Of Mann Film Commission/Keeping Mum Productions/Tusk Productions/Ronald Grant Archive; **p.75** ©.Miramax/Everett/Rex Features; **p.77** PA Wire/PA Photos; **p.78** © Ted Horowitz/Corbis; **p.79** Fox Photos/Getty Images; **p.80** EduardoVerdugo/AP PA Photos; **p.81** Ethan Miller/Getty Images; **p.83** © Reuters/Corbis; **p.84** Daniel Berehulak/Getty Images; **p.85** © Larry W. Smith/epa/Corbis; **p.87** © Peter Macdiarmid/epa/Corbis; **p.88** © Todd Gipstein/Corbis; **p.89** © Grzegorz Galazka/Corbis; **p.90** Matt Cardy/Getty Images; **p.91** Daniel Berehulak/Getty Images; **p.93** *l & r* Circa; **p.94** © Bettmann/Corbis; **p.95** © Jeffrey L. Rotman/Corbis; **p.97** *l* C&M Fragasso/Visum/Still Pictures, *r* © Andrew Fox/Corbis; **p.98** *l* Bob Battersby/BDI Images, *r* © Michael J. Doolittle/The Image Works; **p.99** AP Photo/PA Photos; **p.100** *r & l* Jill Watton; **p.102** © 20th Century Fox/Everett/Rex Features; **p.103** Courtesy of Dawn French; **p.105** St. Bavo Cathedral, Ghent, Belgium/ Giraudon/ The Bridgeman Art Library; **p.108** Tretyakov Gallery, Moscow, Russia/The Bridgeman Art Library; **p.109** The Bridgeman Art Library/Getty Images; **p.110** akg-images; **p.112** © The Art Archive/Corbis; **p.113** © Brooklyn Museum/Corbis; **p.114** akg-images; **p.115** akg-images; **p.116** © Huntington Library/SuperStock; **p.117** © Photodisc/Getty Images; **p.118** *l* © Reuters/Corbis, *r* Jim West/Alamy; **p.121** *t* "The Good Samaratin" by Dr. He Qi (www.heqigallery.com); *b* Rex Features; **p.125** *l* Marco Antonio Rezende/BrazilPhotos.com; *r* Frank Monaco/Rex Features; **p.126** *l* © Tim Graham/Alamy, *r* © Sucheta Das/Reuters/Corbis; **p.127** deshakalyanchowdhury/AFP/Getty Images; **p.129** © Hannah Kolka; **p.131** Mandelngan/AFP/Getty Images; **p.132** Franco Origlia/Getty Images; **p.133** © Nancy Kent/With special thanks to the parishioners of St Columba's Church Chesham; **p.134** © Hannah Kolka; **p.137** World Religions Photo Library/Alamy; **p.138** Kevin P. Casey-Pool/Getty Images; **p.139** VINCENZO PINTO/AFP/Getty Images; **p.140** *l* © Jorge Bai/Alamy, *r* © Design Pics Inc./Alamy; **p.142** © Alinari Archives/Corbis; **p.144** Mimmo Chianura/Rex Features; **p.145** Thomas Coex/AFP/Getty Images; **p.146** *l* © Bettmann/Corbis, *r* Daniel Berehulak/Getty Images; **p.148** Arturo Mari L'Osservatore Romano Vatican pool via Getty Images; **p.150** © World Religions Photo Library/Alamy; **p.151** Carlos Davila/Alamy; **p.152** Simon Watson/Taxi/Getty Images; **p.153** © Hill Street Studios/Walter Jimenez; **p.154** Caro/Alamy; **p.155** Sipa Press/Rex Features; **p.157** Private Collection/Giraudon/The Bridgeman Art Library; **p.159** © World Religions Photo Library/Alamy; **p.160** Circa Religion Photo Library/John Fryer; **p.161** © ArkReligion.com/Alamy; **p.162** *l & r* © Hannah Kolka; **p.164** Canada Press/PA; **p.165** National Gallery, London, UK/Giraudon/The Bridgeman Art Library Photos; **p.166** © Hannah Kolka; **p.167** Manor Photography/Alamy; **p.168** Peter Stiles/photographersdirect.com; **p.170** © Andrew Parker/Alamy; **p.171** akg-images/Amelot; **p.172** © Kim Karpeles/Alamy; **p.173** Anders Ryman/Alamy; **p.174** © Sylvia Cordaiy Photo Library Ltd/Alamy; **p.175** © E&E Image Library/Heritage-Images; **p.178** © P Deliss/Godong/Corbis; **p.179** © Jack Sullivan/Alamy; **p.180** World Religions Photo Library/Mimi Forsyth; **p.181** © ArkReligion.com/Alamy; **p.183** © Hannah Kolka; **p.184** www.thebricktestament.com; **p.186** © Adrian Sherratt/Alamy; **p.188** © Pascal Deloche/Godong/Corbis; **p.189** MarioPonta/Alamy; **p.190** © Hannah Kolka; **p.193** Paul Thomas/The Image Bank/Getty Images; **p.195** akg-images/Rabatti-Domingie; **p.196** © Corbis; **p.197** Spencer Platt/Getty Images; **p.198** © Alex Segre/Alamy; **p.199** Alberto Incrocci/Photodisc/Getty Images; **p.200** © WoodyStock/Alamy; **p.201** Printed by permission of the Norman Rockwell Family Agency © 1961 the Norman Rockwell Family Entities; **p.202** Courtesy of St Vincent de Paul Society (England & Wales); **p.203** *t* Reproduced with permission from Catholic Children's Society, *b* Courtesy of St Vincent de Paul Society (England & Wales)

Acknowledgements

Extracts from What the Churches Say, 3rd edition (Christian Education Movement, 2000); extracts from The Catechism of the Catholic Church (Continuum International Publishing Group, 2002); extracts from The Holy Bible: New International Version Anglicised (Hodder & Stoughton, 1990), copyright © 1979, 1984 by International Bible Society, used by permission of Hodder & Stoughton Publishers, an Hachette UK Company; John Betjeman, extract from 'In Westminster Abbey' from John Betjeman's Collected Poems (John Murray, 1972), reprinted by permission of the publisher.

Every effort has been made to establish copyright and contact copyright holders prior to publication, but if any have been inadvertently overlooked the Publishers will be pleased to make the necessary arrangements at the first opportunity.

Index